REFUGE

To:
DAVID & JOAN
PECK

ON YOUR 40TH
WEDDING ANNIVERSARY
1970 - 2010

FROM: JAMES & TANDRA
M^cLEROY

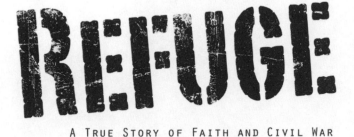

REFUGE

A True Story of Faith and Civil War

John & Bessie Gonleh
with
Bruce Beakley

WINEPRESS WP PUBLISHING

WinePress Publishing (PO Box 428, Enumclaw, WA 98022) functions only as book publisher. As such, the ultimate design, content, editorial accuracy, and views expressed or implied in this work are those of the author.

All Scripture quotations, unless otherwise indicated, are taken from the *New King James Version.* Copyright © 1982 by Thomas Nelson, Inc. Used by permission. All rights reserved.

ISBN 13: 978-1-57921-930-7
ISBN 10: 1-57921-930-6
Library of Congress Catalog Card Number: 2007935557

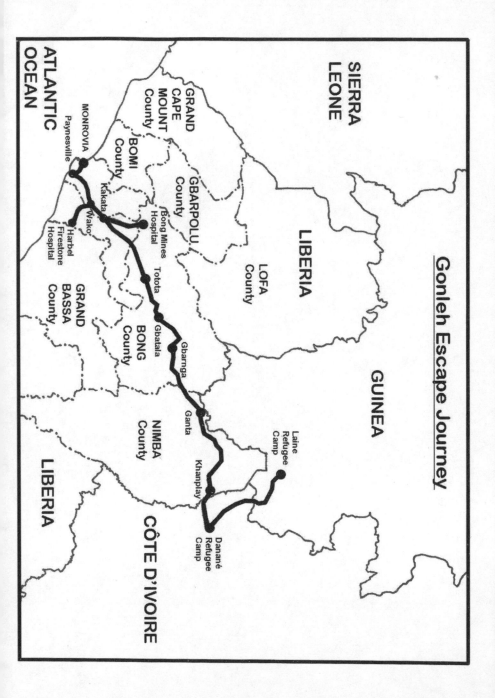

Gonleh Escape Journey

To the One who gives refuge and to our beloved
children—those who remain and those
who have gone ahead

—John and Bessie

CONTENTS

ACKNOWLEDGMENT

J ohn and Bessie would like to thank the Beakley family, Bruce, Debra, and Bryan, for their support and faithfulness in being used by God to bless them. Bruce Beakley would like to extend special thanks to Shane Bolks for her patience, encouragement, and critique of the manuscript. He also extends thanks to John Mark and Betty Carpenter for their keen insights into Liberian life. Their twenty-six years in Liberia as foreign missionaries provided invaluable help to understand Liberian culture and village life.

FOREWORD

During my twenty-six years in Liberia as a missionary and president of the Liberia Baptist Theological Seminary, my admiration for the Liberian people grew. Their resilient spirits and their devotion to family were necessary if they were to survive the horrific civil war that was thrust upon them. My family was evacuated on the very last KLM flight leaving Monrovia as bombs and bullets drew near, leaving behind numerous friends and colleagues. Many dear friends were brutally slaughtered. Others miraculously escaped and survived. John and Bessie Gonleh were among these.

I personally know John and Bessie Gonleh. John and Bessie were active in the Immanuel Baptist Church, which was one of the churches started in our church planting ministry. I got to know them during the construction of their church which was funded by Baptist churches in Georgia. Their story is true and provides one of the most detailed and accurate views of the war from those who lived through it. No book can possibly capture the full extent of horror, fear, stress, grief, and sorrow from this war. However *REFUGE* provides the reader a glimpse of these emotions and the dogged, unyielding faith that was forged and refined by the civil war that engulfed Liberia.

John Mark Carpenter
Former Missionary and President Emeritus
of the Liberia Baptist Theological Seminary
December 2008

PROLOGUE
DIVINE APPOINTMENTS

BRUCE I was a world away from the USA in La Victoria —a sweltering Dominican Republic prison—and I was there with Bill Glass Champions for Life, a Christian prison ministry.

The prisoners were gathered outside, seated on the asphalt listening to the program. One large tree stood by itself, and prisoners crowded beneath it trying to escape the heat. There wasn't nearly enough room for the hundreds of prisoners.

I was seated also, cross-legged and facing the group off on the side. My eyes were closed. The late August sun beat down mercilessly. My water was long gone, and I'd forgotten my hat.

The heat was blistering and the blacktop made it feel like we were slowly roasting in an oven. Heat emanated from the top, the sides, and the bottom so we would be evenly cooked. All I needed was a skewer down through me to complete the scene.

With my head bowed, I prayed I wouldn't pass out in the heat. I prayed for the whole thing to be over soon. Almost as an afterthought, I prayed for the inmates' salvation.

We'd already been two days in Puerto Rico, and today was the second and last day in the Dominican Republic. What in the world was I doing here? I knew the answer well enough. We were presenting information showing how these inmates could receive eternal life by accepting Jesus Christ as their Savior. But Puerto Rico had already taught me my attempts at communicating in Spanish were abysmal.

I was told by Puerto Ricans that Puerto Ricans can't speak Spanish either. They butcher the pronunciation by chopping off all the ending syllables. I couldn't understand a single sentence anyone spoke, and most of the prisoners didn't speak English, only Puerto Rican.

Dominicans were actually slightly easier to understand, but by this time my confidence was shot. It was hard to even muster the effort to try speaking anymore. All my Spanish classes seemed like a waste.

The morning had started out very strangely. Our bus was late picking us up from our hotel. Except for me, everyone else was chatting and waiting where the bus would arrive, a hundred yards away. I was alone, seated just outside the entrance, listening to music from my CD player.

Suddenly, the CD player stopped, and I heard a voice say, "Time to go." I opened my eyes to see who had spoken and simultaneously looked down at my CD player. There was no one around me, and I was sure my hand hadn't bumped the OFF button on the CD player.

Confused, I stood up, walked a few steps to where I could see the bus area, and was shocked to see our bus pulling to a stop. I was freaked out! *What in heaven's name . . .*

Nothing like this had ever happened to me. If I hadn't heard that voice and if my CD player hadn't turned off, I probably would have missed the bus. Roasting here on the pavement, I wondered now if that would have been the preferred alternative.

I occasionally opened my eyes, squinting against the brightness, to take a look around and watch the heat waves rising off the asphalt. All the Dominicans were black but spoke Spanish. They were descendants of slaves carried to the New World by the Spanish explorers. I closed my eyes again.

Why can't that speaker hurry up and finish so we can get out of here?
Bruce, stop it! Stop complaining. You're here.
Sorry, Lord. Help me do what I came here for.

Without warning a voice spoke inside my head: "Tell Michael I want him on my team. I have plans for him." The words struck like thunder.

Where did that come from, and who is Michael? I wondered.

Now, I have plenty of voices in my head. For example, when I fly, as we're taking off, a voice tells me the plane is going to crash and I'm going to die. Then when the plane is safely in the air, I realize the voice was wrong. Therefore, as a general rule, I try to ignore the voices in my head, especially the insistent ones. But this was the second time today I heard that distinct voice. Besides, the first voice had been right.

My eyes popped open with surprise and I looked up. Seated directly across from me was a prisoner. He was the only white prisoner in a sea of black, and he hadn't been there a moment ago. He had come out to the program and sat down when my eyes were closed.

I looked back down at my crossed legs to note the exact direction I was pointing. Then I made a mental line from where I was seated along the blacktop until it exactly intersected the white prisoner. I realized this had to be Michael and to whom the voice was referring.

I instantly started doubting, questioning, and fighting against the voice. *This has never happened before. What is going on? Maybe it's heat stroke. God doesn't actually expect me to go talk to him like I know his name, does he? Speak to me again, Lord. Tell me again if that prisoner is Michael. Give me some reassurance.* I was reeling, but there was nothing else to hear.

If this was God speaking, I knew it was my own fault. I'd been struggling for some time in my prayers. I wanted things to change. I was thirsty. I wanted a deeper relationship with God. It's quite easy for me to tell God what I want or need, to pray for the sick, or even to praise him. All of that gives me no trouble at all. For me the hard thing is listening. Do I really want God to speak? Do I really want to hear what he has to say? Do I want to give him permission to tell me what to do? For me, that prospect is downright terrifying. There really is no predicting what he could say. There's no way to control him. And yet I craved something deeper, more satisfying. I knew I had to open myself up to hear what God had to say to me. I knew it was my choice, but I was scared.

The speaker was finishing. I had to do something. *Should I walk up to this prisoner and tell him exactly what the voice said? No, it can't be. This type of thing just doesn't happen to me.*

The speaker closed with a prayer. Everyone stood up. It was now or never.

I walked up to the prisoner and in English I asked, "Do you speak English?"

"Some," he replied.

"What is your name?"

"Miguel."

My heart sank. The voice was right. Miguel is Spanish for Michael. I had been disobedient. In an effort to salvage the situation I said, "While I was sitting on the ground, through a voice in my head, God told me your name was Michael. He said he wants you and has plans for you."

Miguel looked at me like "Just humor him; the guy is nuts."

Miguel was from Spain. I didn't ask what he was in for. It was probably drugs. I felt awful. I had let down God and let down Miguel. I robbed both him and me of a blessing. And I robbed God of using me to give Miguel a message. I should have just called him by his name. Then he might have believed the message actually came from God. As it was, for all he knew I could have just made up the story.

I felt dizzy and like my head was spinning. A voice had popped into my head, giving me a name and a message. Because I couldn't quite accept it, I didn't act on it, and I failed.

We finished up in La Victoria. The bus ride back to our hotel was long. We unloaded, and I went straight to my room and collapsed on the bed.

I grabbed my little New Testament. I don't know why. Maybe I was hoping for some absolution, some salve to make my failure less painful. But I knew exactly what had happened. I was no Abraham. I didn't believe God. I had failed.

Nevertheless, I randomly opened the Bible. As I did, my eyes seemed to be magnets and the passage was steel. It was Mark 6:50–52: "Immediately he spoke to them and said, 'Take courage! It is I. Don't be afraid.' Then he climbed into the boat with them, and the wind died down. They were completely amazed, for they had not understood about the loaves; their hearts were hardened."

There it was. It pierced like a knife. My heart was hard, hard as stone. I had refused to believe God could speak to me and give me a message for Miguel. I wondered, *Is it even possible for a person to change himself?* I'm not sure it is.

Right there, I knelt beside the bed. "Lord," I prayed, "I can't change my own hard heart. If you want it changed, then you're going to have to do it, because I can't. Soften my heart, Lord."

I left Santo Domingo for the USA and Houston the next day, August 24, 2005.

Seated in the departure lounge at the airport, once again, I heard the voice in my head: "John is sitting across from you. Tell him that even though things seem bleak now, they'll get better soon."

Oh, no, not again. Am I losing my mind? I shook my head as if the words were cobwebs that needed clearing out. But as precise and clear as the words were, they were spoken only once. The voice wasn't repeating itself. The next move was mine.

I was tempted to just shout toward heaven, "Leave me alone," but I was equally afraid he would. I realized there was only one way out of this dilemma.

OK, Lord, I may make a fool of myself, but I'm not going to be disobedient again. If you tell me to speak to someone, then I will.

Even with those words I prayed, I wasn't sure I had the nerve. I looked around from where I was seated. I reasoned it wouldn't hurt just to look around to see if anyone was across from me. I only saw one person who was close, and he was facing me, but he was off to the side.

Well, I thought, *he's the closest one to fit the description. Here goes.* I walked over to him and said, "Excuse me, sir, but is your name John?"

"No," he answered, looking at me like I was a space alien.

OK, God. I hope you're happy. Now, I officially look like a fool. I sat back down. I noticed out of the corner of my eye the man glance at me. I purposely avoided eye contact.

Finally, it was time for my flight. I got on the plane and sat in the aisle seat, 8C, but the voice's message still nagged at me. I leaned over to the guy in the window seat, 8A, and said once again, "Excuse me. Is your name John?" I got the same answer as before and the same look.

Thankfully, there was only one guy across the aisle, seat 8F. Same question. Same answer. Same look.

Well, I was done looking stupid. I had failed God once, and though I felt foolish, I wasn't going to be willfully disobedient again. Of course, neither of these men was technically seated "across" from me, but I had asked anyway, just to be sure.

On top of this, when I landed in Panama to change planes, I called my brother, John, to ask him if he was having any unusual trouble. No, no trouble at all, he said.

Finally, I'd exhausted all the possibilities. "God, I tried," I said. I boarded my plane for Houston and promptly forgot all about this message.

I was home for only a few days. On Sunday, August 28, 2005, I left for Brussels, Belgium, for a new type of hip replacement surgery that wasn't yet FDA approved for the USA. A snowboarding accident a few years earlier had destroyed the cartilage in my right hip, but I was too young for traditional surgery.

The surgery went perfectly and I felt great. I changed my flight to fly back a few days early on September 7.

In the Continental Airlines departure lounge, I sat down to wait. I was early and bored. I'd been bored for days now following my surgery. I went back to a coffee bar I'd passed. By now I was quite proficient with the crutches.

While I drank my coffee, a group of about sixty Africans walked past, sitting down when they got to my gate. I finished my coffee and returned.

A Belgian woman was escorting the group. I caught her attention and asked about them. She explained that her organization escorted refugees from United Nations' refugee camps to Brussels. Then the refugees flew to different destinations, in this case the USA.

There were families with parents and little children. Some were dressed in nice clothes and others plainly. I assumed they all knew each other.

The children played, and the adults talked to each other. Everyone was waiting. One couple, however, seemed particularly quiet. They sat on the edge of the group. He wore a business suit with cleric's collar. She wore a yellow dress suit. They were seated across from me.

Curiosity got the better of me. *I wonder who they are?* I stood up and walked over to the man with the cleric's collar.

"Excuse me," I asked. "Do you speak English?"

"Yes," he answered.

"I was talking to the woman escorting your group. Do you mind if I talk to you?"

"No, not at all. Please sit down."

"I noticed your cleric's collar. Are you Catholic or Episcopalian?" I asked.

"No, I am a Baptist pastor. In Africa, Protestant ministers wear the collar also. My name is John Gonleh, and this is my wife, Bessie."

I sat talking to them for another minute, just small talk. Then I went back to my seat. Finally, we boarded the plane. I settled in for the long flight.

About two hours in, while I was reading a book, without warning, a voice popped into my head: "Bruce, you need to go help them."

My first reaction was a sustained "No-o-o" as I knew exactly who "them" was. Anxiety kicked into high gear and my heart started pounding. I succeeded in calming myself down some when I realized that the voice wasn't insistent or demanding. Somehow, I realized it was more of an offer. It was completely my choice. It was that still small voice of God offering to let me participate with him, but only if I wanted to.

My failure in the prison yard sprang fresh to my mind. I wasn't sure what "helping them" involved, but I sure didn't want to repeat my failure. *Besides,* I thought, *how many times can I say no to God and expect him to keep coming back giving me more chances?* After all, I was the one who wanted a deeper relationship. God was simply responding to the desire of my heart.

I struggled a good fifteen minutes before I finally mustered up enough courage. I unfastened my seat belt, grabbed my crutches, and stood up.

I turned and began to walk down the aisle. Another voice inside my head kept yelling, "Turn back. Turn back. Don't do it." But my feet continued forward. Trying to drown out the negative voice, I whispered to myself as I walked, "Well, here we go."

The book you now hold is a result of that long, slow walk toward John and Bessie—and toward a deeper relationship with God. I pray their story will bless you, inspire you, and motivate you, as it has me.

Bruce Beakley
December 2008

INTRODUCTION

L iberia is a small country on the West African coast. Its most notable feature is its distinction of being the point closest to the New World, the Americas. From that promontory point some five hundred years ago, Spanish slave ships first departed with their human cargo. Slaves toiled till death in the gold and silver mines and the sugar cane plantations of South and Latin America. Later slave labor worked the cotton and tobacco plantations of the United States.

Forty years before the American Civil War, freed slaves returned to Africa to start a new life. Liberia or the land of freedom was born.

The first settlers arrived back on that very promontory point from which their ancestors departed. They died by the droves from tropical diseases like malaria. Undaunted, more settlers arrived and took the place of the fallen. They created a permanent settlement that became known as Monrovia, after James Monroe, the American president.

Arriving ships brought American customs, dress, holidays, the English language, and most of all Christianity. Settlers from America dreamed that Liberia would be instrumental in reaching the entire African continent with the gospel.

By local standards the returning freed slaves and their descendents were rich. The new arrivals soon became the ruling elite over the indigenous tribes. Inequality from America was transported to Liberia. The rich immigrants took advantage of the poor locals. Armed clashes and battles ensued but the Americo-Liberians prevailed and created a democratic government and founded the country of Liberia in 1847.

For almost 140 years the Americo-Liberians maintained power over the indigenous tribes. Then a coup in 1980 brought Samuel Doe to power. He was the first Liberian president to come from an indigenous tribe. But he turned out to be a despot and dictator and used his power to persecute other tribes.

On December 24th, 1989, Charles Taylor, an Americo-Liberian, launched his civil war. The stage was set for a bloodbath.

#72 SOLDIERS' BARRACK

1

July 11, 1990

P utrid aromas from sweat, urine, blood, and infected sores mingled to rouse me from a fitful night. Moans and curses in the dimly-lit room let me know the others were awake.

"You should pray with me, because only God can save us now." I spoke softly but deliberately to the group of eleven men huddled into the cramped, muggy cell. So, as the early-morning sun peeked through the palm trees, I prayed one last time. Our captors had told us today was the final investigation.

"Father, here we are, committing ourselves into your hands. We have no one else but you. Save our lives from these wicked people. And let these men know you are God. In Jesus' name I pray. Amen."

I didn't actually lead the men in prayer. It was just that no one raised any objection. No one had any energy left for theological arguments. Mine was a prayer of unyielding stubbornness. After all God had done for me, I refused to give up on him, like the others.

Our cell was one of ten. Several weeks earlier these had been the living quarters for Liberian army soldiers. The rebels had turned them into a makeshift prison.

About a hundred men were being held in the ten cells. Some were wealthy—government officials or prominent businessmen. I had been assistant prayer leader with a volunteer group at the executive mansion chapel. That was my crime. I was a collaborator with the Liberian government of President Samuel Doe.

After the war began six months ago, I spent many mornings at the chapel with my group. We prayed for soldiers and government employees. Sometimes I delivered the message at the midday service. In the afternoons, I worked at my construction block business. I never saw President Doe.

Years before, I met President Doe once, though I doubt he would remember me. I wasn't one of his wealthy friends, his generals, or his political enemies. I was merely a volunteer Christian. Inconsequential.

I don't think the rebels expected to get much information from me. I was a collaborator and my wife was one-half Krahn. These crimes justified the beatings and torture. I could only hope justice would prevail during the final investigation today. Perhaps, afterward, I would finally be free from the terrible mistake that had brought me here.

We were being held in the #72 Soldiers' Barrack outside Paynesville, an upscale suburb on the outskirts of Monrovia, the capital city of Liberia. My house was close by. It was so near, and yet I struggled to remember details I'd never paid attention to before. I had carelessly placed my house and neighborhood in the background scenery. Now I longed to remember the color of the flowers Bessie planted in our yard. After a brief failed effort, I gave up.

My mind kept going over the events of the past week, the moment when the rebels came for me. I tried to logically process what had happened, but nothing fit together.

Where are you, God? Why are you allowing this to happen?

I alternated between faith and doubt.

Of course he was in control and could save me. But that didn't mean that I, Bessie, or the children would survive.

The rebels had entered Paynesville nine days ago. We heard automatic gunfire in nearby neighborhoods. Three weeks before, we had heard their long-range artillery shells hitting the city center. Everyone knew the rebels were coming, slowly but steadily advancing.

The first two days, we escaped the bullets coming straight down through our roof. Victorious over the government troops, the rebels celebrated by firing their weapons into the air. Bullets fell from the sky like tiny meteors. Our family was lucky. A neighbor's child three doors down was struck and wounded by one of these projectiles.

Bessie and I took the precaution of packing all our important papers into one of the children's book satchels. We included our marriage certificate, the children's birth certificates, school report cards, our deeds, and cash. That was all. There wasn't room for anything else.

Then, on the morning of the third day of the attack, I happened to be looking out my living room window when an army Jeep drove right onto our front lawn. Rebels started piling out.

Wide-eyed, I screamed, "Bessie, get the children and hide." A frantic commotion ensued for a few seconds. Small bodies ran past me as Bessie yelled her orders. In just seconds, it was quiet again. I stood alone, watching.

Four rebels stood on our lawn. Each carried an automatic rifle, a Kalashnikov. They fired their weapons into the sky. They looked crazed and terrifying.

The AK-47 was the favorite among revolutionaries. Firing up to thirty bullets per trigger pull, and outfitted with a wicked-looking and effective bayonet, it was simple and cheap. At only twenty dollars each, it was light enough for a small child to handle.

A month earlier, I had nearly been killed by an AK-47.

I had taken a taxi to the open market to purchase a hundred-pound bag of rice. Food had gotten scarce as the rebel offensive drew near the city, so the rice cost triple its normal price. I placed the heavy bag of rice in a little wagon and turned to pay the merchant. When I turned back, I saw a man walking away, pulling the wagon and taking my rice. I yelled for him to stop and ran toward him. He abruptly halted and slowly turned around.

His face was streaked with white clay, his long hair matted in clumps, and his clothes were filthy. A rebel! Fear suddenly gripped me. Bessie and I had heard from neighbors that rebel excursions into the city were becoming common as their army approached. He had come to the market to get food by any means he could.

He was big, almost a foot taller than I and heavier by thirty pounds. His AK-47 was slung over his right shoulder. Ignoring my fear, I ran up to him and told him the rice belonged to me—as though he didn't already know. He didn't speak but calmly reached into his flak-jacket pocket with his right hand and started to unsling his rifle with his left.

Blinking and dumbfounded, I realized the bullet clip wasn't in the rifle, and he was retrieving it. I didn't know what to do. Should I run? Try to reason with him?

Just then, the clip snapped into the rifle.

Inside my head I heard, *Are you just going to stand there and let him kill you?* Startled by the unexpected voice, I snapped out of my stupor. I mouthed, "Help me, Lord!" Before I knew it, I had grabbed hold of the rifle with both hands.

Now, the rebel was the startled one. We both gripped the gun tightly. We wrestled back and forth, each trying to gain control without success. As large as he was, he couldn't shake me or twist the gun free. After a few moments, a Monrovia policeman saw our struggle and rushed in. He yelled for the crowd of gaping merchants and customers to grab us and pull us apart.

Once we were apart, the policeman quickly ascertained the situation. He yelled at me, "Get your rice and go. Just go!" The merchants released me on his command. I ran, snatched my bag of rice out of the wagon, jumped in a taxi, and sped off. All the way home I trembled.

Whereas that incident had been a chance encounter, the rebels on my front lawn now were not there by accident. After shooting their guns into the sky, they walked across my yard toward the front door. I saw bandoliers of ammunition draped over their shoulders and around their waists.

I've never owned a gun and never handled one other than in the market. I did know, however, those weapons in the hands of the teenagers standing in my front yard had defeated Liberia's national army. The sight of the rebels paralyzed me with fear.

At least when I first saw them, I had the presence of mind to yell to Bessie to get in the back bedroom with the kids.

"Thank you, Lord, for letting me see them," I prayed.

I breathed in deeply and slowly exhaled, trying to control my emotions and thinking of what else I could do.

"Nothing. There is nothing I can do," I told myself.

So, alone in my living room, I sat down in my favorite comfortable armchair. I waited. I watched the rebels through the large front window as they walked toward the door. One wore a uniform. His face and arms were streaked with white clay. I recognized the clay as Juju, witchcraft, designed to make its wearer impervious to bullets. Another wore a crimson church choir robe with an ammunition belt cinched around his waist.

What an odd spoil of war, I thought, *looting a choir robe.*

Choirboy's hair was wild, almost like spikes coming out of his head. It wasn't clear if this was his hairstyle or just happenstance from living months in the bush. Strange, the details we notice in a crisis.

With each step the rebels took toward my house, I grew more frightened. I couldn't move, still paralyzed by fear. At that moment, it wasn't an expression or figure of speech. I was truly paralyzed. My muscles were so constricted, it seemed as if each possessed its own little mind and instinctively knew what to do in a moment such as this. I was a fawn hiding in the Liberian savannah grass and being stalked by a leopard.

There was no chance of escaping. All I felt was stark terror, not breathing, everything shutting down. I couldn't even form a prayer. "Jesus, Jesus, Jesus," was all I whispered. Did those words reach my lips or were they just in my mind? I couldn't tell.

The rebels were at the front door. Suddenly one called out, "Come out and bring your Krahn wife. Bring out the bank money and tell us where President Doe is. Otherwise, we're going to kill you and burn your house down."

I didn't move or speak. I couldn't. I was paralyzed. The rebels didn't ask twice. With a swift boot to the front door, the door jamb splintered and the door swung open. With bloodshot eyes from drugs or sleep deprivation, their eyes locked on mine as they approached. Oddly, my eyes apparently were the only part of my body not frozen. As time slowed down, they followed each movement as the two converged on the helpless creature staring back at them.

It was as if my body floated. I was weightless. They jerked me hard up and out of the armchair. The force must have torn my shirt because I heard a rip. I felt my feet bouncing across the floor, through the front door, across the porch, and down the steps.

My short weightless journey abruptly ended. Once in the front yard, they dropped me. I tried to use my arms to break the fall, but they wouldn't respond. I remembered the saying about dropping something like a sack of rice. Now I knew what that meant.

I fell face forward straight down onto my chest and tasted grass as my head bounced. My eyes saw the bottom half of a small figure approaching. The two larger rebels who dragged me were walking away. The approaching figure had small skinny legs and mismatched oversized boots.

I guessed the child to be about twelve years old. As I started to lift my head, out of the corner of my eye, I saw a sudden blur. The concussion from the butt end of the assault rifle snapped my head back to the ground. My right temple started to throb.

Taking aim a second time, the child struck once more with the ease of someone possessing supreme confidence in his ability to perform this most basic of warfare skills: *Stand over your subject. Hold the barrel in the left hand near the muzzle, the right hand holding the stock just above the trigger guard. Now while keeping a firm grip, arc downward like you're planting a flagpole in the ground, you should hear a good solid crack as you make contact. That's correct. Now try it again.*

At once, their leader demanded again, "Where is your Krahn wife? Where is the bank money? Tell us where President Doe is."

Jarred to my senses, my head now reeling and throbbing from pain, but shocked out of my frozen, paralyzing fear, I once again was able to think.

"I . . . I'm alone in the house. We have no bank money. It stays at the bank. I don't have anything to do with President Doe. I have no idea where he is." The pain loosened my frozen arms and they now hurried to protect my head, but the damage had already been done.

These particular rebels were so ignorant they thought Bessie, a bank teller, brought the bank's money home at night and took it back the next day. While they certainly needed it, they weren't asking for a lesson on the Liberian banking system. They just wanted the money.

I blurted out these answers as fast as I could. If I thought immediate compliance to their demands would preserve me from another head blow, I was wrong. The efficient and skillful assistant found an open spot and replicated his technique. Once a skill is perfected, it is only a natural human tendency to want to show off to your superiors. The child was rewarded by their grinning approval. Rising weightless once more, I was dragged to the jeep and thrown in the back.

The teenage leader was the passenger, of course, as was befitting his rank. He should naturally be chauffeured during these roundup excursions. In the back with me were the skillful assistant and the cherub choirboy. They had successfully bagged their prey, and now it was time to take it home, victorious once more.

Knots were already forming, slowly rising off my skull, and I felt blood trickle down one cheek. The warm liquid mingled in my mouth with dirt and the grass I'd planted when we first built our house. Silently through the pain, I breathed a sigh of relief. As odd as it seems, I also shared in their victory.

Driving away from the house, my prayer and those of Bessie and the children were answered. The rebel soldiers forgot all about searching the house. Bessie and the kids weren't discovered. They certainly would have been found if the search had taken place. In a closet and under the bed aren't exactly unique hiding places. My basic house just wasn't constructed for such a clandestine purpose. It was such a simple mistake really and yet one that would affect everything to follow.

"Thank you, Jesus. Thank you, Lord," I silently prayed as we drove away. I glanced up and noticed the sky. The sun was just starting its climb. It would be another typical summer day in Liberia, hot and humid.

BESSIE'S ESCAPE 2

BESSIE

As soon as we heard the gunfire coming from the front yard, John yelled for the children and me to hide. We all moved like lightning. Huddled in our back bedroom, we made no sound, fearful of giving our position away to the rebels.

There was no crying, whimpering, or freezing in place as might normally be expected. It was as if, for the past six months, the children had been preparing for this very hour. Just as the children had sung in church choir programs, this was now their survival recital. Each child knew the danger by heart.

Having to evacuate the house earlier to avoid the death squads had been practice. Hearing the distant explosions drawing closer day by day had been preparation. Bullets dropping from the sky and landing close by had been the dress rehearsal. And now the biggest performance of their lives, *for* their lives, was upon us.

Rather than involving singing or recitation of memorized lines, this performance demanded the determined concentration to remain completely, totally, and deafeningly silent. All the children had to gain control over their emotions and fear. Even Chester and Comfort, though only four years old, knew what to do. A single cry, whimper, or bump would bring the rebels right into the room.

As frightened as the children and I were by the gunfire earlier and the yelling coming from our own living room, we didn't make a sound. The older children, Gloria and the twins, Annie and Kou, hid in the small closet. Only the youngest children, Monica, Comfort, and Chester, were able to fit under the low bed. I laid down flat behind the bed and away from the door. If anyone opened the door, I hoped they wouldn't see me.

We had been so fortunate. Our four-bedroom house in Paynesville was in one of the nicest suburbs in the city, boasting beautiful houses, water mains, electricity, and a sanitary sewer. There was no storm sewer, but the road had ditches on both sides for the rainy season.

We had only one window air conditioner in the master bedroom. The children liked to spend most of their free time there, drawing, coloring, or playing games under the cool air.

Lying behind the bed in the back bedroom, so still and deathly quiet, I could hear only my own breath and the faint sound of breathing from underneath the bed. With each moment that passed I expected the door to burst open, revealing the terrifying wild rebels. I kept praying.

I couldn't bear the thought of what would happen to my girls should our hiding place be discovered. I kept drowning out negative, hopeless thoughts with words of prayer to Jesus.

For a few minutes my children and I lay motionless in the hot and still, quietly waiting and listening. Then as quickly as the episode began, we heard the Jeep drive away. We waited another minute or two and then emerged from our hiding spots.

Logic told me the rebels were gone, but I slowly opened the door, half expecting one to jump out at me. As we made our way up the hall and into the living room, it was obvious what had happened. The front door was broken and standing open. My husband was gone.

Instantly, my mind went numb. Sixteen-year-old Gloria asked several times before she got my attention, "Mama, what are we going to do now?" The only thing I could hear in my head was a voice saying, "You have to leave." I didn't know if it was my own thoughts or something else, but I heard it several times.

The rebels had just left, and we probably had some time to think things over. I had to think. Otherwise, I wouldn't gather and take what we needed. Still the voice nagged in my head again. "You have to leave now." It just kept repeating itself. Suddenly I decided to listen. We had to get away. Maybe the rebels would come back. Maybe they would steal our things or burn the house down.

Quickly, I went to retrieve the satchel in which we had previously collected our important papers. As I gathered up the children, one asked about taking some food, clothing, or water, but I said no. We had to leave.

We would just have to try to buy what we needed with our money along the road. I talked as if I had a plan of where to go and what to do, but I didn't. I was completely confused, and the children were scared and traumatized. I loaded little Chester on my back, took Comfort by the hand, and we all quickly exited out the back door.

Once out the back door, we ran toward a big field of tall grass and didn't stop until we were safely camouflaged, shielded from anyone watching. It was still early in the morning, and at first we walked slowly. I had no destination in mind, but then I remembered we could go to the Kabas, our good friends and neighbors.

We had only been underway for a few minutes, so I'm not sure what prompted me to stop, turn around, and look back at our house. Perhaps it was a sound or a premonition, given the persistent repetition of the voice telling me to leave. When I looked back and saw my house, I noticed a plume of rising smoke. Before long I saw the flames.

The rebels had come back! Just like that, our worldly possessions were gone, lost to looting, and then torched and reduced to ashes. At that moment I realized whose voice I had heard in my head. It was the Lord's.

We made our way to the Kabas' carefully avoiding the road whenever possible. Walking through the tall grass, I led our little troop very slowly so that any snakes could have plenty of time to hear our movement and grant us wide berth.

As we neared the Kabas' house, I saw smoke rising all over Paynesville. It was clear the rebels swarmed all over Paynesville this morning, devouring everything like a plague of locusts.

We reached the Kabas' house and, thank God, they were home. They quickly gathered us inside. I told our story and how John was taken away. Still peering out their windows, they told us how earlier, they had seen rebels arrive at a house down the street, pull everything outside, take what they wanted, and then burn the house down. The inhabitants were either taken away or killed on the spot.

Corpses were already starting to litter the once-clean streets of Paynesville.

We stayed with Fatta Kaba and her family all day. Throughout the morning, bullets rained from the sky. Later in the afternoon the rebels left our suburb for the evening, and the shooting subsided. People streamed out from their homes. Most had large bundles on their heads and were leaving while they could.

I left the children eating dinner while I went outside and talked with the neighbors. It seemed everyone was evacuating. I determined that we should leave too. The Kabas wanted to wait a while longer before making their final decision.

They hadn't been targeted, so maybe they would be safe. With our house burned down and my husband taken away, there was no reason to stay. We carried nothing except the clothes we wore and my little satchel with the important papers and money. Seeing all the neighbors with their bundles and possessions made me wish that we too had supplies from home.

At six that evening we left the house of Fatta Kaba and her family. They had been so kind to us. With tears and prayers we said our good-byes. We didn't know if we would ever see each other again.

In the gathering dusk my six children and I started walking. I fought to blink tears from my eyes as we proceeded toward an unknown destination and into an unknown future. With a heavy heart

I pled, "Dear Lord God, have mercy on us," and continued leading our small procession down the road.

After a short distance we left the road, cut back across an open field, and waded into a sea of swaying tall dark grass. Risking encounters with snakes or other night creatures seemed safer than encounters with rebels. They were gone for now but would likely still be driving around Paynesville, celebrating.

We walked parallel to the road leading away from Paynesville toward Liberia's interior for about an hour. From a distance, through the grass in the gathering twilight, I saw other refugees traveling in the same direction. They were on the road leading toward the University of Liberia, Fendall Campus, about fifteen or twenty miles away.

Not knowing where else to go, we followed our neighbors. Walking that first evening among the fields, I was fearful and wanted to keep as far away from the rebels as possible. In the dim light I could see them, driving their Jeeps and shooting their guns into the sky. The only cars or trucks on the road belonged to rebels. No civilian dared drive his car. It would surely be hijacked and the inhabitants killed. Everyone fleeing the war walked.

John and I had feared this day was approaching, but we hadn't prepared or planned other than packing our satchel. We had no basis or previous experience that could tell us what would happen or what we should do.

For several weeks I had seen rebel spies coming into the bank. We always recognized the rebels. Some wore ill-fitting children's school uniforms or choir robes, and some even wore women's dresses. They had long beards, raggedy corn-rows, and wore women's wigs. It shocked all the bank employees that they would enter the lobby dressed that way. They walked in and looked around, sometimes asking questions, as though they were from another planet. In their bizarre clothing and the bank employees wearing business suits and dresses, the contrast couldn't have been more striking.

Of course, they weren't really spies. Spies at least are supposed to blend in, but these boys stuck out. I couldn't help but stare at them; that is, until they stared back at me. They carried themselves with a swagger of fearlessness and arrogance. It was as if they sensed their impending victory and wanted to inventory the spoils of war. Even though we knew they were rebels, no one did anything. Government soldiers were nowhere to be found, and the police had ceased all of their patrolling. There was no one we could call.

Inside the bank, they just stared at the tellers, managers, and loan officers. They studied us, committing our faces to memory. Each employee was examined and mentally cataloged before they switched their gaze to someone else. We all knew exactly who they were, and they didn't care. A rebel visit had a chilling effect on everyone's disposition.

Around the city, I noticed new graffiti on the sides of buildings and houses. But it wasn't graffiti at all. It was a claim, a mark of ownership. The rebel soldiers were window shopping.

Now with the children behind me, I peered at the ground through the tall grass, hoping to see a snake before I stepped on it. Stopping for a moment, I looked up to make sure I could see the parallel road off to our right a few hundred yards. Yes, it was still there. The moon was just starting to rise.

John was gone. I had no idea if he was dead or alive. Six children were depending on me to take care of them. I was alone and so afraid. In the dark, in a field of snakes, bitten by mosquitoes, trying to avoid poisonous centipedes, I started to weep. Continuing to walk, I couldn't let the children see me. As tears blurred my sight, I prayed over and over for mercy, for protection, for my children, and for my poor lost husband.

Eventually our trail converged with the road. Now we were part of a large slow-moving parade. Some people had push carts stacked high with boxes and bags and mats. Most carried small bundles under their arms and large bundles on their heads. There was an assortment of animals. I wondered if the exodus out of Egypt looked like this. We had nothing. We joined them.

I was glad to get out of the field. It felt much better to be walking on a real road and safe from the snakes and bugs. The moon rose higher and higher. Then we came to the small village. Immediately I went to the largest hut I saw, owned by the village chief, to ask for a place to spend the night. Praise God he was kind. He offered to let us stay in a small hut located next to his house.

The parade spread out over the entire small village. People continued arriving throughout the night. I was so thankful we had a place to sleep with a roof over our heads. The alternative was outside on the dirt. Inside the little hut, we collapsed, exhausted. Despite sore feet, hunger, thirst, and fear, sleep came as a blessed relief, even if only for a few hours.

Rising the next morning, we thanked the man, blessed him for his kindness, and left right away—though I had no idea where we were going. My only thought was to get as far away from the city and the rebels as possible.

We had nothing to eat and had to find something. We soon came upon farmers and villagers who had laid out little blankets on the side of the road from which they sold bananas, oranges, and even peanuts and sugar cane. My starving children and I devoured everything. Fruit had never tasted so good. While grateful to the enterprising entrepreneurs, I thought how odd that even during war and death, business continues as usual.

Back on the move again, it seemed that just as we made some progress, the procession of refugees came to an abrupt halt. Blocking our way was a checkpoint, an improvised barrier set up across the road by the rebels. We joined in a line of a hundred people. They told us the soldiers were only checking identification cards. It was much more than that.

At the first checkpoint, a soldier shouted at me, "Hey, you, come here." I froze. Just then, the man next to me brushed my shoulder as he obeyed the order. I let out a sigh of relief and kept my eyes down. From the corner of my eye, I watched the man as he was led off into the bush. The line shuffled forward.

A couple minutes later, several shots pierced the morning quiet. A bird flew up from the trees where the man and soldier had gone.

Suddenly, everyone was terrified. The children immediately forgot about their sore feet. At our turn, the soldiers glanced at me and waved us through. We weren't scrutinized at all. "Thank you, Jesus. Thank you, Jesus," I mouthed as I hurried the children in front of me. We walked quickly, and I dared not look back.

Midday came. The large crowd slowly moved away from Paynesville and danger. Because of the sheer number of refugees, we walked close together. Right next to me was a woman along with her husband and several children. We briefly glanced at and acknowledged each other. Neither of us spoke. It wasn't like we were taking a Sunday afternoon stroll in the park. We walked side by side for some distance. Suddenly, the woman abruptly stopped. Startled, I stopped also, turning to look at her. Her face registered a shocked look of surprise. The expression never changed as, if by slow motion, she fell face forward and hit the ground squarely. I couldn't believe my eyes. *Why did she do that?* I wondered. I stared down at her.

Her stunned family rushed around her and turned her over. She had taken the bullet directly into her chest. A spreading pool of blood formed on the ground beneath her. She gasped for air but only produced a gurgling sound as blood filled her lungs. Her eyes, unblinking and staring straight up into the sun, still recorded disbelief.

No one had heard the gunfire. Behind us, the crowd surged ahead like a powerful current, barely parting for the dying woman and her grief-stricken family. Without resisting, the children and I were swept forward. We didn't dare stop. My arms started shaking, then my legs. My breathing became shallow. Wails of pain and anguish reached my ears and followed us down the road.

She was right next to me. Just a little more to the left and I would have taken the bullet instead of that poor woman.

I was so scared, I couldn't think. In my mind, I kept seeing her clothes turning red and the look of surprise on her face. The children seemed to be in shock or confused. They just kept walking close to me, silent and grim.

How long will God continue to protect us? That woman could have been me. That could have been my blood soaking into the road. Then who would take care of the children? God didn't protect her. Why?

All day long we passed through multiple rebel checkpoints. At each gate, several people were pulled out of line and led away. Whether the rebels recognized them or just didn't like their looks, I don't know. I prayed we would be invisible to their stares and scrutiny. I never made eye contact and instructed the children to do the same. I was sure one of the boys would recognize me from the bank, but they never did. At each checkpoint we passed through easily.

Rebels were interested in people with possessions. Possessions meant money. Possessions meant you were "shining," as in having money. Most people carried on their heads or backs as many of their possessions as they could lift. For some refugees, to be "shining" was their death sentence. The rebels hated anyone who had more than they did.

The children and I looked destitute. We carried nothing except for the one small satchel, even though inside it was fifteen hundred Liberian dollars, about one hundred dollars US. Even our clothes were old. Because we left the house so quickly, the children had thrown on the first play clothes they could find. I wore an old blouse and pants. On my way out the door, I had snatched up an old *lapa*, the traditional African wrap garment, to help me carry Chester or Comfort. I had my hair tied up, rather than styled as I normally wore it. I was wearing old house slippers. Sneakers would have been more comfortable had I thought of them, but I was confused, scared, and not thinking clearly when we left. None of this was intentional. These were simply the first things we could lay our hands on. We looked poor.

It occurred to me that our rapid escape from our house was now working in our favor. We were as ragged as anyone could be. The logic was completely counter to my way of thinking. No one leaves their home with nothing. And yet that was what saved us. Possessions meant death. Slowly it dawned on me that God really was looking out for us, protecting us.

We passed five or six checkpoints set up by different factions of rebels. There seemed to be no overall command or structure. Different rebel groups put up their own checkpoints as money-making ventures. All women's purses were searched if the soldiers thought they might contain money. With a sharp command of "Bring your bag and open it; we want to check what's inside for security reasons," the rebel would take whatever money he found during his search.

Rebels wanted more than just money. Young teenage girls were taken as sex slaves. At one checkpoint, a rebel commander pointed at a girl, about fourteen, waiting with her parents and siblings. He said, "Bring that girl over here." One of his soldiers went and grabbed her by the arm. Her shocked parents asked why they were taking her. The commander answered casually, "I need a wife. She is going to cook for me."

At once, the girl started crying and resisting as the soldier dragged her away. Then the mother started screaming. It was horrible and heart-wrenching. They protested, but the soldiers shoved the parents forward with their guns.

"Let's go. Let's go," they commanded, brandishing their weapons to show they were serious. The parents couldn't say anything else or they would have been killed. We heard the girl's screams slowly fade as we continued on the road.

Gloria was beautiful. I prayed over and over that they wouldn't notice her. I couldn't have left her and probably would have gotten all of us killed. But I knew I would never leave her in the hands of these barbarians. Death for all of us was preferable.

At each checkpoint it was if the rebels didn't even notice Gloria at my side. She seemed invisible. The rebels inspected everyone. But they never once spoke to her or looked closely at her, even though she carried the satchel. I carried Chester or Comfort on my back and used my arms to keep the other children close to me. The soldiers asked for my name but never asked for my ID card, which was inside the bag. Sometimes they would look at me up and down and then pass me through. Other times they would ask my name to see how I spoke and what my accent was. They asked me where I came from and which part of Monrovia I lived in. I always answered truthfully, telling them Paynesville, even though it was one of the richest suburbs of Monrovia. I'm sure the rebels knew this fact. But I didn't look like a rich woman.

Still, I felt so conspicuous. I just knew some of these rebels had been in my bank. For whatever reason, we passed through all the checkpoints without problem. To them, I was just a poor woman with six poor children.

After each checkpoint, I prayed and thanked God. But every time we approached another one, my fear returned anew. It seemed my little faith constantly melted away under the hot Liberian sunshine.

Late afternoon came. We were exhausted with fatigue and stress. The children's feet were swollen. We had to find a place to stop. We asked other refugees if there was a village near. They said we were approaching Wako, a small farming village.

As we walked, I thought of the woman who was shot. It seemed long ago. My thoughts were interrupted as the flickering campfires from Wako Village came into view.

TORTURE 3

As the rebels' jeep carried me through my normally tidy, well-kept neighborhood, I was startled to see bodies strewn along the roadside like trash. I suddenly remembered our weekly garbage pickup was today. Seeing the corpses, I concluded there would be no more trash pickup in Paynesville.

Continuing farther, I saw more bodies in the fields. There were so many. They were naked and bloated and lying next to each other. In some places they had been organized, as if they were sleeping side by side in rows. I didn't look to see if they were men or women. All I focused on were their distended bellies and limbs swollen by decomposition gases. They looked like deformed or disfigured manikins, stiff and plastic. Each body had once been a person, a living soul. But now these people were litter. Something for someone to clean up whenever they got around to it.

How did it come to this? I thought. From my schooling, I knew that Liberia was founded by freed American slaves bringing freedom, democracy, and Christianity to Africa in 1822. I had also learned about the subsequent fighting and inequality between the newly-arrived immigrants and the indigenous tribes.

But that was long ago, and nowadays everyone mixed together. I was from the Mano tribe and Bessie was Krahn. We didn't care. Until recently, most people never noticed differences like distinctive last names, telling accents, or facial features.

In Monrovia everyone spoke English; tribal languages were slowly dying out, now spoken only in the bush villages, where technology and modern conveniences were unknown. Life in the villages remained unchanged. That's why my father and other parents sent their children to boarding schools in Monrovia. These parents foresaw opportunities a modern Liberia could offer.

In the village, tightly-held superstitions, grudges, and prejudices persisted as they had for hundreds of years. Witchcraft flourished, preying on the people's superstitions, ignorance, and fear. Juju charms, fetishes, potions, spells, and secret societies abounded. Of course, this is where most of the rebels originated: the bush.

The ironic thing was most of the rebel recruits came from my own tribe, the Mano, from Nimba County. They were the ignorant, the unschooled, the shoeshine boys. They possessed no job skills.

Charles Taylor, the conqueror, was these rebels' hero. Though he himself was a child of privilege, he convinced these "have-nots" he was one of them. He assembled his rebel army, trained them in neighboring Ivory Coast, and then crossed the border and started the civil war.

Mr. Taylor offered these teenagers uniforms, guns, drugs, power. Everything was for the taking if the revolution was successful. It was a chance to finally get rich. So out of the bush they joined up with the rebels, ignoring their parents. Their comrades in arms became their new families.

Charles Taylor was Liberia's Pied Piper, leading the children away from home. Instead of a magical flute, he held a magical Kalashnikov. Children, both boys and girls—as young as seven—were given guns with little instruction. They fell into ranks and marched along with their peers.

And just like the story of the Pied Piper, most of these children would never go home again. Initially, the fighting was fierce against the government troops. The children playing soldiers were slaughtered. The youngest ones had little training. They were too small to understand the officers' instructions and became cannon fodder.

In the beginning, these children were sad, uncounted victims. Abandoned from Monrovia to Nimba County, they were a pathetic lot with maimed or amputated limbs, wretched little creatures no one cared about. They had nothing to show for their grand adventure with the Pied Piper of Liberia. Like the corpses I saw littering the roadside, these children were also discarded garbage. They just happened to still be alive.

Surprisingly, however, as the war progressed, surviving child-warriors developed into first-class soldiers. They rapidly gained experience in battle after battle and became excellent fighters. Confusing play with war, they were fearless and took incredible risks during pitched firefights. Furthermore, lacking the socialization provided by their parents, they made up their own rules of warfare. These youngsters were intensely loyal to their own units. They were unpredictable, ruthless, and would commit unspeakable atrocities at the slightest provocation.

■■■■

The jeep arrived at the #72 Soldiers' Barracks, once a government army barrack and now a rebel prison. I was dragged out and once again sprawled facedown on the dirt. Ordered to get up, I slowly complied.

After I struggled to my feet, I was ordered into the barrack. One guard walked in front of me and another behind. They were taking no chances with this dangerous 130-pound, five-foot-five-inch Christian.

I was led into the barrack, which held a series of locked rooms. The first guard stopped at one, unlocked the door, and motioned with his rifle for me to go inside. At half capacity, it held five other men. I looked at them and they at me. No words passed. I sat down and began to pray.

In the afternoon, an ordeal commenced that would not end until seven days later with the final investigation. Prisoners were called by name and the cell door swung open. Each prisoner was led back outside to stand before a long table. Seated behind the table were rebel officers.

When it was my turn, as I saw their shocking appearance, I drew in a sharp breath. They didn't dress in the color-coordinated sharp uniforms of President Doe's army. Each rebel seemed to be from a different army. The only thing they had in common was a frightening display of arms and ammunition.

Bandoliers of bullets crisscrossed their chests, they wore another ammo belt around their waists, grenades hung from their belts, and sheathed knives hung in the small amount of real estate remaining. Some wore what I recognized as Juju fetishes around their necks or waists. Some faces were streaked with white clay, a charm they believed would stop bullets. One man donned an officer's cap, while two teenagers wore makeshift headbands. Six soldiers sat behind the large table. The one with the hat ordered me to sit down in the chair opposite them.

I felt myself start to shake and immediately mouthed a prayer in an attempt to regain my composure.

Like the hymns we sang in church, the questioning started slowly. Then as the melody came into full force with voices lifted heavenward, so it was with the rising crescendo of questions. First one question was asked and answered. Then a second. As I tried to answer the second question, a third was fired off from another inquisitor. As I shifted to the third, I received a fourth from yet another. Soon, I became confused.

"You're lying. You're lying. You must tell us the truth. We know you have the bank's money hidden in your house. Tell us where it is. Tell us the truth right now," the commander shouted.

I wasn't sure how long this went on. Time quickly became a disposable commodity. It meant nothing. They would take whatever time they needed to accomplish their will.

At one point, I tried to respond to a question I'd already answered several times. One of the interrogators got up and walked around the table, smirking as he approached me. He withdrew his sidearm, an automatic pistol. He held the gun close to my head, allowing me to feel the cold steel brush against the side of my face as if it were the caress of a lover's hand. In the next moment, an explosion of gunfire reverberated in my head. The shock of the pressure-wave concussion entered my ears and seemed to exit directly through my skull.

I stared across the table as the five remaining interrogators broke into smiles and started laughing. I couldn't actually hear them. All I could hear was loud ringing. My senses had shut down in an effort to undo the damage still vibrating through my body.

That last bit of fun apparently signaled the end of this phase of my interrogation. I was jerked up by my arm out of the chair and walked over to another area outside the barracks. Other prisoners were already there, about ten in all. Construction blocks, the kind my company made and used for buildings, lay about on the ground. I was told to pick one up, stand next to another prisoner, and with both arms lift the brick up high over my head. The brick weighed about fifteen pounds. I did as I was told.

Time passed. My arms ached. Sweat poured down my face. I kept my eyes closed against the sun and prayed. Suddenly, one of the ten screamed. Accompanying his screams was the whirring sound of an air disturbance created by a high-pitched vibration. Each whirring ended with a loud slap, followed by the scream. It all happened so fast that I snapped my head around to find the origin of the odd noise. It was a rubber water hose. That was the whip that caused the screams. I began to shake uncontrollably.

Again and again I heard the whirring, the slap, the screams. The prisoner struggled to push his brick higher into the air as if offering it to a vengeful god: *Please take it; take this offering and be placated.* But no, the vengeful god of the rebels was not to be placated. He was never satiated or satisfied. Their god took only the free-flowing blood of humans as an acceptable sacrifice. I felt myself suddenly growing weak. It seemed all my blood wanted to get out of my body to find some safer place.

Despite the aching in my arms, my fellow prisoner's screaming provided fresh motivation for me to push my block higher. I didn't dare risk another look in the direction of the prisoner. There were no screams now, just muffled crying as he lay broken on the ground.

Time passed slowly or quickly in the hot sun. I couldn't tell. My arms began to pound and ache and shake, and finally I could no longer hold up the brick. It was inevitable. This was precisely the point. I heard the whirring first and then the sound of a slap. Oddly, I felt nothing.

Once, I cut my finger in an accident with a knife. It was deep. I looked down at the wound but felt nothing. It was like my body couldn't believe or comprehend what had just happened and there-fore would not react to it. But after about twenty seconds, my body understood. And now, just like with the cut on my hand, my body once again became a believer.

My shirt had been partially ripped when I was taken at my house, exposing my skin. Let neither shirt nor clothes of any kind impede worship to this god of blood. The pain seared through my body as the hot iron branded me with ownership. "Jesus, O Jesus, help me," I cried as my knees started to buckle. I heard the whirring again, then the slap, and once more the whirring.

In that moment, a last thought entered my mind. The god of this world branded Jesus in an attempt to own him once and for all.

"Jesus, don't let—"

Then a fog enveloped me, transporting me to a place where I couldn't be seen or found, not a place of rest exactly, but a place of suspension. My only focus was my pain. I was neither here nor there, neither now nor then. The rest of the afternoon became a whirring blur.

WAKO VILLAGE 4

BESSIE We turned off the main road like we'd been told. A few hundred feet later, we came to the village. Smoke from cooking fires whetted our appetites and boosted our spirits. There was no guarantee we would have anything to eat or even a place to sleep. We weren't thinking about those things. We had reached our destination. Our pace quickened.

Walking into the village I paused. "God, help us. Direct us where you will," I prayed.

Then I asked directions to the house of the village chief. Wako, I noticed, was larger than where we had spent last night. We slowly made our way past the throngs of villagers and refugees, past campfires and the wonderful smells of greens and palm oil boiling in large cauldrons.

I called out a greeting. An elderly man came out of the small hut, followed by his wife. It was the village chief. I asked him if he knew of a place where my children and I could stay for the night. Before he answered, I blurted out what had happened to us and to John and that God had saved us several times getting us to this point.

The stress was all bottled up inside me. I had to tell someone what happened, even a stranger. Then he told me he and his wife were also Christians.

Tears appeared, filling my eyes. He offered his own living room for us to sleep in. We could stay as long as we liked. I was overwhelmed. It was more than we could have hoped for.

"Thank you! Thank you! God bless you. You don't know what this means. We had nowhere to go. Nowhere to turn. We didn't know who would help us. God bless you, sir," I said as I continued to weep.

His wife gathered up the children like a mother hen with her chicks and took them inside. She laid out extra mats, no longer needed as their own children were grown and moved away.

I bought some rice and oil and greens and cooked everything in borrowed pots. That night the children slept well. One crisis had passed. We were safe. God had seen us through. He provided brief refuge here in this small room from the tempest outside.

It's been two days since John was taken. What is he going through? Is he even still alive? Is God protecting him like he has us? Or will he—? I stopped the thought. I drifted off to sleep with prayers still on my lips.

The next morning I rose early while the children slept. I recounted in detail to the chief and his wife everything that had happened. They reaffirmed their offer to let us stay in their house. Because of their kindness, we avoided—at least for a time—further checkpoint horrors and stray bullets. I was so relieved and thankful.

The layout of the village was typical of Graie, in Nimba County, where I grew up and lived until age twelve. A medium-sized village, Wako had about a hundred huts. The village where we had stayed the previous evening had only about thirty huts. I don't even know if it had a name.

Most of the huts had one round room and were made with sticks for walls. Mud was then packed between the sticks to seal out the rain. The mud was almost as hard as concrete and impervious to rain. The roof was constructed of overlapping palm thatches. The palm branches overhung the walls to form eaves to channel rain water off the walls.

Huts with only one room were about ten feet in diameter. All the huts had dirt floors with sleeping mats arranged around the edges against the walls. In the center was the cooking fire. The smoke rose straight upward, due to the slight draft created by the slope of the palm thatches, and exited out of the hut. Each hut had a front door and back door made of woven palm leaves with a stick frame. The houses weren't very sturdy but had sufficed for thousands of years as the typical Liberian house.

There was a large *palava* hut, where the men and women held community meetings. I located the village latrine.

There were several larger houses with two or three rooms, including the house where we were staying. The largest houses reminded me of my childhood home. My parents had a three-room hut before we moved to Monrovia. My father even built our own private outhouse latrine.

In Wako, water was drawn from a well or the nearby river. There was no electricity, which didn't matter anyway. Monrovia's only power plant had shut down weeks before. Kerosene lamps or candles were the norm for lighting. Charcoal was preferable for cooking, but since the war began, I was told, charcoal was scarce and everyone collected wood from the bush.

Observing the village, I was thankful John and I lived in a modern house with all the modern conveniences. Then I remembered our house was gone, along with all of our worldly possessions. A wave of sadness swept over me. Not only was my house gone, I had no husband either.

Tears tried to reassert themselves. I fought them back. I had to keep negative thoughts away for the time being. God had protected the kids and me this far. I would just have to keep trusting him. Six little ones depended on me. There was work to do. I returned to the chief's hut.

After getting the children up and fed, I organized our activities. In the afternoon, I took Gloria and one or two of the others to forage for food. Thankfully, the Liberian bush has remains of old farms all over the countryside where a scavenger might find growing foods.

We saw other refugees foraging in the bush just like we were. I instructed the girls to look for little palm-like branches. Each branch would have twelve leaves, four to six inches long and fanning out from the middle and looking like the tips of spears. Eventually we found enough cassava roots and wild yams to make several meals. Cassava is a cultivated crop, but during the summer rainy season, we could find only wild roots. It was too early for the farm-grown cassava.

We returned with enough food in the late afternoon for our family as well as the chief's family. We were overjoyed to discover the chief's wife had prepared our dinner. I offered a prayer of thanksgiving. We were all ravenous.

After dinner, I offered to lead us in evening prayers. As John and I had grown in devotion to the Lord, we started to have evening prayers and a morning devotional. We had practiced these for the last three years. The chief and his wife were not strong Christians, didn't pray much, and had never studied the Bible. But they owned a Bible and were happy to allow me to lead them. So for the next several days that is what I did.

The children quickly fell into their new routines. I organized chores for the older children to help clean the chief's house and to wash dishes. The villagers had a well, and the chief allowed us to use his buckets and pans for clothes washing. We had to borrow clothes from other people in order to wash the clothes we were wearing since they were our only possessions. The children's governess, Ma Martha, washed our clothes by hand in Paynesville but had three large tubs and a washboard to make her job easier.

I felt fortunate to have spent my first twelve years in a village like this one. Life is different in a village. There are more chores, but we learned more things. For instance, at a very early age all Liberian girls help their mothers in making palm oil. We learn to identify edible jungle plants that form our staple foods. We can identify edible palm cabbages and know how to cut away everything around the cabbage that can't be eaten. We learn to avoid the places snakes hide.

My children didn't know any of these things growing up in the city in a nice house and shopping for food in a grocery store. All my girls know how to make is *fufu* from cassava roots. I remembered that was what we were preparing when this nightmare of a war began six months ago.

Day after day we continued our routine. We looked for food. We fetched water. We searched for firewood. I led the children in Bible studies and verse memorization. In the evenings we had Bible study and devotions.

I prayed continually for John. But in my heart I feared I would never see him again on this earth. Except for the immediacy of surviving in Wako Village, I had no idea of where to go. I had no plan. I just supposed we would stay with the chief and his wife until they told us to leave. We couldn't stay with them forever, but thank God, they didn't ask us to go away.

In the village, I was surprised to see several Paynesville neighbors. Most everyone left the same day John was taken. That was the day the rebels swept into Paynesville killing, looting and burning.

I saw our neighbor Ma Rachel. She had children close to the same ages as Kou, Annie, and Monica. She had escaped with her children. She asked about John when she didn't see him with me. I told her everything.

Ma Rachel told me she would pray for him. It really seemed, though, as if she wanted to get away from me. My loss made her uncomfortable. She didn't know what to say. I felt as though everyone I told already knew John was dead. After all, everyone had seen the dead bodies strewn along the road leading to Wako Village. We all knew what the rebels were capable of.

I'm sure they thought I was in denial. I headed back to the hut.

QUESTIONS OF FAITH 5

JOHN **B**ack in the barrack cell, I was finally able to rouse myself. The other prisoners and I inspected the damage inflicted by the garden hose. Our backs told our stories.

It's quite interesting how each human being is unique. No two of us are exactly the same. We discovered that this is just as true of our backs as it is of looks and personalities. Some of us possessed thick skin and some thin skin. Others were in between.

Thick-skinned prisoners exhibited bright red, raised welts that intersected across their backs. Some of the welts oozed a clear liquid that shone in the dimness when the light hit it just right.

One prisoner with thin skin seemed to be painted with an abstract portrait of colors, textures, and geometric shapes. In some places his skin was laid open as if sliced by a surgeon's scalpel, while in others the cuts were jagged and uneven. His back was a range of colors mixing in different hues against his dark skin. His blood, now dried and crusty, had flowed from one gouged-out valley and stopped at the next. It then took a jog left or right before continuing its journey. In short, his back looked like raw meat.

The contrast between thick and thin skin was great. Distinct lines on the thick-skinned back could have been a road map. A thick-skinned back could be read much like a palm reader examines the

33

hand. Had the back been a palm, a village fortune teller would use the intersecting stripes and creases to predict the future.

Likewise, one look at the back of the thin-skinned prisoner, and I was certain that I could predict his future. Though his back bore no resemblance to a road map, his injuries presented a clear picture of his destination.

I estimated my own stripes were somewhere in the middle of the spectrum. I considered myself fortunate. None of my stripes were sliced or had popped open from the impact of the hose.

Strong, bush-hardened teenagers gave us our severe beatings. Our humiliation beatings, however, were delivered by children, some only slightly older than my six-year-olds, Annie and Kou. These small rebels weren't strong enough to injure us with the rubber hoses. The only purpose was our humiliation and to train them in cruelty.

Many of these children and teenagers looked almost normal except for one thing: These kids possessed a wild, unearthly dull look in their eyes as they meted out sadistic punishment. In odd contrast, later in the week, as we were being herded back into our barracks, I heard laughter. I glanced in the direction of the noise and saw three of them playing tag. Laughing, cutting up, and chasing each other, they could have been the children from my own neighborhood.

Startled at the odd scene of miniature dressed-up soldiers at play, I almost forgot who they were and what they did. As I shuffled painfully toward the barrack I was reminded. Guttural moans sounded from the prisoner directly behind me. Each step produced in him a spasm of pain. Seeing the children at play, I wondered if they themselves forgot what they did.

By this time in the war, killing was easy for them. Their innocent eyes glazed over in an instant as they put on their business face. Dead on the inside, they threatened us in a monotone, lifeless voice: "Give me your watch" or "I want your belt."

Death meant nothing to them. If they wanted something and it wasn't given to them quickly, they just pulled the trigger. The item transferred ownership. What could be easier than that? They'd seen too much death. One more made no difference. Besides, in their new families, killing was the rewarded behavior.

Plied with the drugs their commanders gave them, the children's consciences soon desensitized to atrocities both committed and received. With dull minds and dead eyes, they went about their business of revolution. Life was cheap, ours and theirs. Devoid of hope, they lived moment to moment and instilled fear in all of us.

For days, I never knew what new horror was being concocted in the imaginative minds of my captors. It was a tremendous struggle to encourage my cell mates, to keep praying myself, and to remind myself that God was in control. Fear and anxiety kept fighting Jesus for ownership of my soul.

At the beginning of the week, prolonged prayer was difficult. Now it was easier with continuous practice. Every important thing in my life—food, family, possessions, my health—was now stripped away. Only prayer remained. Prayers lasting seconds the first day now lasted minutes.

With all my praying, I don't think I helped a single cell mate. Most of them ignored me as I prayed. They just didn't care. With others, it caused an argument. "If your God is so great and so loving, then why has he allowed these devils to do this?" asked one.

In another, my prayers prompted complaints against God. He claimed to be a Christian and attended church, but now it seemed his faith failed him. "John, why hasn't God rescued us? You said he can if he wants to. Does this mean he doesn't want to?"

I responded as best I could. "God is not a genie," I said. "Certainly he knows our predicament. But regardless of what happens, you must have faith and trust him." My answer sounded like a cliché.

With rising anger and indignation he responded, "Why should I place my trust in a God that knows I'm being tortured and doesn't care enough about me to stop it? Tell me, John, why should I trust in a God like that?"

I didn't respond. I didn't have an answer. Nevertheless, I would not give up on my own faith. That issue had already been settled.

Three prisoners kept up a tirade of curses against the rebels. They had been government officials and couldn't contain their utter disdain for the "vermin" that now presumed to pass judgment on them.

"Who do these rebels think they are anyway? They are no better than illiterate scum. They're dogs. They'd better hope I don't get free. I will beat these little savage bastards within an inch of their lives. I'll show them."

These men didn't want encouragement. Their intense anger and abject hatred fueled their souls. That the rebels were the ages of their own children or grandchildren was truly galling. It was if their own children had turned on their elders with whips and guns and bayonets. How dare they! It was incomprehensible. It defied logic that these little monsters beat and tortured them for a week under the guidance of their senior leaders. "Just wait till we're free!" they swore to themselves and the rest of us.

Repeating this prayer of vengeance like a mantra stoked their anger. As the possibility of freedom seemed more and more remote, each of the prisoners prayed in his own way to his own god. For me, it was the God of creation, of Abraham and Isaac and Jacob; for them it was the gods of anger, hatred, despair, and hopelessness.

The intensity of our suffering was matched only by the rebels' childlike joy in playing such fun games. That I survived was not my own doing. All the tortured prisoners survived. To kill us meant the rebels' fun was over.

Our interrogations and torture continued throughout the week. They took time to think and discuss, became creative, and enjoyed making up new fun games as children do. They shot rifles between my legs and near other parts of my body, each time laughing at the effect produced by the concussion shock wave.

Another time one threw me to the ground, put his knee on my chest, and gripped my neck to hold me still. Then, taking his razor-sharp knife he carefully carved a slice off my right ear, as if he were whittling a piece of wood. Thankfully, his Juju fetish didn't require the whole ear, just the tip.

Everyone in my cell had similar experiences. I kept telling these men not to curse the rebels or God. "We should all take our complaints directly to God," I told them. "He is just and will fight our battles for us. We have to stay in prayer." No one believed me.

I tried to organize them to have a round-the-clock prayer vigil in our cell, but it failed. Several cooperated the first day. But once the beatings started, no one cared. Their attitude was that God didn't prevent them from getting beaten, so what good was he? On the last day, I was the only one who would pray out loud for the group.

Despite our differences, we still developed a bond of sorts and helped each other. The first night I was in the cell, around midnight, we heard the outer barracks door opened. In the dark hallway guards called several prisoners' names and waited until they answered. It was clear the rebels didn't keep good records of who was in each cell. They opened the cell doors where voices answered and led the prisoners away. Dawn arrived, but the prisoners never returned.

After the beatings the previous afternoon, we guessed that the unreturned prisoners had been murdered—no doubt in some gruesome manner designed to maximize the entertainment value. As a group we decided that if any of us heard our names called out we would remain silent.

Each subsequent night, more names were called out, and more prisoners were taken away. All of us stayed quiet. By the end of the week, all original twelve men in my cell still remained.

We all tried to assist the bloodied thin-skinned prisoner, wiping his oozing cuts and helping him to sit or stand up. It wasn't much. We didn't have any food or medicine or clean dressings.

I thought I had prayed hard when I first arrived. But after living in this hell with constant stress, physical pain, and hunger for a week, I now prayed like a battle-hardened spiritual warrior. Rather than being beaten up spiritually like some of my cell mates, somehow the deprivation reinforced my prayers.

They were simple prayers. My mind could form no other kind. But my spirit had been stripped clean of all pretense and charade before the Father. So over and over I prayed simple, razor-sharp prayers. I would not yield. They would not break me. God was in control. Not them. God would see me through whatever happened.

For the first time in my week of captivity I entertained a glimmer of hope. Yesterday, our captors had told us today would be the final investigation. When questioned what that meant, one rebel responded, "You will receive justice." No one knew what he meant, but it sounded hopeful.

Any fair-minded judge would realize I am innocent, I reasoned. Besides, in Liberia, every accused criminal was guaranteed a jury trial and a chance to present evidence proving innocence.

All week long, the rebels hadn't cared about the truth, but maybe that would change now. I had answered all their questions truthfully, but they wouldn't listen. "God-man," they called me, mocking me as an assistant prayer leader, "where is the bank's money? We know you have it." Perhaps this ordeal would be over soon, and they would release me from this terrible mistake. I thought of Bessie and the children and wondered if they were home.

The sun began its climb in the sky. Before long, we heard a distant noise. We all strained to identify the source of the sound. "It's a truck!" someone exclaimed. He was right. The truck was almost here.

Outside, the rebels were also alerted to the truck's approach. I heard shouts as senior officers gave orders to their underlings.

As the truck came closer, I heard gears grinding as the driver downshifted. I imagined the inexperienced driver was one of the teenage rebels and had no experience shifting the gears on a large truck.

Clearly something was going to happen now. The big truck rumbled into camp and came to a halt. Next, the jailers entered the barracks. Cells were opened one by one, and all the prisoners were ordered to come outside. We slowly stood, trying to stifle our moans and groans.

Whatever we might have been one week ago—government minister, industrialist, or assistant prayer leader—we were all equal now.

Once outside, I saw the large army truck that had been making the noise. I wondered if the rebels had had it from the beginning or if they had captured it from the government troops. It was big, with an open top, and had railings all around the sides, the kind you could carry livestock in.

Other prisoners were already standing in the truck bed by the time our group was led outside the barracks. They bunched near the cab as other prisoners climbed in behind them. Armed guards stood on each side of the prisoners as we exited the barracks. We joined the end of the line as other cells were opened and lined up behind our little group.

I climbed up onto the bed and went to the front, squeezing in with the others. We all stood and waited. No one spoke a word.

It took a long time to get all of us loaded. Injured men moved slowly. Some were helped up by other prisoners. Everyone packed close together to make room for all. Before long, the large truck was full. The last of the prisoners were loaded.

No one knew where the truck was headed. Everyone was ordered to remain silent. No talking or whispering was permitted. We dutifully obeyed. There was nothing to be gained from talking anyway.

The truck ignition clicked and the diesel engine roared to life with a belch of black smoke out the tailpipe. Armed guards were posted around the perimeter at each corner of the truck and in the middle. They seemed to be in good spirits. They held on to the railing and rode like firemen heading off to put out a fire. With gears grinding, the lumbering truck lurched slowly forward and headed off down the road. The #72 Soldiers' Barrack slowly disappeared from view.

CHRISTMAS EVE 6

December 24, 1989

C hristmas was always the best. We had our tree, our stockings, presents, and delicious food.

The freed American slaves who founded Liberia brought all their customs to Africa. Our Founding Day, July 26, 1847, is a different date from America's Independence Day, but we celebrate the same with parades and fireworks.

Every household that could afford it bought a Christmas tree. All Christmas trees were imported from Europe, mainly Norway and Sweden. With all our myriad jungle trees, I thought it funny that we had to get our Christmas tree from another country. Maybe Liberia's equatorial sunshine is too hot for them to grow.

Christmas just wasn't Christmas in the Gonleh household without a real tree, decorated with colored lights, beautiful ornaments we collected or the children made, and fake snow. Of course, no Liberian child had ever seen real snow, located as we are ten degrees north of the equator. We didn't care. Christmas trees were exotic and exciting.

The children loved to open the box the tree came in and be hit with the powerful scent of pine flooding their noses, even penetrating and burning their eyes a little, because some of the tree resin would vaporize in the hot Liberian climate. Once the box was opened, POW! The smell hit you, overwhelming your nose. It was absolutely wonderful.

Outside the store, some trees had been put up and decorated with ornaments, lights, tinsel, and garland to help get everyone in the spirit. The girls stuck their noses right against the pine needles to take in the wonderful smells. Sometimes they got too close. The needles stuck them in the nose or in their eyes making them jump. We all laughed when that happened.

On Christmas Eve morning, 1989, John and I already had our tree up and decorated, but we still had much to finish. Tonight, six children would await the arrival of Sani Claus with their presents in tow. The older girls had stopped believing in Sani Claus, but they played along for Chester and Comfort. It made the occasion more festive that we still had two children who experienced everything with a sense of wonder.

The whole city was preparing. Most shops and businesses would shut down at noon, since people were anxious to get home to their families.

Final trips to the supermarkets or the traditional open-air markets made them crowded; people stood elbow to elbow in the aisles and the stalls. Supermarkets stocked up on special European and American delicacies like exotic cheeses and frozen fruit pies. Any meat we wanted—beef, pork, goat, lamb, chicken—could be found. The open-air markets carried more traditional African foods, such as wild deer and monkey meat, both dried and fresh, and dried elephant meat. Snails were a popular delicacy, as was bonny, a dried salted fish.

Bonny is one of my favorite dishes, but preparing it involves a lot of work. It must be scaled, soaked, and deboned before it can be cooked. I like to make mine with Liberian spices and hot chili peppers and serve it with rice and vegetables. It's delicious.

Life in Monrovia had been fairly stable now for several years, though there had been a real fear about civil war a decade ago when Army Sergeant Samuel Doe overthrew President Tolbert in a coup.

For 132 years, since 1847, all the previous presidents, including Tolbert, were descendants of the freed slave immigrants from America. They came to Africa with last names like Jefferson and Washington.

Then Doe executed President Tolbert and made himself president. He also executed by firing squad thirteen other government ministers and officials down at the beach. Some were still breathing when they were thrown into a burial pit dug in the sand.

Families of the executed officials fled to other countries but mostly to the adjacent Ivory Coast. Thousands of people connected to the Tolbert government were killed or lost their homes. For some families, their only crime was having an American-sounding last name.

For Liberia, the land of liberty, the coup almost started a civil war. But after the initial scare, everything calmed down. Samuel Doe, like most Liberians, was from an indigenous African tribe and claimed to represent all the indigenous tribes against unfair treatment by the upper class African-American descendants. The slave descendants only represented five percent of the population but controlled most of the country's wealth.

In the beginning President Doe listened and learned. It didn't last long. He was an illiterate and violent man with a penchant for witchcraft. Later there was a coup attempt by one of his army generals from Nimba County. President Doe survived but he never again trusted the Mano and Gio people of Nimba County. He trusted only people from his own tribe, the Krahn.

In the two or three years prior to 1989, Doe received counsel only from his Juju mediums and sorcerers. He spoke with Christian words but sank deeper and deeper into the occult darkness. He was paranoid, suspicious, and perceived any criticism as a threat to his rule. Rumors circulated that he ritually murdered and ate the hearts of political opponents as a way to enhance and maintain his power. Trouble was brewing.

Despite the ominous signs, however, life was quite good. We had modern conveniences and everything in abundance. Tomorrow all businesses, government offices, and shops would be closed for Christmas.

John had finished work at his block factory, so he was able to stay home. Meridian Bank, where I worked as a teller, was closed. Life was good. We had more-than-adequate salaries and enjoyed a comfortable home, a nice car, and other good things.

John worked throughout the week at the church. He never was able to go to seminary or college, but it didn't matter. John tells how God put a call on his life in 1985. I was just happy he was so committed to the Lord. Our relationship had suffered horribly over the years. Even though we became Christians as teenagers, sinful living had almost torn us apart over and over. When John truly committed his life to the Lord, he became a new person.

Christmas Eve morning I was busy cooking food for Christmas dinner the next day. The older girls were helping me finish the *fufu*, our traditional Liberian dish made from cassava root.

To make fufu, we started early. I had already soaked the cassava roots in a bag of water for three days. Next, we placed them under a press, and the water drained out. Gloria pounded the roots into a pulp with a mortar. Then I mixed them well with more water, strained the water out, and finally let it settle. Our last step was to bake it in the oven.

While I normally insisted on spoons, eating fufu with their hands was a special treat for the children. Once a year at Christmas, with great laughter, those silly girls invented ever-new ways to lick the fufu off their fingers. Chester and Comfort, who were only four, quickly learned from their older sisters. Monica preferred the one-finger approach—sticking a finger totally inside her mouth and scraping it clean with her teeth as she slowly and with great fanfare withdrew it. Annie and Kou preferred the two-finger-scoops approach and licking off the fufu in layers with their tongues. Chester and Comfort wiped it all over their hands, face, and clothes, all the while squealing with delight. Gloria was a young woman. She had outgrown such silliness.

Besides the fufu, there were many other dishes to prepare. All of these were either started or in the planning phases to be ready for Christmas dinner. Early Christmas morning, everyone would rise and the children would find their presents. With joyous shrieks and laughter, they would tear off the paper to see what gifts they had received. Chester and Comfort were getting into the Christmas spirit. Last year, they weren't quite sure about the presents and what to do, but now they were as excited as their big sisters. Time creeps and Christmas Day just seems like it will never come when you're little. Chester especially could barely stand it, he was so excited. The waiting was torture, just like it is for children everywhere.

After present opening, our family would get dressed and head over to Immanuel Baptist Church for a service. After singing carols, saying prayers, and hearing a short sermon, we would go back home to the feast that we had been preparing for all week long.

After we ate Christmas dinner and spent time with family members who had come over, the children would get ready to sing Christmas carols in the neighborhood. The kids loved this part because at many houses they would be given small gifts or candy or some other unexpected goody after finishing the carols. It was delight upon delight to end this most happy of days. But it was only Christmas Eve morning, and all this fun was yet to come. After all these years, I still think what a joyous time Christmas was in our house.

There had been rumors. Trouble was brewing along the border with Ivory Coast, in Nimba County. In response, President Doe sent his interior minister to find out if there was any truth to them. He had returned a week ago with his report: All was calm. The rumors were dispelled.

That morning, the Christmas music on the radio was interrupted for a special news bulletin. We abruptly stopped everything we'd been doing.

It was President Doe. "The country should pray," he said. "Our nation has been attacked through Nimba County. We are at war. Everyone should watch for strange persons in your community. If you see anyone who looks like they don't belong, you should report it to the authorities."

That was it. Nothing else was said. And with those few words, the whole country was thrown into panic.

A moment before, we were anticipating Christmas. I looked at John. He stared back at me. With the briefest of words, our ordered lives, our schedules, our plans, and our preparations were transformed into question marks, fear, and confusion. And as it was in the Gonleh household, so it was in the suburb of Paynesville, the capital of Monrovia, and all of Liberia.

John and I simply stopped. We stopped decorating. We stopped cooking. We stopped laughing. All activities ground to a halt.

No one knew what was happening. There was no information, just rumors and President Doe's cryptic announcement. For all intents and purposes, Christmas was over before it began. There was no Christmas dinner, treats, or fufu. We stopped preparing after the bad news. There was no SaniClaus, no Christmas tree lights, no candy, no caroling, and no church. Even the service scheduled for Christmas morning was cancelled.

Everyone stayed home and prayed just as President Doe had told us. Though Christmas had effectively been cancelled, ironically, Jesus Christ, born two thousand years before, heard more prayers on Christmas Day, 1989, than had ever been uttered on any single day before in the country's 150-year history.

I remember vividly that Christmas Day was overcast and gloomy. A dark cloud had formed over Liberia.

AFTER CHRISTMAS 7

BESSIE

The week after Christmas was total confusion. The interior minister was fired for not seeing the danger brewing. At work, bank customers brought in the latest rumors. With each good rumor there was an offsetting bad rumor. And the bad news was always worse than the good news.

At first bank customers related the latest rumors to us tellers with almost gleeful concern. Rumors added a spice of excitement to everyone's otherwise mundane life. Early on, the war was distant and abstract. We had faith that our army would stamp out the troublemakers and things would return to normal.

This attitude soon changed. As days passed the bad news accumulated like rotting garbage. Before long, we couldn't escape the smell pervading the city.

In stores and markets, people conducted business like always but things were more deliberate, more urgent. Absent was the small talk between the clerks and customers. It was straight business. It was as if no one wanted to speak the fear that everyone felt, for to do so would hasten the arrival of its source.

Prices suddenly rose. Gasoline lines grew. Store shelves were bare. Initially, food shortages were caused by hoarding rather than lack of food. However that soon changed as sources dried up. Most of the farmers lived inland, away from Monrovia. They also lay in the path of the advancing rebels.

Gasoline prices were stable for a few weeks. Then the refinery shut down. Liberia had only one refinery for the entire country. Tanker ships that had arrived periodically with crude oil from the Middle East stopped coming. Some gasoline was trucked in from neighboring countries, but it was very expensive. In time, almost all the cars in the city were parked indefinitely or abandoned by the roadside.

On December 31, John came home earlier than usual. He looked shaken and scared. That in turn scared me.

"What happened?" I demanded in a frantic tone.

I followed John inside and he sat down. He started explaining.

"I was working when a government army truck pulled up. Three soldiers got out of the truck. I greeted them and asked them how I could help. They wanted to buy a truckload of blocks. I told the workers to load and stack the blocks."

At this point John's hands started to shake. He stopped for a moment. When he began speaking again his voice sounded strained.

"When I came out of my office with the receipt, the truck was pulling away. I couldn't believe what I was seeing. They were driving off without paying. Without thinking, I ran after the truck, shouting at them."

By this time, John's voice had reached a high pitch and his face was taut with tension and anger. I could see a vein in his temple throbbing.

"The truck stopped. But then one of the soldiers aimed his rifle at me. He said, 'Stay where you are or I'm going to spray you.' I couldn't believe it—this from one of our own country's soldiers."

John had a look of disbelief on his face. Gathering himself and trying to calm down, he furrowed his brows and said in a low voice, "As the truck drove away, the soldier said to me, 'This is only the beginning. We'll be back.'"

I couldn't even imagine anything like this. I reached over to hold his hand. Never before had he been threatened like this, he said, his voice filled with indignation. He told how his workers and foreman quickly gathered around him to simultaneously express their shock and outrage.

After angry voices died down, they conferred. They all determined that it would be best for John to stay home for a few days.

Staying home was safer than working, but that merely allowed John to listen to the radio and television news all day long. Together, we began to pray harder than we ever had before.

Only God himself knew what else lay in store for us.

New Year's Day was ruined along with Christmas. Fireworks and firecrackers were banned. The last thing anyone needed or wanted was to hear what sounded like gunfire. We adults understood the logic, but the children loved fireworks and didn't understand.

John and I tried to maintain a semblance of normalcy for the children. We tried not to look too worried, and we didn't talk in front of the children about atrocities we heard on the news.

Gloria, being older, knew things were bad and was frightened. We consoled them, telling them God would protect us. Together as a family, our habit was to pray three times a day whenever we were home. This new crisis generated a new intensity and fervency to our normal prayers. We prayed at church and gathered more often for prayer meetings.

One prominent spiritual woman in Monrovia, Mother Dukuly, prophesied she saw in a vision a dark cloud gathering over Liberia. In her vision she saw that Liberia would experience a storm of untold bloodshed. She said the coming storm was punishment from God. Many in the nation professed to be Christians, but they continued to dabble in Juju sorcery and witchcraft. They did not worship the true God. They did not love their neighbors. Therefore, God would give them over to their own evil desires.

Another member of our church said he also saw the dark cloud in a dream. Our pastor urged everyone to pray and fast. Our entire congregation of the Immanuel Baptist Church assembled daily for prayer and fasted for an entire week. It was agreed that Psalm 91 should be prayed daily and memorized by every member. Everyone who was old enough should make these verses part of their day. Breathe out one verse and breathe in the next.

HE WHO DWELLS IN THE SECRET PLACE OF THE MOST HIGH SHALL ABIDE UNDER THE SHADOW OF THE ALMIGHTY. I WILL SAY OF THE LORD, "HE IS MY REFUGE AND MY FORTRESS; MY GOD, IN HIM I WILL TRUST."

SURELY HE SHALL DELIVER YOU FROM THE SNARE OF THE FOWLER AND FROM THE PERILOUS PESTILENCE. HE SHALL COVER YOU WITH HIS FEATHERS, AND UNDER HIS WINGS YOU SHALL TAKE REFUGE; HIS TRUTH SHALL BE YOUR SHIELD AND BUCKLER. YOU SHALL NOT BE AFRAID OF THE TERROR BY NIGHT, NOR OF THE ARROW THAT FLIES BY DAY, NOR OF THE PESTILENCE THAT WALKS IN DARKNESS, NOR OF THE DESTRUCTION THAT LAYS WASTE AT NOONDAY.

A THOUSAND MAY FALL AT YOUR SIDE, AND TEN THOUSAND AT YOUR RIGHT HAND; BUT IT SHALL NOT COME NEAR YOU. ONLY WITH YOUR EYES SHALL YOU LOOK, AND SEE THE REWARD OF THE WICKED.

BECAUSE YOU HAVE MADE THE LORD, WHO IS MY REFUGE, EVEN THE MOST HIGH, YOUR DWELLING PLACE, NO EVIL SHALL BEFALL YOU, NOR SHALL ANY PLAGUE COME NEAR YOUR DWELLING; FOR HE SHALL GIVE HIS ANGELS CHARGE OVER YOU, TO KEEP YOU IN ALL YOUR WAYS. IN THEIR HANDS, THEY SHALL BEAR YOU UP, LEST YOU DASH YOUR FOOT AGAINST A STONE. YOU SHALL TREAD UPON THE LION AND THE COBRA,

THE YOUNG LION AND THE SERPENT YOU
SHALL TRAMPLE UNDERFOOT.

"BECAUSE HE HAS SET HIS LOVE UPON
ME, THEREFORE I WILL DELIVER HIM; I
WILL SET HIM ON HIGH, BECAUSE HE HAS
KNOWN MY NAME. HE SHALL CALL UPON ME,
AND I WILL ANSWER HIM; I WILL BE WITH
HIM IN TROUBLE; I WILL DELIVER HIM
AND HONOR HIM. WITH LONG LIFE WILL I
SATISFY HIM, AND SHOW HIM MY SALVA-
TION." (PSALM 91)

Food in the market was scarce. There was sufficient food in the countryside, but the problem was transportation. There was little gasoline. Everyone was frightened. The rebels attacked trucks and killed the drivers. This left the farmers too afraid to risk getting their produce to the city markets. What little that did come came with a steep price. Businesses shut down all over the city.

Things were awful for John and the block factory. After several days of staying at home, he returned to work. His business was rapidly deteriorating.

So far, the war had remained in the outer counties, still far from the capital. Even so, construction projects all over the country ground to a halt. Every project John's business depended on shut down. Eventually he had no choice. John had to close the block factory and lay off all his workers.

That was one of the saddest days of his life. The factory may have been small by some standards, but it was his. He'd started it; his employees respected him and depended on him. He fed their families. From Christmas to closing his business was no more than two months.

Thankfully I was still able to work. The bank manager lived near our neighborhood in Paynesville. Meridian Bank made sure he had money for the expensive gasoline. So he picked me up for work in the mornings and then dropped me back at home in the evenings. It was a blessing that the bank remained open as long as it did. Eventually, however, the fighting reached the city, and the bank, along with all the other businesses, closed.

The situation in Monrovia was worsening. News reports brought bad news every day. The rebels had advanced another ten kilometers one day, twenty the next, and so forth. Fighting was vicious. There were tremendous casualties on both sides. Hospitals that had been gradually filled to capacity now overflowed. They were like a lake whose level had risen from too much rain and spilled over the top of the dam. People now spilled out onto the streets surrounding the hospital. The few operational cars and trucks carried the wounded and the maimed trying to gain entrance in the hospital. Gazing at the wounded, all of Monrovia got a good look at the progress of the war.

The children's classes were cancelled, so through April, May, and June, John stayed with the children. I kept working in the bank, though there was little to do.

For her safety, we sent the children's governess, Ma Martha, back to her home village. Thankfully, my job allowed us to keep saving money. Through those lean months, we were able to help out John's ex-employees, our neighbors, and other church members with food when they ran low. God had blessed us, and now we had to help others.

My biggest problem during this time was my own family. President Doe had initially rallied the country back to God. He asked us to remain in prayer. For a few Sundays, churches all over the city were packed. But as the wounded returned from the front and the rebels gained recruits, President Doe shifted from prayer to revenge. He was furious with the Mano and Gio people in Nimba and blamed them for the war.

The hatred was ripping families apart. President Doe hated all the Mano, even those in Monrovia. He suspended Liberian laws and arrested all Mano government employees as potential traitors. Several of these men had wives of different tribes: Krahn, Lorma, and Kpelle.

To make a big show for the television, the wives publicly denounced their husbands and divorced them. President Doe congratulated each woman for her loyalty and solidarity with the government.

Seeing this on television started a rush of similar actions throughout the city. All over, husbands were leaving wives and vice versa to follow the good example. Newspapers carried stories about families that were destroyed, always adding the appropriate propaganda justifying the action.

"Yes, it was a difficult decision to leave my wife," stated one man.

"Certainly, the children will miss their father, but loyalty to stand with my country comes first," declared a wife.

It was sickeningly cynical and transparent. The press was being pressured and manipulated to act as the president's pawn. Everyone knew the truth, but the truth was no match for the hatred being spewed by the president and those who obeyed him or curried his favor.

With the success of his forced declarations of loyalty, President Doe stepped up his haranguing against the Mano tribe. In regular radio speeches he repeatedly berated the Mano. He blamed them for the lack of food, gasoline, and fresh water. They were the cause of every bad thing.

Then it was my turn. The phone rang.

Bessie, it's your aunt. How are you? Good. And the children? Good. Listen. Your mother and I are very worried about you and the children. You know I love John, but maybe you should ask him to move out for awhile. After all, he's putting you in danger by staying. OK, OK. Don't get angry. Just think about it. But don't wait too long.

Then my mother called. Then my aunt called again. First one and then the other, growing to several phone calls a day.

Oh, I know John is loyal to the government, but they don't know that. Look at all the horrible things the Mano people have done. Is it any wonder that our president wants to know who is loyal and who isn't?

I couldn't tell John about the calls. He would be furious. Slowly, their relentless pressure began to wear me down.

Bessie, you're acting recklessly. Yes, I know John has done nothing wrong, but listen to me. You're putting yourself and the children in grave danger. Don't you realize that? Actually John is being quite selfish, don't you think, to put you in this position. He should leave voluntarily.

I prayed, but it was so confusing. I didn't know what to do. I wished I could tell John. My father wanted my mom and aunt to leave me alone. But they didn't listen to him. The calls came over and over, week after week.

Bessie, you're going to die for nothing. They'll kill you and the children when they capture him. John is selfish. If he really loved you he would do the right thing and leave.

Slowly, bit by bit, their phone calls wore me down. Each discovery of mutilated Mano bodies around the city brought more calls. After two months under their pressure, I couldn't take it anymore. I made my decision.

DESCENT INTO CHAOS 8

JOHN My business was gone. Food was scarce. Prices skyrocketed. I was an enemy of the state. Today I was leaving the prayer chapel for the last time. Words and prayer were all I had. Whatever good might come from them, I didn't know. The results belonged to God.

"Trust in God and his protection," I often said. "He knows your situation. He hasn't forgotten you." The words sounded hollow and trite. I was tired.

I thought back to the vision I'd had in 1985 when God called me. I saw in my mind God speaking to me, telling me to serve him as a pastor. He said he had something for me to do. I realized it was time to repent, stop sinning, and fulfill the plan he had for my life.

I had questioned this and wondered if it was my conscience convicting me of the bad things I'd done or if God was really speaking.

The very next Sunday, I was shocked when a woman at church said she'd had a vision about me and described for me the very things I heard. I was convinced. From that day forward, my life began anew.

In reality, God really was our only hope. No other nation wanted to get sucked into Liberia's morass. We were three million people in sixteen tribes, who now hated each other. We would have been grateful for some country to come in and protect us from ourselves, but we were cut off and alone. I had to believe that God hadn't forgotten or given up on us.

While counseling others, my faith and my words contained power, conviction, and reassurance. When they left, I wondered how many of these poor frightened souls would survive this war. Would my family and I be among them? Only God knew that answer.

Nimba County people couldn't stop Mr. Taylor. Cheap shotguns for hunting bush meat were no match for AK-47s. Besides, villagers weren't going to fight against their own children from the same tribe who had been recruited by Mr. Taylor.

The tragedy in this was how easy it was to start a civil war. The people of Liberia were willing pawns in a chess game between power-hungry thugs.

Muslim Mandingo merchants living throughout Nimba County, eager to curry favor with the government and avoid persecution themselves, helped the soldiers against their Mano neighbors. They led government soldiers down narrow jungle paths to hidden Mano bush villages deep in the jungle.

Once discovered, the government soldiers raped and murdered the rice farmer inhabitants and burned village after village to the ground. The Mano then turned on the Mandingo, slaughtering them for their betrayal and treachery.

With these tactics, President Doe proved to be the best recruiter of all for Mr. Taylor's fledgling army. The rebel army quickly swelled in size to unmanageable proportions as government retaliations rivaled the rebels' actions.

In Monrovia, for weeks, the government-controlled news berated the Mano people from Nimba County. Bessie and I only watched after the children were in bed as the television news delivered the latest government denouncements. Newspapers reported arrests of Mano government employees for spying.

Injured soldiers and civilians returning from the front lines filled the hospitals. They carried back stories of limbs hacked off with cutlasses and soldiers beheaded. Never before had such barbarism entered the minds of our people. We could hardly believe it, yet the reports kept coming.

What became evident was that the rebels were inching closer and closer to Monrovia. It was clear that our army was losing the war to the "Liberator" Charles Taylor.

Unable to win on the battlefield, President Doe turned his fury against scapegoats to blame the troubles on. With little effort, he found an enemy he could defeat. He and the government commenced to wage war against their own citizens, the Mano people of Monrovia.

With the rising denunciations, I decided it was too dangerous to continue my work in the chapel. Just as I was about to leave for the last time, a Krahn soldier opened the door and came in.

His brother had been killed in battle with the rebels. He was grieving and sought comfort. If he only knew who was praying for him, I wondered if he would erupt in rage or harm me. Placing my hand on his shoulder, I prayed for him. My words of faith and hope seemed to ease his distress. He thanked me and left, his head a little higher, I thought, than when he had come in. God help him. God help us all.

Turning to leave the chapel, with a final glance, I thought what a strange journey had brought me to this moment. Twisting and turning through the events of my life, God had somehow worked his plan.

My sins, my hypocrisy, my unbelief, together with an occasional good deed all intertwined. Through each good and bad act, God somehow used them to draw me near. Reflecting on my life reminded me that it was about his plan, not mine. "Lord, what do you have for me now?" I asked as I walked out the chapel door.

My car was parked several blocks away, so I had time to think and reflect upon my long, strange journey that had brought me to this point.

1962–1969

I am Mano, born in Nimba County in 1953. At nine years old, the eldest of five children, I came to Monrovia to attend boarding school. I saw my father twice a year but never saw my mother or siblings for seven long years.

My father wanted more for his eldest son than to travel long distances on foot to virgin rainforest, cut down large trees with an axe, burn and clear the bush to create a small jungle field that would yield just one year's crop of upland rice. The soil wasn't that good for crops. The topsoil was only four or five inches deep, and below that lay primordial clay. Without treatment by expensive fertilizers, the shallow topsoil was exhausted of its nutrients by a single year's rice crop. Only the majestic mahogany, ebony, and other hardwoods could penetrate this layer of clay and create the towering rainforest canopy.

Due to a variety of reasons—topography, monsoon rains, low crop yields, limited access to capital, and lack of transportation—Liberian farmers farmed the way they always had for hundreds of years. While they didn't possess the modern farming methods of the West, they did possess the rain forest. But that too was slowly going away.

To feed his family, my father, like other farmers, first cut down the tall trees to expose the forest floor to the sun while leaving the stumps intact. He possessed neither the farm implements nor the need to remove stumps. All that was needed was a sharp axe and a cutlass (machete). I can still remember as a child accompanying him to clear the field. He let me swing the huge, heavy axe against a large tree. I so wanted to chop it down, but my mighty swing barely scratched the bark. He just laughed, rubbed my head, and took the axe.

Farms in Liberia didn't resemble those I saw pictures of in my schoolbooks from America. There were no long, straight, plowed rows with amber waves of grain, no automated planting or mechanized harvesters. All farming was done by hand with strong shoulders and stooped backs. Besides, the soil was too shallow for plowing. Farms in Liberia were pocked by stumps and intersected by fallen trees too large to remove.

In truth, farms in Liberia didn't really look like farms at all. Despite this, my father and the other farmers still possessed a level of science with regard to successful techniques and practices that were passed down from their fathers. The day he would pass them down to me never came. Instead they went to my younger brother, Alfred.

I remembered the only time I helped my father farm. I was eight, and Alfred was six. When the field was clear, my father took Alfred and me to help him plant the rice. My father lit a fire and burned all the plants that had managed to survive on the glints and occasional streaks of sunlight that passed unobstructed through the high canopy.

Gone were the species that nature had adapted to thrive without direct sunlight. Now that I'm older, I think destroying the flora and fauna of Liberia's rainforest to plant poor-yielding upland rice seems tragic. Perhaps my father foresaw all this and knew his way of life was unsustainable. Perhaps that's why he sent me away to the city.

Nevertheless, burning all this vegetation produced a nutrient-rich ash, full of valuable minerals that would contribute to a plentiful harvest.

I remember working on a newly-cleared field early in the morning. This occasion was special because my father let me use the cutlass for the first time. Normally, we children were forbidden to touch it. I felt very responsible and grown up.

My job was to dig little shallow holes every few inches. I pushed the tip into the dirt at an angle and then gave the handle a twist to pop up a dirt clod. Alfred would use his hands to clear the dirt and debris out of the little hole. My father would follow us, dropping a few kernels into the hole, covering them up, and gently tamping down the dirt. Hole after hole, we dug, cleaned, planted, and covered.

Alfred and I were exhausted, and our hands ached by the time the day was over. That day, however, I was a rice farmer just like my dad. I never felt so proud or important.

That experience was my only recollection of home. Almost everything else, I'd forgotten.

Upon graduation from the sixth grade at age sixteen, I boarded a bus bound for Garnwe, my home village. Then I saw her. She was slender and wore fashionable jeans and a nice blouse. Bessie!

Never very shy, I maneuvered to sit in the seat directly across from her, introduced myself, and struck up a conversation.

I learned that she was a little younger than me, a Christian, and a very pretty one at that. Like me, she attended a boarding school and was traveling to her home village, Graie. She was three grades ahead of me, having started school younger. We talked the whole way to Ganta, where we would board separate buses. Once we arrived we had a little wait until our buses left, so I bought us some juice and talked until the last moment we had to board our respective buses.

I had just become a Christian myself at a crusade a few months before my trip home. And then I saw her again, exactly one week later, changing buses in Ganta. We both were heading back to Monrovia. It had to be divine intervention.

I ran up to her. "Bessie, what are you doing here?" I gushed. She replied coyly, "I'm catching the bus back to the city, same as you." Then she added, "I guess we can ride back together."

Joy of joys. That sealed the deal. It had to be God. He had arranged all this. I think we both felt awestruck from the whole God-arranged-coincidence feeling of our reunion. This time, we sat on the same bench for the return trip and talked nonstop.

Arriving in Monrovia, the bus unloaded, and she was set to leave with her aunt, who picked her up.

"Bessie," I said, gathering up my courage, "I really like you and want to see you again. Would that be all right?"

Glancing over her shoulder to see where her aunt was, she turned back and in a soft, almost whispering voice, she said, "Yes, John. I would like to see you again too. But I have to go. Here's my number."

Retrieving a piece of paper out of her pants pocket, she shoved it in my hand. She quickly turned and left. I watched her until she was gone. Opening the paper, I saw her telephone number and realized she had planned ahead for this possibility when I wasn't looking. Praise the Lord! She felt the same way I did. I reveled in my good fortune.

April 1990

I reached my parked Renault, unlocked it, and got in. I sighed and turned the ignition. The sound of the engine roaring to life felt good. What a wonderfully common sound.

This would be the last time I would drive it.

I was almost out of gas, and every station I passed coming to the chapel from Paynesville was closed. It was too risky to drive not knowing if I would run out and get stranded. Few cars were on the roads, but I saw many that were parked, deserted by their owners. One final trip home and it would be silenced.

Driving slowly through Monrovia toward Paynesville, dodging abandoned cars, I saw many people outside, some with possessions on their heads evacuating to somewhere, scattered soldiers looking confused, people scurrying to buy what little food the open markets had left.

Life was disintegrating in Liberia. But in my mind's eye, I remembered and saw Bessie again for the first time on that bus bound for Ganta. It nearly brought tears to my eyes. Now, twenty years later she was waiting for me at home.

How blessed I was. We'd had awful problems in our relationship. But through my sins, Bessie stuck with me. So many times I fell short of my own standards, let alone God's. I was a Christian, but for years I lived like a total hypocrite—I owned a nightclub; I had affairs and children with other women.

Pulling into my driveway, I sat in the car a moment reflecting. Everything was changing. Life had been turned upside down.

I wondered how these events all fit together in God's master plan. I had to believe he had one. Without the hope or comfort of knowing God is in control, I couldn't imagine how to make sense of the chaos in my life.

Greeting Bessie inside the kitchen with a big hug and kiss, I gathered our children together in one giant hug. We had each other and our faith. Pressed between the government and the rebels, it would have to be enough.

DEATH SQUADS 9

JOHN

At first it was just a murmur overheard in the market while waiting in line or from a neighbor who heard something from a coworker. Rumors of President Doe's death squads reached our ears, as strange and unwelcome as a winter blast in equatorial Liberia. Icy chills coursed through our bodies, constricting our breathing. Bessie shuddered and trembled uncontrollably at the news. I held her tight, trying to warm her and drive away the bitter terror. We could barely comprehend that this man, our president, who only a few months before had asked God for protection, now sought to kill me and everyone like me. We thought tribal affiliation made little difference in modern cosmopolitan Monrovia. Now it was the sole determiner of friend or foe. Mano were enemies of the state. Bessie was safe as a Krahn. I was a criminal and a traitor, trapped between Doe's assassins and Taylor's bloodthirsty rebels, high on drugs, revenge, and plunder.

"Jesus, is this the end?" I asked heaven. Heaven wasn't answering that question. With my body trembling from fear and uncertainty, the Spirit within told me to believe, to follow Christ wherever he leads. *Easier said than done,* I thought.

Stories circulated slowly at first but then with frequency. Nightly death squads freely roamed Monrovia hunting their prey. Mano people were taken away in the darkness, and they were never heard from again.

One evening, through the tiny slits in closed window blinds, I saw a black Jeep drive past our house followed by a van. This ominous sign meant a victim lived in my neighborhood. Thank God they hadn't come for me. The next day, I heard our neighbor, Moses, had been taken and his house burned down.

According to another neighbor, they arrived at his house two hours after dusk, forced their way inside and took him away in handcuffs. The next morning, our battery-powered radio reported twenty to thirty bodies absent their heads laid out in orderly fashion on the beach. Bessie and I wondered if one of those bodies was Moses. He was an important government minister, but however important he may have been no longer mattered.

For now, I was still safe. Without knowing for sure, I guessed that as one of the volunteers, no one in the government would take notice of me. My employees and immediate neighbors knew I was Mano, of course, from my last name. Anyone could have turned me in anonymously, and that would seal my fate. Thankfully, we had good relationships with all of them.

Over the next few weeks, rumors and stories swirled around the death-squad killings. One particular incident, related by eyewitnesses, stands out. Bulldozers dug a large pit on the beach, almost twenty feet deep. Mano citizens rounded up in the dead of night were ordered to walk down into the pit at gunpoint. Once inside, men, women, and children alike were buried alive. The bulldozers covered them up one bucket full at a time. Screams of the hapless victims slowly fell silent under a sea of sand, removing all traces of their existence. By morning there was no sign of them.

One evening, after the children were in bed, Bessie said she had to tell me something. Before the words came, she started to cry. She confessed that even before the death squads appeared, her mom and aunt had pressured her to leave me. They told her for the safety of her and the children, she should divorce me like so many others were doing to prove their loyalty to the government.

Through her tears, she admitted they had pressured her for weeks. Bessie said she finally cracked under their pressure and screamed at them. There was an awful argument. Horrible things were said. Now they weren't talking at all.

Until that moment, I hadn't realized the strain she'd been under. I knew her mother and aunt hadn't been over in awhile, but I hadn't really given it much thought. Now I understood why.

"What demons have cursed us that marriages must be broken to prove loyalty?" I asked Bessie. She shook her head, drying her tears with a tissue. All I could do was to hold her.

One afternoon about a week later I just happened to glance out through our front window. Seeing a soldier in uniform standing in the middle of the street, I ran to the window and peeked around the edge so I couldn't be seen.

Several soldiers had pulled up in their Jeep. They spread out up and down the street. Suddenly I realized I recognized the soldier in front of my house. Unfortunately I knew him well. It was the Krahn soldier from the car accident.

Peering out the window, I saw the Krahn soldier motion to another soldier hidden from my view. Catching the hidden soldier's attention, the Krahn soldier then turned and pointed at my house.

I watched with horror. It was as if he had used his finger to paint an invisible bull's-eye on my chest. Luckily, he couldn't see me or into our house due to the time of day and the angle of the sunlight. I knew I'd been found and marked for extermination. Many had been murdered. Now it was my turn.

The accident had happened a few months ago, at the start of the war. I was driving past the outskirts of Monrovia where shanty shacks crowded the road. All of a sudden a woman bolted out of a shanty, stumbling and running backward. She was trying to turn around while running without falling or stopping. Something or someone was chasing her. She clutched something in her hands and couldn't catch her balance.

Just as I was going past, she turned and ran right into my car, into the right front bumper. I slammed on the brakes, but it was too late. I heard the loud thump as my car hit her.

I jumped out and ran around to find her under the car. The right front tire had rolled over her leg. She lay under the car groaning and whimpering. Still clutched in her hands was a pair of shoes, men's shoes.

Right then out of the shack he came. It was the Krahn soldier. And right behind him emerged another woman. We carefully pulled the woman out from under my car. An ambulance was called.

Slowly the story was pieced together. The soldier was the injured woman's husband. He had been having an affair with the woman in the shack. The wife had followed her husband to the shack, run in, snatched his shoes, and was just emerging as I drove by. I suppose she wanted hard evidence. It turned out he had left her two or three weeks earlier. The whole thing didn't make much sense to me, but that was what happened.

The police were called. The ambulance came and took the woman to the ELWA (Eternal Love Winning Africa) hospital, and the police took me to the station. That is how it works in Liberia: People are presumed guilty until they can prove their innocence.

I called my "foster" mother, the woman who had helped raise me until I was an older teenager in Monrovia and someone who could vouch for my character. She worked for the Justice Ministry in the court section. She came to the station and the police allowed me to be released into her custody. Thankfully, after the facts came out the police didn't charge me with any offense.

Nevertheless, Bessie and I went to the hospital to visit the woman. We agreed to pay for her surgery because she had nothing now that her husband had left her. We bought her and her children a hundred-pound bag of rice and delivered it to her house only to discover that the husband had returned. He demanded money from us.

I refused. But after one week he called and wanted more rice. He said they had used it all and needed more. That was impossible. We knew he was lying and merely trying to extort food and money from me.

Shortly after this, he and I had a very heated argument, and Bessie and I stopped visiting the woman. I initially paid for her treatment and continued to pay for it, but no longer was there any direct contact with either the woman or her husband. I never saw the husband again until he stood in my front yard pointing at my house.

I realized he knew my name, knew I was Mano, and had looked up my address. He had a vendetta against me and was now coming for revenge for not giving him money and rice.

After another minute, the Jeep returned, picked up the Krahn soldier and the others, and left. Thank God. Immediately, I called out to Bessie and told her what had just happened. I said we must leave the house for the night.

A brief panic ensued as the children ran to us. Calming and soothing them as best we could, we began to make our preparations. I left to go two blocks to our trusted neighbors, the Kabas. I explained the situation and asked if our family could spend the night. Fatta Kaba and her husband instantly agreed. The Kabas were from Lofa County, which was considered to be neutral, so they had no fear of the government death squads.

Returning home, Bessie fed the children. Then, as darkness settled on Paynesville, a procession of eight people—two adults and six children—could be seen taking an evening stroll. As we made our way down the street, I turned to my wife and whispered, "Bessie, what if I hadn't seen them? What if I wasn't sitting in my chair looking out the window?"

I realized at that moment it was no coincidence or stroke of luck that I had seen the Krahn soldier on the street pointing at our house. What man was smart enough, rich enough, powerful enough, or clever enough to safeguard and preserve his own life? I realized my life was not under my own control but under that of a higher power. Only by his protection and intervention were we taking our evening walk. Together we breathed a prayer of thanks and praised God despite our fear.

We turned up the street and continued on toward our sanctuary for the night. We spoke to no one as we walked, which wasn't difficult. Anymore, people rarely ventured out at night. Death lurked in the dark, and to go out was merely to tempt it.

The death squad came later that night, our next-door neighbors reported to us the next day. They heard the Jeep arrive a little after midnight. They dared not look out their windows for fear of being seen. They heard the crack of automatic gunfire coming from our front yard. After a minute or two of noise, all fell silent.

Next morning, the neighbors came around to check on us. The Gonlehs were nowhere to be found. Not knowing what had happened, they assumed our entire family had been taken away. There was nothing to do except to go back to their houses. Who would they call? The Gonlehs were hunted enemies of the state. During these days, even the police were afraid of the government soldiers. They were helpless, both the neighbors and the police. Where were the Gonlehs?

The next morning, Bessie stayed with the children while I returned to check out the situation. Neighbors were outside talking with several other neighbors when they spotted me coming toward them. They thought we all must be dead and were astonished to see me walking calmly up the street, but surprised expressions quickly gave way to joyous hugs.

I described to them how the Lord had saved us, and the neighbors quickly recounted the night's events. After thirty minutes I returned to the Kabas and retold the neighbors' tale. Joined by our good friends, the Kabas, we once again praised God for his protection.

That morning, more than a few neighbors saw the Gonlehs walking down the street with six children dressed in their pajamas slowly making their back home. We prepared food during the day, and the next night we followed the same routine. Our friends were happy to let us sleep over for the entire week.

Thankfully, the death squad came for us only the first night our neighbors reported. After a week we thought it was safe enough to return permanently to our house.

Days wore on, and the rebels inched closer to the city. Government soldiers grew reluctant to carry out their death raids in outlying suburbs like Paynesville. There was a growing likelihood that they would encounter the advancing rebel troops. They didn't want to risk their lives fighting an enemy that could fight back.

Fortunately, the death squads operated only at night to hide their identities. Government soldiers could have just as easily murdered the Mano in daylight, except they preferred the night. Perhaps the reason for this was the looming threat to their safety. It was becoming apparent the rebels were going to take the city. The last thing these soldiers wanted was for any citizen to be able to identify them and what crimes they had committed. That would have meant certain torture and a horrible lingering death at the hands of the rebels.

Time was running out for President Doe and all of Monrovia. The rebels continued to advance on the government positions. Street by street and block by block they came. Suffering terrible losses didn't deter the rebels. All of the conscripts were expendable, and with enough drugs, guns, bullets, and bodies they would eventually win. By late June it was all but inevitable the suburbs like Paynesville would fall. President Doe and his death squads had retreated to the city center, leaving the outskirts unprotected. For us, it was just a matter of days.

THE FINAL INVESTIGATION 10

July 11, 1990

W e didn't have to travel far, only ten or fifteen minutes in the large truck. During the short trip I kept praying and pleading with God, over and over, to take control of the situation. We turned off the main paved road onto a dirt side road, and from there into a small field.

The field was savannah bush grass. It may have once been cleared of trees, but there was no sign of a farm. The bush grass had grown high as it always does during the rainy season. It was about seven feet tall. The truck turned in and made a tight circle, further matting down the already flattened grass. Apparently this wasn't the first time the truck had been here. The truck circled completely around until it was pointed back out the way it had come in. Once again, with gears grinding, the truck jerked to an abrupt halt.

I couldn't really see very well, just glimpses of the scenery around the standing men but I knew we were near Paynesville. I had recognized some of the landmarks we'd passed along the way. Much of the journey, however, I had my eyes closed, continuing to pray. I didn't have to worry about falling as the truck hit potholes in the paved road or uneven ruts in the dirt road.

We were all squeezed in together, arms pinned at our sides. There was no risk of anyone falling over. There was nowhere to go. We all just swayed in unison right or left and front or backward like our choir did at Immanuel Baptist when they performed.

Once the truck stopped, we didn't have to wait long. Soldiers removed the rear gate, and prisoners carefully jumped or climbed down off the truck bed. Shuffling slowly toward the rear, I think we were all glad to be finally making some progress. At least it was a nice change of scenery from the pain and torture back at #72 Soldiers' Barrack.

I arrived at the edge and was able to jump down without assistance. Some of the prisoners were suffering so from their injuries that they needed the help of their cell mates to get down without stumbling and sprawling on the ground.

Once on solid ground I turned and looked around, confirming my earlier assessment. We were standing in an open field, about eighty feet across, of matted-down bush grass. It was clear that people had been here before. I assumed that the size roughly coincided with the turning diameter of the large truck. Other sections seemed like they had been driven over by heavy earthmoving equipment. In some spots near the center of the small field I saw the red dirt mounded up in a pattern as if a tractor had been there. The large tractor wheels must have sunk into the moist earth and disrupted the matted bush grass.

As I continued to look around while the remaining prisoners disembarked, I was suddenly struck by another thought: *There is nothing here. There is no table. There are no judges. There is no jury. It is just an empty field.* I started to get a sick, sinking feeling.

I looked at the prisoner next to me and caught his eyes. The look I saw in his eyes was confusion and shock mingled with a growing recognition of why they had actually brought us to this particular spot. I'm sure he saw the same reaction in mine.

Whether beneficial or not, the human brain actually has a "mind" of its own that is not subject to the will of its owner. It will refuse to react to situations and circumstances that violate its own deepest core beliefs. For instance, this brain has trouble with statements like "Your child was playing outside and died after being bitten by a green mamba," or "Your wife has just been diagnosed with terminal cancer; she has only weeks to live." Any thought or notion so repugnant the independent brain cannot accept, it simply rejects, at least temporarily. I remembered that denial is one of the first steps of the grieving process.

So it was with us prisoners looking around a stark and empty field. We all experienced a kind of shocked disbelief. One part of our brains was in denial, while another part knew exactly why we were here. I'm sure we all recognized what the signs meant, but our brains wouldn't cooperate. One part tells you you're about to be killed, and another part says that's impossible; *I can't be about to die.*

Without agreement in our own brains, the soldiers did our thinking for us. For this reason, when we were ordered to make a circle in the center of the clearing, everyone dutifully complied. No one tried to run or make a break for it. *They all like sheep have gone astray,* I thought.

I don't know if anyone could have run and gotten away before he was shot down, but in any case no one tried to run. Down to a man, we all did what we were told. Nervously, all one hundred men slowly made a circle, shoulder to shoulder. The circle was about twenty to thirty feet across. Just as we all got in place and our circle formed up, the commander spoke. "God-man," he said, calling to me as he edged back away from the circle.

I turned, and when he saw I was looking, with a half-smile curling his upper lip, he once again said, "God-man, get in the center of the circle and say a prayer for these men." I left my spot in the circle and went to the center. I looked at the men and they looked at me. By now the commander had joined the guards, all standing back near the truck about forty feet from the edge of the circle. Then I bowed my head and said, "Let us pray."

With those words of mine commenced a loud crack as the sound of automatic rifle fire pierced the calm. Startled and jerking my head up, I saw a prisoner across from me register a shocked look of surprise and pain. Looking past him, past the matted-down grass, I saw a rebel standing up in the tall grass.

Where did he come from? I thought. In my peripheral vision, I glimpsed several more rebel soldiers with automatic weapons standing in the tall bush grass. They had not been there a moment before. They must have been hiding in the grass. They were stationed every few feet apart. Deafening sounds filled the air. The circle collapsed toward me as the men rushed, were struck, and stumbled toward the center. Instinctively, their unthinking minds propelled their bodies forward as if to outrun the bullets. The roar and crack of bullets shot continuously from twenty to thirty automatic rifles now filled the air.

Crowds of men were all around me. I couldn't move. It was as if each man's mind gave him the same message: Run away from the danger. Their unthinking minds driven by instinct didn't comprehend that the rebels had planned this well ahead of time.

We were surrounded and taking fire from all sides. Men were falling, mortally wounded, as they stumbled forward. In the next moment, I too had hit the ground into the dirt and matted grass.

The rebels continued to rake the prisoners with machine-gunfire from all sides. Rebels practiced overkill. Prisoners' bodies were filled with bullets well beyond any lethal level. I don't recall anything else that happened on a conscious level.

For all intents and purposes I died. Along with all the other unfortunate victims, my brain shut down. I don't know how much time passed. I don't remember hearing any last gasps. I never heard all the moans of the dying as life slipped away. I don't remember anything.

But then, with a start, I returned. The shooting stopped. Going from the air filled with the roar of continuous gunfire from AK-47s to dead silence was just as much a shock to my system as the opposite had been.

It suddenly occurred to me then that I was alive. I didn't know if I was shot. I didn't know if anyone else was alive, but I was alive!

I couldn't move. As I lay there it slowly dawned on me that I was buried. Something was pressing down on me. Something else was poking me in my back, in my left arm and on my legs. I could turn my head a little but at first dared not.

I'm not sure how much more time passed, but then I heard the large truck drive away. "They've left! The rebels are gone!" I whispered as my heart leaped inside of me.

While I believed they had left, I actually couldn't know for sure. That a rebel could still be posted on guard never occurred to me. Thankfully, it didn't occur to them either. Clearly, this wasn't the first time they had used this field, and their skill with weaponry was proven. Dead bodies stay put.

I tried to move and squirm. It was difficult. My left arm was near my face, but my right was pinned to my side. What was holding me down? I looked but couldn't see clearly. Something was in my eyes, something wet.

Opening them a little and squinting, I saw an arm. Cracks of sunlight illuminated small parts of the burial scene. Straining, I lifted my head, and twisting it, my eyes rested on part of a leg and then a face. The face was lifeless and pale, eyes staring intently at me but no brain functioning to process and interpret the picture.

I tried to wipe away the wet in my eyes but couldn't get my arm close enough. Ceasing my effort for a moment I lay still, thinking what to do. Then in addition to the sound of my own breathing, I heard a short soft wheeze quickly followed by a slightly louder gurgling sound.

That was it. I started to panic. Instantly, I twisted, turned, clawed, pushed, and struggled upward. I realized now that I was covered with the dead or dying bodies of my fellow prisoners. As I fought to get clear, their bodies slowly complied with my will just as they had complied with the will of the rebels.

Fighting my way up through bodies piled on top of me, I finally got out. I scrambled to my feet. My hands instinctively wiped my eyes. I stumbled as I tried to get my footing.

As I was falling I saw in my peripheral vision the blood covering my hands and arms. I went down and landed with one hand on a neck and the other on a back. No objections were raised. Regaining my footing and balance, I stood up again. I listened carefully. No more sounds were forthcoming from the pile. Save my own, all other striving had ceased. Scanning the scene of carnage, I saw all one hundred bodies of my fellow prisoners. Every prisoner lay dead except for me.

I looked down at my shorts and my legs, my feet, my torn shirt; I saw that I was soaked in blood and dirt. I started to panic again and fought to bring my emotions under control.

Surveying the scene, I saw the personified definition of "blood-bath." Bodies were strewn on the ground, intertwined with other bodies. One corpse hugged another around the torso, and it in turn had a hand grasping its ankle. It almost appeared that we men who typically shun intimate friendships in life embraced them as our last dying act of humanity.

The slaughter that began with the twenty-foot circle had collapsed to an even tighter kill zone. In the center bodies were stacked several feet high. Being sent to the center to pray, I was under that pile.

For the rebels, it was like shooting fish in a barrel. They couldn't miss, especially with an automatic rifle. Just as they had been trained, the rebels raked their initial fire back and forth horizontally. Vertically, they kept their elevation range from knees to groin so they wouldn't shoot across the circle and risk hitting each other. Mid-section shots to their legs incapacitated the victims, causing them to fall—seriously injured but not necessarily dead. Once the victims were on the ground, the soldiers lowered their fire angle to take in upper torso and head shots. Proven techniques like these ensured no survivors.

It was obvious now that the rebels had used this spot before, bury-ing the previous victims in a mass grave. My group would soon join them. The earth would reclaim and receive back what had been taken from it years before in the form of living beings. Before long, even the bones would decay and be returned to the rich, thick clay of Liberia. Anonymous mass graves would soon disappear under the prolific Savannah bush grass, and all traces of the atrocity would disappear under a field of green.

Not thinking clearly, I tried to step over or around the bodies. It would have normally been a case of "Excuse me, pardon me, sorry about that." But now no one took offense and graciously permitted me to step on their hands and fingers as I stumbled outward from the center.

With one glance back, I recoiled at the amount of blood and grime gleaming in the sun. I couldn't help but stare. Some of the blood was still gathering in small streams and rivulets, flowing into the large pools and puddles that disappeared under the main center pile of bodies.

Soon, all remains of human life and vitality would become dry and caked. After that would come the front-end loader to scoop them all up and take them to their final resting place. I now understood the tractor-tire prints in the grass. Without looking over my shoulder, I ran into the tall grass.

POST MORTEM 11

JOHN

I ran like a wild animal pursued by hunters, crashing pell-mell through the grass, past the trees, and into the swamp. There, I slowed down and then finally stopped, wheezing and panting from the exertion. Bent over with my hands on my knees, I caught my breath. Slowly I straightened up, looked around, and got my bearings. Checking behind me now, I didn't see anyone following. Dead men don't get up and walk away.

When I realized I knew this area and where I was, I turned and aimed for home. Thank God it was only a few miles away. The swamp held serious dangers, including poisonous snakes, scorpions, leeches, and ticks. Liberia has some of the most lethal poisonous snakes on the planet: black and green mambas, Egyptian and black spitting cobras, the West African bush viper, the gaboon and rhinoceros-horned vipers, and puff adders. In addition to poisonous snakes were the boa constrictors and the dwarf crocodiles, which can grow as long as six feet. All of these once terrified me as they do all Liberians, but now, they were nothing to me. Somehow, miraculously, I had just survived attack from the most dangerous animals on the planet. God's lesser swamp creatures held no fear for me now.

Slowly I made my way through the marsh. I looked back occasionally to make sure I wasn't being followed. Logic told me this wasn't necessary, but I looked anyway. I hadn't really noticed anything else around the field before I ran away. The bodies held my attention as I escaped.

I now ran as fast as I could to reach my house and find Bessie and the children. I ran and ran, cutting through fields, ditches, and small farms cultivated by squatters. I guessed that the killing field was only five miles from my house.

I slowed down to catch my breath and then tried to run again. Even though I'd been gone a week, it now seemed that time was of the essence and every moment precious and irretrievable. I had to get home as fast as possible.

Finally, I came through some trees and saw my Paynesville neighborhood. Another minute and I'd be able to see my house. Anticipation helped drive my weary legs forward until I at last saw it.

I stopped as I took in the full image. Only a blackened frame stood where my beautiful house had once been. I must be looking at the wrong house, my brain told me. So I used the edges of my worn shirt to carefully wipe my eyes free of blood and dirt. Then I looked again.

There was no mistaking the charred rubble that had once been my house. It sat, burned to the ground, between my two neighbors' houses that remained intact and undisturbed.

After all I'd been through, now this. It was too much. Bessie and the children were dead. I dropped my face into my hands and sank to my knees. I began to sob. It was all my fault. I was responsible for their deaths. I had gotten them killed. My beautiful Bessie. My beautiful children. All dead. I wept bitter tears.

Had I been thinking rationally, I might have decided to kill myself at that point. I had miraculously survived the massacre in the killing field and had everything to live for in Bessie and the children if I could just get back to them. Now, surviving seemed like a cruel irony. My only reason for my living was now dead.

And yet I still lived. I had depended on God entirely during my ordeal, and miraculously he had brought me through it. And it was for this; my wife and children dead. "How Lord? Why? Jesus? Jesus?" I pled.

What could I pray now? What could I say? I had no idea. I was completely drained of life, emotion, feelings, and rational thought. My mind became clouded with jumbled images of all the traumas of the last six months. Like a movie reel, my mind played them—the news flash that ruined Christmas and started this madness; the looks on the faces of my employees when I told them I would have to shut down the block factory; the rebel dressed in his choir robe as he came through my front door and directly toward me.

God is punishing me. That's what this is all about, I reasoned. "Dear God, I didn't do anything wrong. I'm innocent. Why me, Lord," I pled toward heaven. Heaven wasn't talking. Exhausted, I remained in my kneeling position, not feeling much of anything. *Why? Why?* Just then another thought flashed through my mind and jarred me out of my stupor: *My Son didn't do anything wrong either. He was completely innocent.* That thought sank slowly and deeply into my psyche.

And then I repented. I could not comprehend the reasons for what I had been through. With no understanding, I understood that God was God. He had chosen his own Son to suffer much more than I ever would, and he was truly innocent. I was not.

Sick with grief, loss, and hunger, I started to drift off. Shaking myself, I forced my mind to refocus on the immediate task of survival. After a little while longer on my knees, I decided I had to do something; I couldn't just stay on my knees forever.

I hadn't eaten in a week, and now my stomach started to reassert its demands. For a week living in fear, continual stress, and the pain of the torture, I hadn't thought much about food. At the barrack there had been a water well with a hand pump, so we had plenty to drink, just no food. I now know why our captors felt no need to feed us. I immediately felt guilty. My wife and children were dead and my thoughts turned toward food. Still, this most basic of human needs drove me, and I decided to look for my next meal.

I didn't know where to go. I could go south and track along the coast highway. That road would lead me toward Grand Gedeh County and Krahn militia or soldiers loyal to President Doe. To go back toward

Monrovia was unthinkable. That would just put me going toward President Doe and the army who had already tried to kill me.

That left my only option: to go north from Paynesville on the Ganta Highway. If I walked far enough on that road, I would eventually reach Nimba County. One group of rebels had just tried to murder me. Hopefully, I would fare better in areas where no one would know who I was. Additionally, I could still speak Danh, the Mano dialect. That should help protect me if I encountered rebels who were coming from Nimba County.

My decision was made. With one last look at my burned house, I struggled to my feet. Pain shot through my body as I stood up. So with my world destroyed, my family dead, I set off. It was not yet midday, but the hot Liberian sun beat down. Along with my sweat, the blood that still clung to me was sticky and filled my nostrils with the stench of my comrades' remains.

As I walked I didn't know how I was going to get anything to eat. My clothes and body were covered in blood. Anyone who saw me would be terrified. They would take me for a rebel or a criminal. I didn't have a weapon, and without one people who encountered me might try to kill me. I resolved I had to avoid everyone if possible until I found something to eat, different clothes, and a place to get cleaned up.

If anyone was still left in Paynesville I didn't see them. No one was outside. Leaving Paynesville, I made my way to the Ganta Highway and turned north.

I stayed in the bush grass and fields off the main road. I was far enough away from the highway that I couldn't see it, but I could still hear cars as they went by. I dared not venture closer to get a better look. I was sure rebels were all over, and I still heard frequent gunshots as I walked.

I was able to remain well hidden in the tall grass. While being unseen was a comfort to me, the going was slow. I had no machete. There was no trail. I had to just push the grass over or part it with my outstretched arms as I slowly advanced. Insects didn't seem to bother me much. All the dried blood and mud coating my arms, legs, face,

POST MORTEM

and neck must have provided some protection against mosquitoes. Mosquitoes liked fresh blood, not the caked blood that covered me. My constant movement also kept the flies to a minimum.

The landscape was low forest and savannah grass. Palm trees were everywhere, but there was nothing I could get any food from. I would just have to keep going until I came upon something.

I had been walking for hours and still had not come across any farms. I was starting to get desperate as I gradually weakened. Fighting the savannah grass without water or food was sapping my little remaining strength. I had to find something to eat.

After some four to six hours of walking I came across a bush trail. I knew there had to be a small village nearby, and near a village were always some small farms. Trails always indicated people and with people, villages, and with villages, food.

In Liberia, during harvest season from November to January, farmers who normally live in the city with nice houses will relocate to small thatched-hut villages near their farms. As harvest approaches, they move close to their crops to prevent thieves from stealing their produce. Unfortunately it wasn't harvest time. It was July and there was no crop to be had. Crops had been planted in March and April, but they wouldn't be mature.

Nevertheless, traveling down one of the trails led me to an old cassava farm, and I started to look for food. No one else was around. I didn't expect to see anyone. Farms only yield one crop and then are abandoned for six years to allow the earth time to replenish its nutrients. Either everyone had fled, or the nearby village was only occupied during harvest.

My only hope was that perhaps some cassava roots had been overlooked during the last harvest. I scoured the ground looking for a telltale sign or clue of anything that could be considered edible. I saw the tender leaves of fledgling cassava roots left over from last year's crop but knew I would find no sustenance from digging them up. The ground was overgrown with weeds as the bush slowly reclaimed the land. It had rained recently, and weeds grow quickly. The bush grass reached heights of eight feet in some places. Seeing the tall grass, I thought once again of the rebels hiding in the tall grass with their automatic weapons.

I hoped the old farm would yield scattered seeds of cassava, pota-toes, bananas, or watermelons that had taken root and grown. But as hungry as I was I had no luck in finding anything. I knew it was the wrong time of year, but I didn't know where else to look. I had been looking for some time when a feeling of despair slowly started to envelop me. I was so hungry. I sank to my knees. "God, please help me. I have to have something to eat."

As tears filled my eyes I wiped them away and kept scouring the ground, looking past the weeds for anything edible. Then, in my peripheral vision, a movement made me stop.

Looking up, I saw a woman coming around a bend in a trail. Forgetting my appearance I shouted out to her. "Sister, please help me. Help me, please?" Startled, she looked up, stared at me for a moment, and then let out a horrible shriek of fear.

Whirling around, she started to run away. I was too exhausted to chase her. I cried out, "Please, sister. I'm not a rebel. I'm not going to hurt you. I'm hungry. I've been tortured by the rebels. Please help me."

As I kept shouting, I noticed my words had an effect on her. She stopped and turned warily toward me. As I looked at her, I realized that I recognized her. She was one of our Paynesville neighbors. She lived on the next block over from ours.

She didn't recognize me at first but stared at me as one might stare at a slaughtered animal for the first time. I looked down at myself and remembered that I was covered in dried blood from my hair to my clothes, legs, and arms. She had been terrified by my appearance and now, horrified, couldn't take her eyes off the remains of my fel-low prisoners.

She still didn't recognize me. I said, "I know you from Paynesville. I'm John Gonleh and my wife is Bessie. We lived near you in the same neighborhood." She looked closer, past the blood and then at my face as recognition slowly dawned.

As quickly as I could, I blurted out what had happened to me, that I'd been tortured, and how the rebels had burned my house down and killed Bessie and the children. I was the only one left alive in my family. Everyone else was dead.

I only hoped that she would have compassion and assist me. If she refused to help me then I would probably die. The act of telling another human that my wife and children were dead finally drained me. Fully spent were the last traces of strength and willpower I'd exhausted fighting death for the past week. She was my last hope.

At my words, she registered a look of puzzlement, trying to make sure she understood what I was saying. Interrupting, she exclaimed, "Bessie and the children are not dead. They're alive. They are in the same village as me just a short ways away. I left the village to come back here to look for food. Here, I'll take you to them."

I couldn't believe my ears. Could it be? I couldn't take it in. I was in shock. "Not dead? They're alive? Are you sure?" I gasped.

"Yes, of course I'm sure. They're alive and in Wako Village. I'll take you to them," she said again.

I was stunned. Once more, tears welled up, and I fell to my knees. I didn't know what to feel. I just wept from renewed hope. "Jesus, Jesus, Jesus." I repeated the Lord's name over and over. "Thank you, Lord. Thank you, Jesus." They weren't dead. They were alive. I couldn't believe it.

Before we started for the village, my appearance had to be dealt with. My neighbor told me I couldn't go to the village looking like I did. Covered in blood, she said, the villagers would think I was a rebel and, being alone, might attack and kill me.

In an unoccupied thatch roofed hut near the field the woman found a bright and colorful *lapa*. I first wrapped it around my torso. Then I secured the garment by tying the corners around my neck. I'm sure I looked a sight with a *lapa* worn over my blood-soaked clothes and body.

With the *lapa* secure, I started to follow her up the path. After walking just a short way she stopped, turned around toward me, and said thoughtfully, "You know, you're really lucky that I found you when I did."

With that she turned back and started up the trail again. As the tears rolled down my blood- and mud-streaked face and fell onto the *lapa*, I kept close behind her as we wound through the lush Liberian countryside. With this most recent turn of events, as hungry as I was, I completely forgot about my stomach.

After walking about twenty minutes or so, we finally came to Wako Village. We entered a few hundred yards from the chief's hut. As we strode through the village, past huts, past people milling about, more than a few stared and then followed as they called out to their friends.

I had forgotten about my appearance, but the villagers no doubt thought they were seeing an apparition of a Juju spirit in the form of a walking human. I started to breathe hard from the anticipation.

My neighbor called out as we approached the chief's hut. I couldn't speak. Lack of food and water, along with mental and emotional exhaustion, had rendered me a spectator to my own life.

Bessie emerged from the hut, followed by the children. A look of puzzlement registered on her face. What was so important that Ma Rachel would call out for her in a loud voice? She looked at our neighbor but didn't see the strange creature straggling close behind her.

I still couldn't speak. Even though I had been anticipating this very moment, I was overcome by shock. My brain wasn't connecting the image of my precious wife and blessed children to my voice. My body and senses froze, just like when the rebels had burst into my house, only my eyes now were able to process the scene unfolding before me. I heard nothing as I watched my wife. Her mouth opened slightly as her eyebrows lifted. She gasped in a lungful of air and her eyes grew to enormous proportions as recognition spread slowly across her face. Mercifully, at her first shriek my eardrums and senses broke free from the shock that had bound them. Her screams pierced the air, penetrating the surrounding village activities just as if it had been gunfire. Bessie and the children rushed me all at once.

Villagers jerked up and ran toward us to discover the source of the commotion. In my mind flashed a reminiscent picture. This morning, death surged toward me in the form of a hundred fellow prisoners throwing their dying bodies at me. Now life rushed at me with equal desperation and intensity.

Bessie's screaming continued as she embraced me, not noticing my horrific appearance. Snapped out of my stupor, I embraced her and croaked out unintelligible words. By this time the children surrounded us, holding me while jumping up and down. Time seemed to slow down as we embraced, hugged, kissed, laughed, and cried in one gigantic release of emotion.

Our collective unburdening of pent-up stress over the events of the last week was overwhelming. We remained for minutes in this rapturous state and soon accumulated a large crowd of onlookers. Bessie eventually calmed down enough to notice them gawking. Turning to them, she said, "My husband was lost, but now he is found. God has delivered him." No truer words were ever spoken.

WITCHCRAFT 12

June 1969

My first trip back to my home village of Garnwe occurred when I was sixteen. It was also my first encounter with witchcraft. It wouldn't be my last.

Stepping off the bus on the outskirts of Garnwe, I encountered an idyllic village scene. All was peaceful and calm. It was quiet except for the occasional chirps of rice birds flitting about or the laughter of children going about their afternoon chores, having returned from walking their three-mile trek to the government school.

Smoke rose lazily from the crest of the kitchen huts, combining with other plumes high overhead and forming a low-hanging cloud over the entire village. Stripes of sunlight would break through the smoke blanket, softening as they passed through almost so as to not strike the ground too harshly.

Absent from the scene was the loud harshness of the city. There were no cars, exhaust, honking horns, or blaring stereos or televisions.

Diminutive but hardy bush chickens pecked at the ground all day long. Roosters performed their daily jobs of announcing the new day repeatedly, each in a daily competition with his fellow fowl for volume and duration. Now, in the late afternoon, however, only an occasional rooster would continue to announce his self-proclaimed supremacy over the village.

The few scrawny cows that belonged to the rich families wandered on the edge of the bush grass. As herd animals, they kept close together, but any natural predators—leopards, for example—had been long ago dispatched. Now predators found refuge from hunters only in the deepest rain forest. The cows didn't want to take any chances, however, and never ventured far from the village. Cud was plentiful from the bush grass and low forest vegetation growing in the fallow fields near the village.

Finding my family's hut, I announced myself and received a rambunctious greeting with hugs and kisses from my parents, brothers, and sisters. I only vaguely remembered my siblings. They had changed just as I had.

Stepping into our hut, I noticed the fetish at the top of the doorframe. My father had carefully secured it so that all who entered or exited would pass under the fetish and receive either its positive protection for family and friends or negative magic against a neighbor with hidden evil intent. I imagined that my father, taught by his father and grandfather, must have thought constantly of the spirits and demons that inhabited the jungle. It seemed so foreign to me that anyone believed these superstitions.

Later, I inquired about the Juju fetish, and my father explained that it had been purchased from North African traders from Morocco. The fetish was expensive, almost the price of three cutlass sharpening files, but if it performed its job of protection, then it was worth the cost. I said nothing.

In fact, my father was the village *zo*, the headman of the secret Poro Devil Bush Society. It was a position passed down from generation to generation through the eldest son. The bush society offered protection and instruction in appeasement of the spirits. You never knew when you might unwittingly offend a spirit, so Juju fetishes were owned and rituals were carefully followed.

I immediately felt uncomfortable as I realized I would have to deal with this, being the oldest son. Beneath the peaceful exterior appearance of rural village life lay another realm of spirits and demons that must be appeased. As a new Christian of several months, I knew I could not accept these beliefs.

From the time I was nine years old, I had been taught about the Bible at the Carver Mission School. I believed that these Juju fetishes and secret ceremonies were nothing more than superstitions designed to keep people captive and slaves to their irrational fears.

Fetishes and secret practices only had power because people believed they had power. Sometimes a fetish consisted of nothing more than deer's cud wrapped in a banana leaf and tied with a vine. It had no power.

The next morning I arose early. My mother was already up, minding the fire in order to fix "tea," the family's first food of the day. For tea, my family was prosperous enough to have a small meal, and my mother would prepare farina, oatmeal-like cereal made from ground cassava powder, or perhaps roasted plantains or roasted cassava slices.

As tradition dictated, at every meal, my father ate first, and whatever was left was eaten by my mother, and then whatever was left from that went to the children. My father never ate with my mother or the children but would often eat dinner, the evening meal, with his friends.

It sounds harsh and unloving of my father, but it was just customary to eat in this manner. Village life held many customs that were now foreign to me.

After tea, my father emerged from our hut to check the sharpness of his cutlass, or machete, for the daily task of clearing the bush or repairing the hut. If the blade was dull, the store-bought file would be carefully taken out to sharpen the edge.

Hard currency was difficult to come by in a subsistence farm community, but there was no substitute for a good file and a sharp cutlass. These constituted the main and only tools needed to effectively survive in the bush. Proper care was taken.

As the village *zo*, my father was more prosperous than most of his neighbors. His position allowed him certain latitude to make a little more money by those who curried his favor. He was also a successful farmer and had been able to scrape together enough cash to send me to boarding school in Monrovia since I was nine.

Later that morning, we took a walk around the village, greeting the neighbors, and made our way down to the river. That brought forth an interesting story about the local spirits and demons.

One neighbor related how a man in another village had drowned in the river. This man crossed the river back and forth every day in a dugout canoe to go to his work. One time his canoe tipped over, dumping the man into the river, and the man subsequently drowned. His family, as well as this neighbor, believed that the "Nigi" people pulled him under the water and drowned him. The Nigi people are supposedly spirit demons that live under the water, and they would certainly kill you if they could by drowning you. You have to be careful around the water, and for this reason most Liberians never learn to swim.

This unfortunate man, however, had to cross the river to get to work. On the day he drowned, he was wearing large rubber boots that filled with water, weighing him down. However, this man's family and our neighbor were convinced that the Nigi had drowned him, not the water in his boots. Perhaps the Nigi knew the man had these boots on and chose that moment to attack the canoe and tip it over. You could never be sure about these things so it was better to avoid the water, pray to the Juju, and observe all the rituals needed to placate the forest spirits and demons.

Walking back to the village, my father told me that this particular Nigi story was probably told in every village in Liberia. He had heard it many times himself. No one actually knew the man that drowned, but everyone knew the story.

Why did my father send me to the Christian school? I asked myself. *Didn't he know that Christian beliefs are completely at odds with these traditional beliefs and the practices of the bush society?*

My second day back, the news that the bush devil would be passing through the village that evening spread quickly through the village. All women and children had to close the blinds tight and not look out. Only those initiated in the bush society were permitted to gaze upon the devil.

Normally boys are given to the bush devil by their fathers when they are between six and ten years old. Boys are taken by the bush devil into the jungle for a minimum of three months. There they are instructed in the secret ways of the society—witchcraft and herbal medicines—and are circumcised as a right of passage. Once initiated, no one can ever leave the society.

Occasionally, a boy taken for initiation will not return at the end of the initiation period. The only explanation given to the parents is that he was given the honor of staying in the jungle, "putting fire in the devil's pipe," a euphemism for being made a human sacrifice.

Perhaps, deep down, my father wanted his firstborn son to break free of the traditional ways, even though he himself was both captive to and a leader in sustaining and continuing the ancient traditions. Perhaps God intervened in some mysterious way to influence my father's decision. I don't know.

It was common in those days for Liberian families to send a child to school in Monrovia. Powerful *zoes* of the bush society may have recognized that the traditional ways were fading away and being replaced by education as the new path to importance and status. But when my father made the decision for me to go to Monrovia, my life would follow a very different path from anything I could have imagined.

Now I had a problem. Everyone in the village, including my father, would expect me to join the society. But I was a Christian. I decided I would not leave the hut. I would stay inside with the women and children. To go out and gaze upon the bush devil meant acceptance of the society. To stay inside meant I rejected it.

When I told Alfred, my brother, and my other old friends that I wasn't going outside, they thought I was joking. Then, when they realized I was serious, they were incredulous and couldn't believe I would defy my own father, the village *zo*.

But I had made up my mind. The bush society practices were incompatible with my new Christian faith. I could not compromise.

Before my decision, I was destined to be *zo* in the village bush society. My father was *zo*. My grandfather before him was *zo*. What my father had not reckoned on, however, was the consequences of his decision to send his eldest son to school in the city years earlier.

The devil's power operated in secret and usually at night. There were many devils of various ranks, and my father was a devil himself. Most people in the village knew the identity of the devil, but fear kept them from talking about it. The real power of the devil however was when he donned the *kru* mask, a large, carved wooden mask depicting a spirit or demon. The man and mask each held some power individually, but it was amplified when these two were combined. Then the man became the devil, and everyone in his own and surrounding villages both respected and feared the power he could wield.

That evening, all windows and doors were shut tight and the curtains drawn. A little after midnight, I heard the drumbeat a long distance off. Only my mother and sisters and I were in the hut. My father and brothers had left earlier in the evening.

When I told my father my decision that afternoon, he looked deeply into my eyes, saw the determination on my face, and then nodded in acceptance. I wondered if he knew this was the inevitable result of my schooling in Monrovia. Perhaps he wanted it for himself but couldn't break with his role in perpetuating the bush society. I thanked God that my father accepted my decision without argument.

The noise reverberated in my ears as it steadily grew near, penetrating the bush for miles in all directions. As they came, the jungle drums grew steadily louder, and eventually I heard the sounds of chanting. It was clear that the procession had grown larger, picking up members as it passed through the bush. Now they were at my village.

Winding throughout the village, they came to my family's hut. I couldn't tell for sure, but it seemed that they slowed to a near stop, perhaps to give me one last chance to change my mind, one last chance to follow in my father's and grandfather's footsteps.

I felt my heart beating in unison with the pounding of the drums just outside the thin hut walls. It was as though the drums called to me to come out, join them, and receive the acceptance of the group. Instead, I bowed my head in prayer, asking for strength. I wanted to remain a Christian, but I didn't want my family to reject me for rejecting the bush society. After a short time I heard the drums moving on past our hut and through the remainder of the village. My test was over. God had given me the strength, and I had successfully resisted.

The rest of my weeklong stay was a happy time. No one mentioned the bush society or my decision or tried to force me to justify myself. For that I was thankful. At the end of the week I returned to school in Monrovia and didn't return to Garnwe for many years.

CHESTER 13

BESSIE July, 1990

John's strength slowly returned over the next few days. After his arrival at Wako Village, we seemed to exist in a dream state. Ordinary village scenes took on a new dimension of detail and clarity. The smell of yams cooking, smoke from the meager fires, and the familiar scent of John lying next to me on the mat all conveyed familiarity but with a new sense of discovery. The children were more animated and expressive than they had ever been. Overall, the situation was bad and worsening daily, but my heart was fresh and renewed.

Other refugees arriving from Monrovia and Paynesville had swelled Wako from 150 people to more than 350. With so many, it became more difficult to find food in the bush. We had to forage farther and farther from the village. Hardships abounded, and yet a sense of wonder and awe suffused the scene.

As he was able, John gradually related all the details of his horrendous ordeal. God had delivered John as surely as he had delivered Jonah. Like Jonah, John could have prayed, "In my distress I called to the Lord, and he answered me. From the depths of the grave I called for help and you listened to my cry."

The Lord had surely saved my husband, the children, and me. I did not fear the rebels. Who were they compared to our God? Who was Charles Taylor that we should fear him? Just a man. God had answered our prayers. Jesus had delivered John. The Holy Spirit had demonstrated his power in our lives.

So surrounded by suffering and death in the village, I felt a quietness in my spirit. For me, calm permeated Wako Village. A deep and lingering joy dwelled in my heart that the God of the universe knew and cared about my family and me. He had heard our cries and in our distress had saved my entire family. Praise be to God!

While I had no doubt that God had saved our family, we couldn't ignore our deteriorating situation. More and more refugees streamed into the village from Monrovia. Wako happened to be next to the main highway and was the first village where, it seemed, everyone stopped.

Compounding the danger were the increasingly frequent—sometimes several in a day—raids by the rebels. A Jeep would arrive, and five or six soldiers would pile out. The soldiers would grab people tending their laundry and lead them away at gunpoint. Others would be taken away as they were walking back into the village after foraging for food in the bush. Perhaps someone looked too rich from their clothes or shoes. There never was any rhyme or reason. It was just senseless killing.

A general panic ensued. You never wanted to be caught by the rebels out in the open. That made you a prime target. It was better to remain in the hut most of the time.

John and I spent more and more time systematically teaching the girls the traditional chores and skills of village and bush life. They hated it, and I didn't blame them. I had been glad to escape this way of life when my father took me to Monrovia at the age of twelve to attend school. But being city girls, my children didn't know the first thing about country life.

Thankfully, though, both John and I had spent the first years of our lives in villages, and now those long-dormant skills and knowledge were put into use. Danger from the rebels was constant, so we knew our children's lives could well depend on how well they learned their lessons.

We started with firewood. The girls were afraid to venture into the forest. They had never actually been inside a Liberian forest and needed reassurance that their parents and their heavenly Father would protect them. We taught them to look for dry sticks or branches that had broken off trees and fallen to the ground. We warned them to be careful and watch out for snakes. Snakes like to curl up around dry sticks more than green sticks because the dry sticks get warmer in the sunshine.

We also had to teach the girls to be careful when walking along bush paths during the hottest part of the day. When the sun is high, snakes like to come out of their holes for a sun bath. They lie alongside the bush paths to watch for frogs. The clear paths give the snakes a long unencumbered view to see potential prey they can't see in the overgrown bush grass. This also made walking those paths dangerous, so extreme caution was necessary.

John didn't let the girls use the borrowed axe for fear they would hurt themselves. Gloria tried to use a cutlass, but after a short time, it gave her blisters and she complained. The wood had to be split into pieces to make it easy to carry. I showed them how to collect vines wrapped around trees as rope to tie up the bundle of firewood.

Then I showed them how to make a *kata*, a green branch of palm leaves woven and formed into a wreath for the head. The *kata* cushioned our heads underneath the firewood bundles we carried. The older girls and I collected wood twice per week.

Next, we taught the children to pound cassava and pine nuts and how to make palm butter. We started by boiling the palm nuts to soften them and then pounded them in a mortar. Next, we showed them how to use their hands to knead the palm nut to work the seeds out. They made a game of this and enjoyed it because it was messy.

Inside the seeds is the actual palm butter. The children had to squeeze each seed to cause the butter to ooze out. Then we filtered the water to remove all the remaining chaff and debris. The result is a consistency as thick as heavy cream. This would take about thirty minutes for someone with experience. It took Gloria one hour. The little ones took even longer.

With our money, we bought some fish. There was no meat to be had around Wako Village. The palm butter together with the fish and a little water made for a satisfactory meal of palm butter stew. Nevertheless, the children constantly complained of hunger and never had enough to eat.

God was faithful, though, and throughout our six weeks in Wako Village we never went a day without something to eat. Many other people weren't as fortunate. I was willing to share some of our food. But John would only give them money. His attitude was that he worked very hard converting our money into food. He figured they could do the same.

We had to teach the girls how to go for water at the river, which was several hundred yards away. We needed the water for drinking, washing dishes, and bathing, so fetching it was a daily necessity. This proved very hard for them. They complained a lot. The buckets were heavy, and carrying them hurt their heads. They didn't want to do it.

Two weeks after my arrival at Wako Village with the children, and one week after John was reunited with us, Chester began to run a fever in the night. During the day he felt fine, but each evening he looked and acted run down and ran a low-grade fever. This continued for several weeks without changing, so we didn't think too much about it.

In order to purchase food, John had to walk forty-five minutes to the University of Liberia, Fendall Campus. The rebels allowed the Red Cross to set up a free food distribution center. In addition, farmers and merchants gathered there to sell what food there was. Arriving at the campus, the rebels set up a gate at the entrance. They appropriately named it the "God Bless You" gate. The rebels' attitude was that if a person was fortunate enough to get this far and be allowed to enter without their killing him, well, then God had blessed him.

The gate itself was of macabre construction. It wasn't actually a gate at all but consisted of two wooden posts, one on each side of the road. Atop each post was a freshly chopped-off head from some hapless victim. The heads had been crudely severed. Hanging down from the skulls were the remnants of the spines, ligaments and tendons, veins and arteries, and muscle. John told me later the rebels' machetes must have gotten dull from overuse. Apparently they hadn't had time to resharpen them.

The message to the refugees was unmistakable. Our lives meant no more to them than an ornament to be displayed and enjoyed for one day before it was discarded. John said the rebels joked the heads were replaced on a daily basis. They continuously taunted refugees passing through the gate: "Hey, you! How you like your head on my pole? No? Don't you think your head look nice? I think it is a very good head. You sure you no like make donation?" Then he and his friends would laugh heartily.

The rope barrier consisted of human entrails, intestines, stretched from one post to the other. Everyone entered and left through the "God Bless You" gate.

Inside, a market developed near the main administration building. Farmers and merchants spread out cardboard boxes or *lapas* on the ground to display greens, roasted corn, sugar cane, or rice on a round platter.

John never actually received any of the free Red Cross food. So great was the demand for the free food that people waited all day in long lines to get one or two cups of rice and a little cooking oil. People pushed and shoved. There was cutting in line and cheating. This led to many fistfights. Soldiers would come and stop the fighting, but it would start up again after they left. John used our money to purchase what we needed.

He left Wako early in the morning for the walk to Fendall. Several days when he arrived, the small amount of food for sale was gone. He returned home, dejected, and left earlier the next day.

During one of John's trips to Fendall, he recognized a cousin from Nimba County. His cousin was a rebel soldier manning one of the gates leading to the campus. This gave a boost to John's spirit. Perhaps his cousin could help us if we got into trouble with another group of rebels.

Atrocities abounded at Fendall. Rebel soldiers patrolled the university grounds, scrutinizing the refugees. They were looking for ex-government soldiers or members of the Krahn or Mandingo tribes. Rebels forced refugee men to lift their pants legs to see if they had any hair growing on their ankles. If they had been soldiers, then they previously wore socks and boots and wouldn't have much hair. No ankle hair was the equivalent of a death sentence.

Mandingo tribes people were Muslim, so the rebels would look closely at their foreheads. Mandingos prayed to Allah five times each day and bowed, touching their foreheads on the ground. Over time the slight rubbing from contact with the ground left a spot that was a little darker than the rest of their skin and identified them as Mandingo. Being a Mandingo meant death.

As far as John could tell, the rebels were never at risk of running out of fresh heads for their God Bless You gate. He was very happy to have found his cousin.

At the same time Chester's fever started, we noticed that other small children in the village were experiencing similar symptoms. What was puzzling was that all of the sick children were refugees from the city. The Wako village children were fine.

Then, we heard that first one and then another of the refugee children had died. Chester's condition had not worsened, but we were scared. Next, we heard rumors of witchcraft being practiced in the village. Going from one campfire to another, we heard all the latest gossip and news. More and more refugee children were getting sick. Some were dying. Mistrust grew between the refugees and the villagers.

We had no reason to suspect that the elderly village chief and his wife, whose hut we shared, harbored any ill will toward us. But then something changed.

John and I had been out all day foraging in the bush for food. We arrived back by late afternoon. When we got back, Chester and the girls were standing outside the hut. The girls explained that Chester had awakened from a nap screaming and run outside. He had refused to go back in until we returned. We held him for a little while and then all went into the hut.

That night Chester couldn't sleep and cried that people were chasing him. John held him tight, and during the night his fever soared. By morning Chester's skin was hot, and his complexion was so pale that he looked like a white person. We immediately thought of the witchcraft rumors that had been circulating throughout the village. We dismissed them because we don't believe in such things. Still, Chester was deathly ill.

Immediately, John and I set off for the Firestone Rubber Plantation Hospital ten miles away at Harbel. I knew we could stay with my uncle, a rubber tapper, who lived in one of the Firestone employee camps. We left the girls in the hut when we set out.

We arrived after two hours and got Chester into the hospital. Rebels were in control of the hospital but thankfully didn't prevent us from taking him inside once they saw how he looked.

A doctor took one look at his pale skin and announced that Chester needed a blood transfusion. The doctor took Chester out of John's arms and told us he would take care of him. The doctor arranged for a blood transfusion of type-O blood. Then he told us to leave, prepare food for Chester, and bring it back the next morning.

We made our way to my uncle's house near the main road leading to the hospital. Uncle Dahn was happy to see us, though he felt very sorry for Chester. We used the last of our cash to buy the best food we could, spent the night, prepared the food, and then made our way back to the hospital the next morning.

When we arrived, we couldn't find the doctor or Chester in the children's ward. We found a nurse we recognized from the day before and inquired where Chester and the doctor were. She wouldn't answer and just looked at the ground and mumbled something we couldn't understand. With rising apprehension, we quickly located another nurse and asked again where Chester was. Again, there was no answer.

We finally found the doctor, who confirmed our worst fears. Chester died on August 20, exactly six days before his fifth birthday. They hadn't been able to find enough type-O donors. Chester had received one pint but needed several. Without the blood, he died only a short time after we had left him. The doctor was very sorry.

We couldn't believe our ears. In one day Chester had gone from a healthy child to a dead corpse. How could this happen? We were told they had already taken Chester away and we couldn't see him. It was a rule the rebels instituted—to immediately remove dead bodies to prevent the spread of disease. We were reeling. Chester was our baby, our son, and now he was gone. *Oh, God.* There were no more words or prayers. We were too stunned.

We tried to ask the doctor more questions, but he didn't know what disease Chester died of. He also had no idea how a seemingly healthy child could die in only one day.

Grief-stricken, we didn't know what to do and ended up back at Uncle Dahn's. He was surprised to see us back so soon. With tears, we told him everything that had happened leading up to Chester's getting so terrified and sick in the night. We only wished we knew what had happened to our precious Chester. What had killed him?

Uncle Dahn listened to everything we said, and then he said something that shocked us to the core: "I can take you to a prophet nearby. He is a man of God and can tell you what caused Chester's death. Do you want to go to him?"

Amazed, John and I looked at each other and didn't know what to say. We had never heard such a thing as this. We said yes.

We followed Uncle Dahn and found the prophet. As a favor to my uncle, he didn't charge us anything. He had a Bible, used Bible verses, and people regularly came to him for prayer. We were told he had a reputation for being able to explain supernatural things.

The prophet started by asking us what was wrong with Chester. We explained everything that happened leading up to his death. We even told him about the low-grade fever Chester ran for several weeks. To us, there seemed to be no connection between the two fevers, but we wanted to be thorough with our description.

After hearing our story, the prophet told us it was a shame that we hadn't come to him sooner. He explained that he could have done something earlier to start a "treatment" that would have saved Chester. John and I didn't know what to say. It was all too much to hear.

The prophet explained that Wako Village was known for its witchcraft. The kindly elderly headman and his wife were the chief practitioners of this type of witchcraft.

I asked, "What type of witchcraft? How can this be? They are Christians the same as us."

The prophet explained that they were merely pretending to be Christians to gain our confidence.

Then he explained that the headman and his wife had written all our names on a list. Then they took the list down to the river and put it under the water. In this way our entire family would be killed one by one until we were all dead. Chester was just the first because he was the smallest and weakest.

Finally, the prophet told us that the headman and his wife were able to contact the Nigi people, who hold meetings under the water to decide whom to kill. The Nigi then go and capture the spirits of their victims and drain their blood. This is what happened to Chester. That is why he looked white. The only thing that was protecting the rest of our family was that we prayed to God. Otherwise, he said, more of us would already be dead.

John and I sat stunned. We couldn't believe our ears. We left the prophet and went back to Uncle Dahn's house. We tried to make sense of what the prophet had said. John said the last time he heard of the Nigi was on his trip home when he was sixteen. Also, from our limited knowledge of witchcraft, we knew that demon spirits required human blood.

Liberia's history and its present was drenched in human blood sacrifices. In only one day Chester's blood had been taken out so that his complexion became similar to a white person's. Yet, there wasn't a mark or needle prick on him to suggest that someone had physically drained his blood. Together we concluded that it had to be only witchcraft that could do this.

We didn't even believe in witchcraft, but in the bush, witchcraft was a daily fact of life. Overwhelmed and not thinking clearly, we couldn't arrive at any another explanation.

We recounted the recent events that had happened in the village. There were rumors of witchcraft activities in the village. Other refugee children had gotten sick and died before Chester did. And they were all small, around Chester's age or younger. All the evidence seemed to fit. It had to be the witchcraft of the headman and his wife.

The more John and I talked it out, the angrier we became with the elderly couple. How dare they do this to our family! We were enraged. We would make them pay for murdering our son.

That night we once again stayed with Uncle Dahn. The next morning, we decided to catch a car or Jeep with the Nimba rebels who patrolled the main road that was visible from Uncle Dahn's house. Rebel patrols drove back and forth, every twenty minutes, all day and night.

John's plan was to catch a ride with a rebel patrol with the small amount of money Uncle Dahn had given us. John would pay the rebels patrolling the road to take him to his cousin at Fendall. Then he would tell his cousin what happened. Finally he and his cousin along with his AK-47 would go exact revenge on the elderly couple. John knew his plan would work.

John and I had seen people accused of witchcraft be killed on the spot by the rebels. While many of the rebels bought Juju fetishes and practiced witchcraft for their protection and to enhance their power, they killed others who engaged in the very same activity. Many innocent people were killed by the rebels after being accused of witchcraft. A witchcraft accusation was a very effective means to settle an old score with an enemy.

John and I sat on the side of the road, waiting for the first patrol. Oddly, no cars came. We continued to wait all morning, but several hours passed without a single patrol car or Jeep going by for us to flag down. We were confused; at least ten vehicles should have passed by in the time we had been sitting.

Toward noon, I began to be convicted by the Holy Spirit and thought that what we were doing wasn't right. Yes, the headman and his wife had killed Chester, but we should leave revenge to the Lord. It wasn't for us to take matters into our own hands.

I told John what I was thinking, and he nodded wearily, agreeing that I was right. God had done so much for us. It would be sinful to murder the murderers. Justice belongs to the Lord.

With that decided we got up and trudged the three hundred yards back to Uncle Dahn's house. Once inside, we dropped into chairs and stared blankly out the front window just in time to see a rebel Jeep passing by on the main road we had just left. John and I looked at each other and realized that this was surely a sign from God.

A few minutes earlier and John's plan for revenge would have been implemented. The passing car was confirmation that God indeed had saved John and me from becoming murderers ourselves. Now we were just the grieving parents of a dead child.

Note: Years later we learned that during the war many adults and children died of a disease called acute anemia. The symptoms are a low-grade fever for a period of weeks that can appear to suddenly rise to a rapid climax as the disease overpowers the body's immune system. It turns the body white as the red blood cells are destroyed. What causes this? We will never know for sure, but we have learned several things.

Our house in Paynesville used chlorinated city water. Additionally, our front yard had a water well, and we manually chlorinated the well. The water in Wako village was unchlorinated. Chlorine kills many disease-causing microbes. This is one possible explanation why only young refugee children from the city died, and not Wako Village children. The Wako children had built up some immunity to these diseases, whereas refugee children had not.

Another possible explanation is malaria. The children, along with John and I, took malaria prevention pills every Sunday afternoon until we were forced from our house. Malaria can easily strike down healthy adults in a matter of a few weeks. Natural immunity is quickly lost when taking antimalarial medicine. Only the village children constantly exposed to malaria-carrying mosquitoes would maintain immunity.

The poor nutrition in the village could also have contributed to Chester's death. While we ate something every day, the combination of poor nutrition along with these other factors could weaken the immune system of both the young children and the elderly.

The headman and his wife showed us nothing but kindness, and our family reciprocated this kindness. They shared their house with us. We studied the Bible together and had devotions. In truth, we had already murdered them in our hearts when we were told they killed Chester. Only God's direct intervention prevented John and me from murdering these two innocent people. Even in the midst of our sin, God had mercy on us and stopped us from committing a horrible crime as bad as any the rebels had done.

Of course, the prophet was a fraud. God doesn't share his supernatural power with humans who can't be trusted with it. John and I were deceived. The prophet used the Bible. He quoted Scripture. He prayed. His explanations seemed reasonable at the time. We were reminded that the best lies contain at least some truth.

Is witchcraft real? It's hard to say. It has been practiced in Africa for thousands for years. But the primary lesson we learned about witchcraft was its power to destroy. Witchcraft sows distrust, anger, envy, revenge, jealousy, and all the worst human emotions. It provides an illogical explanation of cause and effect that led rebel soldiers to buy Juju fetishes that can supposedly stop bullets from penetrating their bodies and deceive Christians into killing other Christians. Only by the grace of God were John and I rescued from its clutches.

KAKATA 14

JOHN Chester was dead, and we'd barely gotten to know him. He loved to play with his sisters and other neighborhood children. And whenever I was around, he made a game of whispering secrets in Bessie's ear. Then, I would try hard to get him to tell me the secret and playfully act angry and frustrated. I would plead and beg with him to tell me. He just giggled and laughed and reveled in his power over his daddy. What a wonderful spirit.

Now he was gone. We never even got to see his body before they took him away. The only money we had was what Uncle Dahn gave us. We had spent all of ours on food for Chester he never ate. There was nothing left for us at Firestone.

We walked quickly back to Wako Village, I in front and Bessie behind me. It seemed we took turns grieving as we walked. I would occasionally have to stop when Bessie's silent weeping turned into uncontrolled chest-wrenching sobs. Then I would turn and hold her tightly in my arms with her weary tear-stained face buried in my shoulder. After a minute, she would be able to walk again. Then after awhile she had to comfort me in the same manner as my emotions and grief passed their breaking point.

While we walked I decided we couldn't stay any longer. It was time to try to travel to the border and escape Liberia. I was sure that the longer we stayed in Liberia, the more of us would die. Bessie heard

109

the United Nations had set up refugee camps in Ivory Coast. It was a long way by foot, but we had to try.

When we reached Wako Village, we immediately retrieved our remaining children. Grim-faced we related how Chester died and thanked the elderly chief and his wife for their hospitality in letting us stay with them, all the while hiding our true feelings of anger toward them. I wanted to leave as quickly as possible. It was already afternoon. We must reach another village tonight. Otherwise we would spend the night in the bush or on the road.

The girls started crying when we told them Chester was dead. But there would be time for mourning later. Now we needed to leave before I said or did something I would regret later. We said goodbye to our friends and neighbors from Paynesville and started down the road.

In a small, sad procession, we trudged out of Wako Village with only a direction in mind. There was no plan. We would just have to depend on God's grace. But that didn't seem quite as certain as it had only two days before.

Tens of thousands were dying. Whole villages were wiped out— men, women, children indiscriminately slaughtered, their bodies left to rot. Now the war was personal.

How difficult a thing to comprehend is the mind of God. He saved me alone out of one hundred men executed in cold blood. He saved Bessie and the children from the rebels and their checkpoints. He reunited us. He provided shelter at Wako. He kept Bessie and me from committing murder. And yet Chester was dead.

Without a doubt I knew God could have saved Chester, but he chose not to. Why? What questions could I ask him? He is the Creator and owes no human an explanation. I wasn't angry. He had already saved us several times. But who can comprehend his infinite mind? His ways are mysterious.

I formulated my plan as we walked up the Ganta highway. This road would eventually lead to Ivory Coast, some two hundred miles distant. I couldn't fathom how we would survive the journey.

Another of my cousins lived in Kakata, about fifteen miles up the highway. Our girls were quiet as we walked under the scorching sun. I drove them forward. Soon physical deprivation overcame their sorrow. Thirst, hunger, cramps, and sore swollen feet cried for relief.

We arrived in Kakata after dark and dragged ourselves to our destination. Joseph owned a large house with a smaller adjacent cottage on his lot. Electric lights were burning in both buildings. How surprising! The entire town was completely dark. I didn't think my cousin owned a generator. Who was there?

Going to the door, I knocked. It was answered by several young rebel soldiers. They were no older than the teenagers who had tortured me. "My name is John Gonleh, and this is my cousin's house," I said, introducing myself. "Where is my cousin, Joseph Cooper?"

One boy answered authoritatively, "We are part of Taylor's army. These houses are being used by Taylor's brother. Your cousin is not here."

"Friend," I said, "we are Mano, same as you. I come from Garnwe in Nimba County. Will you help us and let us stay in my cousin's house?"

He glanced over my shoulder looking at Bessie and the girls sitting exhausted on the edge of the street.

"Wait a minute," he replied. He closed the door, leaving me on the porch. Bessie, the children, and I were all praying as hard as we knew how. "Please, God, give us favor with these rebels," we implored.

After a minute, the door opened and there was an older rebel, an officer apparently. Staring intently at me in the dim light, he sized me up, looking for signs of my tribal ethnicity. For a moment, I wasn't sure what he was thinking or going to do.

Then his demeanor changed, and he broke into a smile. "Of course, for our fellow Mano brothers and sisters we can help you. Only for Manos can I make this offer. Otherwise we would most certainly kill you," he said, still grinning as he winked at me. "My soldiers will move into the big house and you can have the small house."

I thanked him for his generosity, and we all praised God. That night we enjoyed the first electric light we had since the power plant shut down months before. It seemed Charles Taylor's brother lived close to my cousin's house and owned a large generator. It was his generator supplying the electricity.

We had only three light bulbs, one for each small room in the house. Electric lights were a small thing but all power plants in Liberia had fallen victim to the war. The entire country was dark. The only remaining sources of light were either candles or a small cloth strip sitting in a cup of oil. By the time we reached Kakata, we later learned, you couldn't find either candles or oil.

How ironic, I thought. *Rebels from Charles Taylor's army tortured and tried to execute me. Now, Taylor's own resources are blessing the Gonlehs with light.*

Late into the evening, completely surrounded by darkness, three little lights burned in a small cottage on the outskirts of Kakata. I decided this must be God's way of reminding us he hadn't forgotten us. I couldn't help but admire the irony and humor. I thanked God for helping Mr. Taylor perform at least one good deed.

The next morning I set out to find a way to feed Bessie and the girls. I had seventy-five Liberian dollars, about five US dollars. God would have to multiply that meager amount in the same way he had the loaves and fishes. Otherwise, we'd starve.

Walking into town the next morning, I saw a small sidewalk market. There, I spied a man selling fresh crawfish. I stopped to talk. He was a local and friendly. His friendliness was a little surprising. I related some of our story and then asked if he was Christian. He was. He attended the Evening Star Baptist Church. Would we like to attend services with him? "Of course," I replied.

Next, he asked if I would like to accompany him into the bush to buy crawfish to sell the next day at the market. I couldn't believe my good fortune. That morning, I had no idea how I would feed my family. I rushed back to tell Bessie the good news.

So the following day at noon, I met my new friend. First, we paid rebels to take us to the hydroelectric dam at the Firestone Rubber Plantation, about a forty-five-minute drive from Kakata.

Rebels controlled all the gasoline and therefore controlled all the transportation.

Mr. Taylor couldn't pay his conquering army after they destroyed Liberia's economy. This meant each group of rebels operated independently to pay themselves. Some small groups systematically stripped siding off of buildings, removed the roofs, and ripped down the copper wire from the power poles. This was sold in Ivory Coast or Guinea for a fraction of its value. All of Liberia was plundered and looted.

Mr. Taylor, for his part, didn't bother with such small transactions. He cut deals permitting wholesale destruction of the rainforest. Foreign companies came in and clear-cut vast sections of virgin forest. Timber, diamonds, and other raw materials were ruthlessly exploited. This wholesale rape of Liberia prolonged the fighting, as rebel factions fought one another, each vying for the rights to exploit the country's natural resources.

Our rebel group in Kakata, with their headquarters in Cousin Joseph's house, ran a taxi service. For ten Liberian dollars, my friend and I made the trip to Firestone. Next, we crossed the river just above the dam in a canoe. Afterward, we made a two-and-a-half-hour trek to the small remote villages on the edge of the river.

We carried large woven rattan baskets. At the riverside villages we located fishermen using traps baited with palm nuts and cassava. A trap consisted of a woven rattan tube like an oversized sock. The trap was placed in the river. There was a small opening at the top entrance where crawfish swam inside to get the bait. Once inside, they couldn't get back out.

My friend showed me how to negotiate and how much to pay for the crawfish. As valued customers, the fishermen gave us mats for the night.

Our fisherman set out his traps at dusk and all night long collected the river's produce while he slept. Every fisherman used from twenty to forty traps. The next morning, all of the small traps were collected and emptied into one large holding basket. Situated in the shallows, the river lazily passed through the rattan weaving, keeping the catch alive until we arrived.

Using the fifty Liberian dollars I had budgeted for this business, I carefully picked a selection of fish and crawfish. Large crawfish sold three for five dollars, and small ones, one dozen for seven dollars. Fish were individually priced.

Then we made the long trek back to Kakata. The entire trip took ten hours. A shorter walk would have been nice, but we had to go deep into the jungle, past other people with the same idea.

Returning by midday, my friend and I set up our food on a *lapa* spread out on the ground. In a short time, we sold out. I had doubled my money. Then, except for Saturday night, it was back to the bush.

Day after day, I returned deep into the bush to repeat this commerce. Slowly I made more and more money for our upcoming journey. God provided the connection. My friend provided the knowledge. And all I had to do was provide the energy for the daily journey.

We attended services at the Evening Star Baptist Church on Sunday. We were happy to go into the house of the Lord. In the midst of the war, the preacher reassured us God's Spirit is everywhere. He will never leave us nor forsake us. I thought to myself, *the Gonlehs are living proof of this fact.*

During the day, Bessie spent a lot of time visiting and talking with the young rebel soldiers next door. They missed their mothers, many of whom were dead from the government attacks.

Bessie became a surrogate mother, extending a woman's compassion, tender touch, and soothing voice. They shared their fears and problems with her. Bessie prayed with them, hugged them, and offered words of comfort.

Many of the rebels were younger than Gloria. Sometimes, they played with the girls. Bessie marveled how they could switch from soldier to child and back again.

A week into our stay, one young rebel knocked on our door. It was Saturday evening. I answered the door and asked what he wanted. He said he had gasoline for sale. Would I like to buy some?

I laughed and said, "Do you see a car around here I could put it in? If you find one for me, then maybe I'll buy some gasoline, but otherwise I don't need it. But thanks anyway. It's good to know that you'll sell your gasoline to normal people like me."

He looked nonchalant, said OK, and turned and left. I thought, *How strange he would ask if I wanted gasoline.* They all knew we had no car. Bessie and I thought it was the funniest thing.

The rebels emptied all the service stations of gasoline so they would have the only supplies. All remaining gasoline in Kakata was stored around my cousin's house in fifty-five gallon drums. The rebels used a hand pump to pump it into any container their customers possessed. The whole operation was incredibly dangerous, but if they didn't blow themselves up, they would make a lot of money.

Even other rebel groups were forced to come to them for gasoline, and they charged an exorbitant price. I supposed the rebel boy who approached me decided I was the easiest potential customer since I lived right next door. I had no car and no need for gasoline, but that didn't seem to be something he had thought through.

My legs were my transportation. Every bit of their strength was needed daily as I carried a large plastic basket filled with crawfish back from the jungle. To increase its capacity, I built up the sides using sticks and leaves woven together. With this modification, I was able to carry thirty-five to forty pounds of crawfish.

Once the basket was filled, it was so heavy I needed help to lift it. I squatted down on my haunches, got balanced, and positioned my *kata.* Then two fishermen hoisted the basket up and carefully set it on my head. Next, I tested the balance and adjusted the load slightly if needed. Then I slowly summoned all my strength and stood up. Upright, I once again tested the balance. Then I was off.

Our time in Kakata was an oasis. God had replenished and multiplied our money. He'd given us plenty to eat. He gave us a place to worship and blessed us with the convenience of a house and electricity for light. And he had even provided our own security force next door. Finally, after the horror of Chester's death, everything seemed to be going our way.

GLORIA 15

BESSIE For two weeks, Kakata was wonderful. Then Gloria became sick. She started vomiting. Next, her temperature dropped, making her skin cold to the touch. Finally, she started having female bleeding. This continued for two days. She was worsening and John was in the bush.

Kakata had a medical clinic but it was only staffed with nurses. All the doctors had left. They were taken by the rebels to the Bong Mines Company Hospital, one hour's drive from the town. Bong Mines Hospital was a German operation and contained the most modern technology and advanced equipment in all of Liberia.

Rebels conscripted doctors evacuating from Monrovia at the Bong Mines Hospital to treat their wounded soldiers. At least the doctors were able to live in the opulent villas vacated by the German mine managers and engineers at the start of the war.

Nurses at the clinic were unable to diagnose Gloria's illness. Just like Chester, albeit with different symptoms, her illness was unexplainable, symptoms pointing to no specific disease. The nurses couldn't stop the bleeding. They thought she was pregnant and was miscarrying. But she wasn't pregnant. Gloria became sicker, weaker, and colder with each passing hour. John was gone and I soon grew frantic.

Right away my thoughts turned to the words of the prophet. Witchcraft! My rational, Christian mind tried to reject this notion as unfounded superstitions, but witchcraft surrounded us. Liberia was filled with it. From the soldiers smeared with white clay, to the Jujus worn around the necks, and the rumors that swirled among refugees, who knew what was true or could be believed. I was so afraid. I'd just lost one child. Now I faced the prospect of losing another.

The nurses recommended I take Gloria to the Bong Mines Hospital. They didn't know how to help her. There was nothing else they could do. I agreed immediately. But then I was told that while the clinic had a Jeep that served as their ambulance, there was no gasoline for it. If I wanted to take Gloria to the hospital, I would have to come up with my own gasoline to make the trip.

Suddenly, I remembered the young soldier trying to sell John gasoline. I ran out of the clinic and raced all the way back to our house. I prayed I wouldn't be too late. Sucking wind in and out of my lungs, I thanked God for the child soldier we had laughed at earlier.

Reaching the big house, I knocked on the door. When they answered, I quickly explained the situation. The good will we'd established immediately became evident as they sold me as much gasoline as I needed. They charged me half the going rate and even provided the container.

They too wanted Gloria to pull through. Just as I was their surrogate mother, Gloria was their big sister. We cooked and shared our food with several of the boys. All the girls had gotten to know the rebel boys and become friends.

I hurried back to the clinic and poured the gasoline into the Jeep's tank. Then I ran inside. Gloria's blood had soaked through the bed sheets. An intravenous drip needle and bag were still attached to her arm. Gloria was listless and nonresponsive.

With the help of a nurse, I loaded Gloria on my back with her arms draped over my shoulders and carried her out to the Jeep. Gloria was so weak that I had to support her head to keep it from flopping around. The nurse held the saline solution bag for the IV drip. Death's fingers were reaching out to claim my oldest child. Thank God she was still clinging to life.

An orderly drove the jeep as fast as he dared. The bone-jarring journey to the Bong Mines Hospital couldn't have been worse. The road was graded clay but now scarred by deep ruts and potholes. There had been no maintenance since the Germans left. The ride threatened to shake the last life out of Gloria's limp body. With each huge pothole, the Jeep bottomed out, scraping the oil pan and the muffler against the road. I was amazed that we didn't puncture some vital engine part or blow a tire. Despite my and the nurse's best efforts, Gloria was being tossed about like a rag doll. All of us were thrown around. The nurse tried her best to keep the IV needle steady to prevent its puncturing an artery. I tried to keep Gloria's head steady so she wouldn't strike the roof or side, giving her a concussion along with all her other problems. Gloria, for her part, was only able to muster low moans and grunts with each shock of pain.

The torturous hour finally came to an end as we saw the hospital. In the gathering twilight, the orderly stopped the Jeep at the darkened emergency entrance. The nurse and orderly jumped out and helped hold Gloria while I got out and ran around to her side. With their help, I once again carried Gloria on my back into the hospital. It seemed a miracle that she was still alive.

There was no one about inside. The orderly ran down a hallway and found a nurse. She directed us to bring Gloria into an examination room. She looked Gloria over and then left.

We arrived at eight o'clock, and the hospital was dark. A few candles had been mounted in the hallway and the exam room. The nurse explained that the hospital had a generator, but it was only turned on at ten. Until then, only the faint yellow glow from candles staved off total darkness.

I waited for thirty minutes without anyone coming to look after my daughter. All the while, my anxiety and frustration were growing. To make it this far, to survive the trip here, to now lose Gloria would be too much.

I held Gloria's hand and lightly stroked her face. She made no sounds. It was as if the Jeep ride had shaken all the moans and groans out of her. She had no noise left to give.

Finally, the nurse came back. Only then did she ask what was wrong with my child. I explained as best as I could, but I didn't know any more than the nurses at the clinic in Kakata.

The nurse took Gloria's blood pressure, sighed, and then turned to us and with a reluctant look said, "I'm sorry, Mrs. Gonleh, but there are no doctors working on shift tonight. We only have nurses. I'm very sorry. There is nothing I can do for your daughter."

It was more than I could take. My head dropped as my hopes for Gloria began to fade. Tears flooded my eyes as anger and frustration welled up inside. *The unfairness of it all*, I thought. "God?" I pled. "Not another one . . . Please, Lord, please save Gloria." I had to leave the room. I left the dim candle-lit exam room and stumbled down the hallway.

Indeed, it was a fine hospital. With beautiful tiled floors and polished wood doors, it was first class, except there were no doctors. Gloria was going to die.

I didn't blame the doctors for not coming back. Death in Liberia was everywhere. People were dying or being killed by the tens of thousands. Was Gloria's life worth more than the rebel soldiers they treated during the day? What made her life so special that they should have to work all day and all night? It seemed so hopeless.

In the darkened hallway, I leaned against the wall for support under a small candle holder. Its shallow flickering light barely illuminated the pain etched on my face. I prayed that God would send a miracle and somehow save Gloria.

"Please, Lord, don't take Gloria," I begged. "It's too much to bear. Chester was my youngest, Lord. Please have mercy and spare my oldest."

It seemed that Gloria's own ebbing life force mimicked the dim flickering candle.

"Please, Jesus. Don't let Gloria's light be extinguished."

Free-flowing streams of tears traveled down my cheeks, past my lips, and gathered on my chin before falling and forming a small pool on the fine polished ceramic flooring.

I stood in the hallway two or three minutes, praying as hard as I ever had or knew how. Then, from the direction of the hospital entrance, I heard a voice.

"Bessie, what are you doing here?" the voice said.

Startled, I turned. Blinking, trying to wipe away tears, I couldn't recognize the face. I wiped my eyes again with my palms. Looking again, I searched my memory for first the face and then the name that had apparently easily recognized me and called me by name.

It was Dr. Joseph Klekpo, my obstetrician from Monrovia! I'd last seen him in the hospital when John and I visited the woman injured in the car accident. Before that, it was when Chester was born.

I'd known Dr. Klekpo for at least fifteen years. What was he doing here? I stared at him, wide-eyed, like he had just landed from outer space. "How? Why?" was all I could muster. I was so stunned to see him.

"Bessie, what are you doing here?" he repeated. I snapped out of my shock but still couldn't speak coherently. I just motioned for him to follow me.

I regained my voice as we approached the examination room. "Quick, Dr. Klekpo, it's my daughter Gloria. She's dying and needs your help."

Dr. Klekpo immediately took control. The hospital nurse was stunned to see him. Dr. Klekpo barked orders at the nurse, who jumped, opening cabinets and drawers, pulling out various bandages and boxes. All the while, I stood back, my eyes taking in the scene, but my mind still dazed.

Questions raced through my mind: *How did he come to be here at the Bong Mines? How did he come to be in the hallway at exactly the same moment as me? Did God plan for the gasoline and the Jeep? Would Dr. Klekpo have recognized me if I hadn't been standing under the candle?* My small human mind couldn't hold all the events that converged into this moment.

Dr. Klekpo was one of the doctors pressed into service by the rebels. Why did he come back to the hospital tonight? The nurse said no doctors were coming in. The answer popped into my head: *It is impossible for man, but with God, all things are possible.*

"Bessie, Bessie!" said Dr. Klekpo, snapping me out of my thoughts. "I'm taking Gloria to my house. This hospital is in bad shape. I can treat her better there. I'm going to get her stable tonight before I leave but will be back first thing in the morning."

He spent the next hour examining and treating her, giving orders to the nurse on duty.

Before leaving, he told us his own story. He was working in the ELWA hospital when the rebels attacked. He and the other hospital staff escaped minutes before they arrived. With only their clothes and no medical equipment, they ran out and kept running.

A group of them first made it to the Firestone Plantation Hospital. Then, he was able to make it to the Bong mines. Being Mano himself proved a benefit. The rebels allowed him to treat their wounded rather than killing him.

His wife and four children had tried to escape to Sierra Leone. He hoped they were safe. There was no information, and he didn't know when they would be reunited.

I thanked him profusely and then, exhausted, made my way to the deserted hospital lobby. I sank into a cushioned couch that was more luxurious than the couch we'd purchased last year for our living room in Paynesville. *What a long time ago that was,* I thought.

Before drifting off, I got on my knees, bowed my head, and gave one last prayer of thanksgiving to the One who held us tightly in his hands.

The next morning Dr. Klekpo, true to his word, returned at eight o'clock. He checked Gloria to satisfy himself she could be moved and then helped me raise her up. She could muster no strength of her own and hung limp wherever there was no support.

This time, Dr. Klekpo loaded Gloria onto his back. We trudged down another pothole-filled road to one of the fine villas vacated by the Germans.

Dr. Klekpo had already prepared a room for Gloria and me. Once we arrived, he eased Gloria onto the bed, and she settled into the plush soft mattress with a groan. Dr. Klekpo set up a new IV bag.

Gloria needed several medicines to get her bleeding and vomiting under control. I gave him all of the money John had earned from selling crawfish, so he could buy her the medications. That money had paid for the food our family ate and some to share with the rebel boys. It paid for the gasoline and the medicine. God provided the means and the opportunity. John supplied the sweat of his brow, his strong back, his time, and energy. It was a good combination.

I decided to stay with Gloria at Dr. Klekpo's, but I went back to the hospital and found the nurse and orderly from Kakata. I told them about Gloria and the miraculous appearance of Dr. Klekpo. They were just as amazed as I was.

The nurse agreed to go over to Cousin Joseph's and tell John and the children what had happened. I knew they'd be worried about us. I was so thankful we had good relations with the rebel soldiers next door.

I thought of Chester. I had so many questions. Did he die because of John and me? Had we not prayed enough or in the right way, saying the right things? And yet, Dr. Klekpo appeared out of nowhere at exactly the right time. My prayers for Gloria were no different than for Chester. And further, why were any of us still alive in this war?

We stayed one week before Gloria was well enough to travel back to Kakata. Dr. Klekpo never did diagnose a specific illness. It was just one more mystery. When the clinic Jeep let us off at our house, my girls let out eardrum-splitting shrieks. Rebels ran out of their house, their weapons at the ready, thinking someone must be attacking. But when they saw their substitute mom and big sister, they started yelling also.

I filled the family in on Gloria's recovery and Dr. Klekpo's kindness. Food was difficult to buy at Bong, just as it was everywhere. But under Dr. Klekpo's care and a diet of eggs, V8 juice, collard greens, and potatoes, Gloria's health gradually improved. We were all just so happy to be reunited once again.

That night at our family devotions, we all spoke of how much we had to be thankful for. True, we had lost Chester and all our worldly possessions. But even so, God had sheltered us under his wings time and time again.

JOURNEY TO THE BORDER 16

JOHN

Tensions in Kakata were escalating. Three months before, Taylor's rebel army had passed through Kakata on their way toward Monrovia. As a result, Kakata had emerged largely untouched and unscathed. Now, after conquering the capital, roaming groups of unpaid rebels were returning from Monrovia with unfinished business.

Taylor had lost control of his army. Each faction operated under its own authority and competed with other groups. The wholesale destruction of the country left the economy crippled, and with no way to pay his army, his commanders turned on him. Each had his own following of loyal soldiers. Each wanted to claim the spoils. Their intent was to strip and plunder anything of value from the town and sell it in Guinea or Ivory Coast. Kakata had survived their first visit. It would not survive the second.

Our adopted children soldiers next door kept Bessie apprised of the latest rumors. I continued going into the bush day after day. I had to earn as much money as possible. We had a long journey ahead. But time was running out.

Groups of twenty to fifty soldiers arrived in Kakata. The only thing keeping these packs of wild animals from tearing Kakata to shreds were the other packs. There were negotiations. The soon-to-be corpse was divvied up. Like hungry hyenas, each pack demanded its fair share.

A few local inhabitants, store owners, and refugees remained. There were no police, no government army soldiers, and no law.

Noncombatants hurriedly packed their belongings. The bus stop was crowded and frantic. Families tried to hire any available bus, car, or truck out of Kakata. I asked several refugees their destination. No one would tell me. They were too afraid to divulge any information.

Markets and streets were deserted by noon, leaving the impression of a ghost town. Finally, negotiations concluded. The city had been divided, and the rebels dropped leaflets warning everyone to leave.

They were about to attack defenseless buildings and stores, stripping them bare. Rebels weren't opposed to killing all remaining stragglers. They'd done it before. It was just less messy if everyone left voluntarily. Massacring civilians resulted in piles of stinking corpses, rendering the task of plundering unnecessarily unpleasant.

So four weeks after arriving in Kakata, it was time to leave. Our finances had been restored, then lost with Gloria's sickness, and then restored once again. We were fortunate.

Bessie and I prepared head bundles for ourselves and each of the children. Everyone had to carry their own change of clothes. Next, I distributed our palm oil, rice, bonny fish, and salt into small plastic bags. Each person carried a little of each staple. This way, if one of us was killed during an attack, we would only lose part of our food.

Finally, illuminated by our three lightbulbs, we prayed and ate our last supper together. Tomorrow we would set out toward the border. No one slept well. Random gunfire pierced the darkness in anticipation of tomorrow's events.

We rose a little before dawn. Bessie and I placed *katas* on the girls' heads and then balanced their loads on top. They had never done this before. Thankfully, it became a game of sorts for them, trying to balance their load. It was a good way to start. We prayed and then off we went.

Single file, carrying Comfort, I led Bessie, Gloria, Monica, Annie, and Kou through the darkened streets. On the outskirts of town we met up with three more refugee families from Paynesville whom we knew from Kakata's market.

We were happy they had gotten out of Paynesville alive. We swapped survival stories and, after hearing ours and how God saved us and reunited us, I suppose they weighed the odds and threw their lot in with us. Perhaps they thought by traveling with us some of God's protection would rub off on them as well.

As the sun rose, gunfire came from the city. Kakata, filled with supermarkets, stores of every kind, fine residential homes, and government buildings, was now ripe for plundering. More staccato gunfire interrupted the new day. It sounded like a firefight. Perhaps there was some ownership disagreement that needed resolution.

We just kept walking forward as hyenas and vultures picked the town clean. At first we walked on the main road. We were soon passed by trucks carrying the flesh, bones, and entrails of the dead city. Mattresses, construction equipment, bed frames, windows, appliances, corrugated roofing, copper wiring, furniture, televisions, refrigerators, stoves, lamps, and even paintings passed us on the highway.

Goods from Kakata, like those from hundreds of other Liberian cities and towns, were being stripped and sold for pennies in Ivory Coast or Guinea. The wealth of Liberia, my nation, my home, slowly bled away.

We discussed it and decided it was safer to travel in the bush. Rebels were absolutely unpredictable. Anything could happen while we walked on the highway. Like a cutlass clearing brush, on a whim we could all be cut down by AK-47s from a passing vehicle.

I became the unofficial leader of our little troop. All together we had three men, seven women, and about twenty children. We adults devoted considerable attention to encouraging the children. Two hundred miles was a long way to the border.

Long before cars sped over paved roads, Liberia had bush trails. For thousands of years these trails crisscrossed plains, rain forests, and mountains. Connecting small remote villages, the trails formed the transportation grid for communication and commerce. There were no beasts of burden. Only strong backs and necks carried heavy loads precariously balanced on people's heads.

Walking in the lead on a well-packed clay rut, I kept alert. The bush trail was only eighteen inches wide and flanked by Savannah grass taller than our heads. The grass had reached its maximum height after a summer of drenching rain.

My eyes watched the trail ahead for that tell-tale appearance of a broken stick, which just might turn out to be a snake basking in the warm sun. Most of the time the stick slithered away with our approach. Sometimes the dark stationary form really was a stick to be kicked aside. However, one snake must have been especially sleepy. It didn't hear our approach. I didn't recognize him as a snake, either, until I was almost stepped on him.

It awoke startled, coiled itself, and reared up into striking position. He was ready for battle. Simultaneously jolting to a stop, my load almost tumbled off my head. I froze.

The snake slightly swayed its head back and forth as his tongue flicked in and out. I tried to balance the load without so much as twitching a muscle below my neck. I remained still as a statue, my eyes locked on his weaving head and his eyes locked on my leg.

My heart was pounding. I could feel reverberations from its beating, pulsing in the veins of my neck. Beads of sweat from my forehead dripped into my eyes. I felt them roll down my cheeks, collect, and then drip off my chin. One after another, drip, drip, drip, they hit my shirt. I just hoped sweat wouldn't drip right in front of the snake, triggering his strike.

The snake seemed to be considering his options: *Should I strike? This prey is obviously too large to eat. What if it attacks me after I strike?* All of this the snake must have been carefully weighing, because I wasn't yet bitten.

The load was teetering. With all my concentration, I kept flexing and bending my neck muscles like steel springs trying to keep the load balanced. Every muscle in my body was taut. Behind me I heard a commotion.

"Why have we stopped?" asked one child.

"What's happening?" went another.

I remained frozen.

After a few interminable seconds the snake stopped bobbing.

Here it comes, flashed through my mind. But no, he dropped his upright pose. He backed down, his natural instinct for self-preservation overcoming his anger at being disturbed. Rapidly, he withdrew into the impenetrable tall grass. I slowly exhaled relief. Reaching up with my hand to support my load, and gulping lungfuls of air, I turned around.

"It was just a snake," I yelled back. "He's gone now."

No sense in alarming the others as to what might have happened. A poisonous snakebite in the middle of the bush with no doctor or medical facilities for miles around would have been disastrous. Quietly under my breath, I mouthed, "Jesus, thank you," and to myself, "John, be more careful."

After that first encounter, I considered making more noise on the trail. I was tempted to lead a choir of thirty voices to let the snakes know we were approaching. Singing was a big part of our services at Immanuel Baptist Church. We sang African Christian songs in addition to those from the Baptist and Methodist hymnals from America. Unfortunately, any noise also risked letting the snakes on two feet carrying AK-47s know we were nearby.

I decided we had to take our chances with the reptilian version and keep quiet. In total silence, we trudged forward, mile after mile of trail from morning till evening.

We stopped every hour for a few minutes to rest and get a drink. We checked on each child, delivered encouragement, examined sores, doctored blisters, and massaged their weary little muscles.

After attending to our physical needs, we addressed our spiritual needs. All the men and women took turns leading our group in prayer. After that we would recite the Lord's Prayer.

Some of our neighbors were not even Christians, but that didn't stop them from praying. If there was a God or higher power that could deliver them from death, disease, or injury, they had no problem praying to him. Some of our adults had engaged in witchcraft but now prayed to God anyway. Their attitude was that it may not help, but it can't hurt.

It was useless to think too much about our final destination, the United Nations refugee camp in Danané, Ivory Coast. That was where we were heading, but we might not live to see tomorrow, let alone next week or next month. Danané was only a direction, though, not yet a destination. Survival was measured one day at a time.

By nightfall we reached a small village. Just as Bessie did in Wako, we went to the village chief and asked for his permission to stay for a few days before heading out. Liberian hospitality still existed despite the war. The village welcomed us, total strangers, into their homes to sleep for the night and remain a few days if needed.

We rested all the next day. Little feet were swollen. Joints and muscles ached. Kind villagers helped treat blisters and open sores. We washed our clothes. We replenished our bodies.

That evening the village chief gave his permission to conduct a worship service. We sang songs, and then I delivered a few words of hope and encouragement and exhorted everyone to trust God. I told my story, and then others shared theirs.

This first service set a pattern for every village we stopped in during our nearly three-month journey from Kakata to the border. Through our own shared experiences and those others told, it became clear that our refuge lay more in the supernatural realm than the natural.

We stayed two days more recovering. Then we set out. Each day we covered about ten miles. It was all the littlest children could handle. Since we were traveling on zigzagging bush trails, our journey was longer than the two hundred miles using the main highway.

While the highway would have been a more direct route for us to take, it also would have taken us directly through all the rebel checkpoints. There were checkpoints before and after every town for the entire two hundred miles from Monrovia to the border with Ivory Coast with additional checkpoints in between. We couldn't get to Ivory Coast on the main road without passing through ninety to one hundred rebel checkpoints.

God had protected Bessie and the children at six checkpoints from Paynesville to Wako Village. Was it reasonable to assume he would protect our group of thirty for perhaps a hundred more? It didn't require the wisdom of Solomon to realize that total avoidance of the rebels whenever possible was the safest approach.

Because we stayed a good distance from the road, the rebels neither saw nor heard us. Walking in silence along the narrow trails, we heard their passing trucks and cars.

At times we were forced to travel near the adjacent highway. Then we were the most fearful of being seen. We marched quickly, exhorting the children to hurry. We were only safe when we retreated into the sanctuary of tall cover.

We listened carefully for approaching vehicles. At the first distant rumble of engine noise, we dove into the tall grass. Parents clutched little hands, pushing past tall stands of elephant grass with sharp-edged blades that scratched arms and legs.

There was no time to look down for hidden dangers such as lounging venomous snakes, columns of driver ants, or scorpion nests. Whatever the danger that lurked in the grass during our pell-mell scattering was no comparison to the danger approaching in the vehicle. There was no question that the car or truck contained rebels with a thirst to feed their bloodlust.

One refugee related a story about a rebel at a checkpoint. The rebel went up and down the line of waiting refugees, taunting them. He told them that his gun, whom he talked to and caressed, wanted to kill them because he (the gun) hadn't tasted blood that day. The rebel, on behalf of his AK-47, was asking their permission to kill them. This terrorizing went on until the refugee made it through the checkpoint.

Anyone foolish enough to drive his own personal car was soon stopped at a checkpoint. We heard stories from survivors who attempted this because of an elderly parent or crippled relative who couldn't walk the trails. Each time, the story ended in tragedy. The car was taken, they were robbed, and often one or more family members was killed, including the elderly relative they were trying to help.

The lucky ones escaped, and we heard several of their stories as we encountered each other at rest stops along the trail and swapped the latest news or rumors. Unlucky victims were killed on the spot or were simply led off into the bush and died in anonymity, their passing recorded only by heaven along with the sparrows that fell from the sky that day.

From refugees on foot, the checkpoint rebels demanded their names, identification cards, destinations, origins, place of employment, occupation, and any other bits of information designed to ferret out any government connections or to determine whether the refugees were too wealthy or "shining." They scattered belongings on the ground and took whatever struck their fancy. They demanded bribes, and abused, terrorized, and murdered at their discretion.

Thankfully, we could easily hear approaching vehicles at a distance. Rebels tore the mufflers off confiscated cars. Mimicking teenagers all over the world, a loud throbbing car is a universal macho symbol. Without a muffler, even a sad, pathetic old four-cylinder 60hp Datsun sounded like a 400hp muscle car that existed only in Liberia from imported American television programs.

In addition, they removed the doors and windshields. Soldiers stuffed themselves into the stripped-down chassis and hung out from every direction. Like television programs of fraternity boys stuffing themselves into a Volkswagen, they could quickly deliver fighters wherever needed.

Bypassing all these checkpoints I estimated would add about fifty miles to our journey. That would add time. Would my money buy enough food or would we starve?

Then I remembered the Old Testament story of the prophet Elijah, the widow, and her son. There was a severe famine in all the land. The visiting Elijah asked the widow to pour her last remaining oil and flour from her jars and bake him a loaf of bread. She agreed but knew they would all then die. With that one loaf of bread, there was no more. However, to her surprise, each day afterward, there was just enough oil and flour to make bread for one more day. Starvation was kept at bay during the entire famine, one day at a time. I prayed God would do the same with my money.

JOURNEY'S END 17

Throngs of refugees crowded the trails. Everyone traveled the same direction as we did: toward Danané. At times traffic jams on the narrow bush trails were as bad as downtown Monrovia during rush hour—before the war, anyway.

We held our children's hands tightly when passing another refugee group to keep them from getting lost. Groups passed each other day and night. We encountered several groups who had taken in lost children. They found them wandering aimlessly, dehydrated, and half-starved.

Each group asked us if we had lost any children. With enough chance encounters, they hoped the child could be reunited with his or her parents, if they were still alive. The lucky ones were cared for by the refugee group they ended up with. The unlucky ones, pitiful and forlorn creatures, simply died alone in the bush as if they had never existed.

Whether these children were lost by accident or simply abandoned was difficult to say. From the start of the war, death by starvation or disease was rampant. Perhaps a dying parent abandoned the child beside the trail, hoping someone with more resources would have pity and take in the little one. Or maybe the parent was just distracted as groups squeezed past each other on the trail and the child became lost.

Aside from these covert, stealthy assassins were the overt killers, the rebel soldiers. Women were routinely gang raped. Then the woman was forced to watch while her husband's still beating heart was cut out of his chest to be eaten later. Sometimes, the husband's genitals were sliced off and stuffed in his mouth before they shot him. Mothers who survived encounters with the rebels were never the same, some driven totally insane and unable to care for their children.

Rebels were especially cruel to pregnant women. Their favorite game was to bet on the sex of the fetus. First, they beat the woman's husband into a bloody heap—but made sure he remained alive so he could watch what came next. Then, one rebel held the woman with her arms pinned behind her back while the other sliced open her belly with his bayonet. Releasing her, she collapsed, dying, next to her husband. Finally, they reached down and pulled out the baby to inspect the sex and determine the winner of the bet.

The game ended when the baby was smashed against a tree, crushing its tiny pliable skull. Both parents were dispatched with bullets in the head while any remaining children scattered into the bush. Whatever the reason, the war orphaned many children.

Lost children were terrified. Their parents were gone. Who would protect them now? Who would feed them? Who would take care of them? They were alone, confused, tired, cut off from everything familiar. Abandoned or just lost on the trail, they didn't know which way to go, forward or back. They had no idea. Whenever we encountered another group of refugees, we made a special point to gather up our children and hang on to them tightly.

The farther our distance from Kakata, the greater the suffering as groups slowly expended their energy. With each contact, we began to notice a contrast between our group and others. For some reason our children weren't deteriorating or getting sick like so many others.

Just as our Chester died from mysterious causes, at each village, passing refugees left one or two dead youngsters behind, felled by symptoms as mysterious as those that had killed Chester. Many blamed witchcraft. It was impossible to tell.

Not only children, but many adults we encountered were sick as well. They were malnourished and diseased, with cloudy sunken eyes and leathery sallow skin. Each scene was so sad. There was nothing we could do for them except pray.

Groups were amazed and remarked how healthy we looked. There seemed to be nothing different about our group except that we prayed continually. We were aware that at any moment jungle diseases—malaria, yellow fever, dysentery, cholera—intestinal parasites, or a host of virulent microbes could strike and decimate all of us.

We followed a set pattern as we moved slowly toward the border. Each walking day started with praying as a group. Then we found something to eat for the children and then ourselves. If there was food for sale, we would purchase some. Food was more valuable than money because staples were so scarce. Sometimes there was none for sale regardless of price. Therefore, we always tried to carefully maintain our reserves.

Our worst problem was swollen feet. We stopped at a village for two or three days once to let our feet recover before setting off anew. We were walking by nine o'clock and continued until dusk at six-thirty or seven. As evening approached, we hunted for a place to spend the night.

Sometimes we were lucky. The information we received at the last village guided us effortlessly to the next. Sometimes we weren't. Then we spent hours searching in pitch blackness, often staggering into a village near midnight.

I saw the effects of despair on several groups we met on the trail. The adults had no patience for the children and sometimes abused them by yelling or hitting them. The children were whining or crying, sapping their energy in the process.

Enveloped in a cloud of despair, the adults made poor strategic decisions. They didn't properly ration the group's food. They stopped too long, or not long enough, at rest stops. They ran out of food or water and had to make lengthy detours to find some. Any unnecessary expenditure of energy left the group more susceptible to the debilitating effects of the bush.

Each day required making a number of decisions, and the well-being of the group depended on the clear thinking of the group leaders. Bad decisions led to more bad decisions, which eventually led to weakness, fatigue, sickness, and ultimately death. Together with the decline of the group's health was the group's spirits. Poor decisions led to arguments, anger, recriminations, back-biting, and mutiny.

Constantly taking our needs, concerns, and problems to the Lord in prayer may have been the prescription for our group's health. Communal prayer throughout the day led us to an increased spirit of unity and a sense that we traveled under God's protection. Each encounter with refugee groups that were falling apart reinforced this belief and gave us an acute sense of the spiritual nature of our physical struggles.

One day, more than a month after we'd left Kakata, we stopped to rest by an abandoned coffee plantation, and I led the group in a song. The trail gradually climbed as we made our way upward into the low mountains. We could see Mount Nimba, Liberia's highest point, in the distance.

"My Lord has done it again," I sang out in a low voice.

"He has done it again," came the group's soft refrain.

"My Lord has done it again," I responded.

"Hallelujah," came the reply.

In unison we all joined together, "He heal the sick, He raise the dead, He has power to save, He never change."

Then once again I led, "God has done a miracle," followed by the group, "He has done a miracle."

We all finished the song together with, "And he will do it again."

I thought about Chester. I missed him. Perhaps it was for the best. So many little ones died during this arduous journey to escape Liberia. With his death, maybe God spared him.

Refugee children in groups we encountered suffered painful and lingering deaths. Death was inexorably coming for them; tomorrow or next week, no one knew. But it stalked them as a leopard stalks a herd of antelope. Soon the weakest members would be culled from the pack.

With so much rampant killing and death, my questions were not so much why did bad things happen, but why did anything good happen? Why did God save us, when whole families, sometimes four generations at once, were snuffed out for no reason? Why were we still alive? What made us so special?

It certainly wasn't anything good I had done. As I walked, I reflected on my past.

———

Even though I was a Christian at sixteen, going to church soon became just one more activity, like going to work. Any fiery zeal I felt at the beginning soon enough burned away.

Right after I asked Jesus into my heart, I had the strength to defy my father and the Poro Devil Bush Society. Then, on the trip back home, seeing Bessie a second time seemed like a sure sign from God. He had picked her out as my own Eve. I was her Adam.

Slowly, however, things changed. I still went through the motions, but Jesus Christ was someone separate from me. It didn't seem like he was part of me.

At eighteen I was living alone, renting a room, working, and going to high school. I loved my independence, my freedom, and being my own man. Bessie was my steady girlfriend. Then she became pregnant.

We told her parents. They were upset, of course. I told them she was now my responsibility. I would take care of her. Bessie and I moved into an apartment. Gloria was born while we both were still attending high school. I graduated and went to work. It was hard work, but slowly our finances improved.

With success in my career, I had free time and joined a soccer team. Soon I became a popular player. Being short and wiry, I was quick and possessed the endurance and stamina for constant running. I never played sports growing up and relished my newfound popularity. Soon, my teammates and I attracted a following of fans.

Sometimes Bessie came to the matches, but often she stayed home to take care of Gloria. Our fans included some pretty girls who enjoyed partying after the game with the players. Following my teammates, I soon enjoyed several girlfriends on the side. I wasn't ashamed. I was just doing the same thing as my teammates.

Before long, Bessie learned about my girlfriends. She cried. It hurt her deeply, she said. Over and over we had arguments. I wanted my freedom to do whatever I wanted. Anyway, we weren't married, just living together.

During one of our many arguments, I told her that if she didn't like what I was doing to get out. She replied, "If you want me out, then you have to put my things outside the house." She refused to leave voluntarily. She was making me kick her out. I wanted to. I really did. I was sick of her complaining. I wasn't doing anything any other Liberian man wouldn't do. Besides traditionally, Liberian men can have as many wives as they want. And yet I couldn't kick her out. I don't know why.

Bessie got pregnant again. Dennis was born in 1982, the same year as Prince. Prince's mother was one of my girlfriends. One year later, Dennis was stricken with polio. He survived, but I sent him to live with my aunt in Totota, where there was a polio clinic. In 1984, Bessie and I had our twins, Annie and Kou. That same year I fathered Monica with yet another girlfriend, Viola.

I now had six children from three women. Whatever else I was, I took seriously my responsibility to care and provide for my children. Prince and Monica often stayed with us along with our other children. By the war's start I didn't see Prince much. His mother had moved to another town.

Monica stayed with us every other week. She was with us in 1990 when the rebels came for me. There was no way to reunite her with Viola. Monica escaped along with Bessie and the other children.

In 1985 I was invited to play on Liberia's national soccer team but turned them down. The team traveled almost constantly. I made a decision and quit soccer. Taking care of Bessie, all my children, and running a business were more important.

That was my turning point. A few weeks later, the Lord spoke to me. It happened one morning when I was in the bathtub. Out of nowhere, I heard a sharp, clear voice in my head, surely inaudible to others. The voice said, "I have something for you to do." That's all. I don't know how, but I knew it was the Lord's voice.

I wasn't thinking about God or church or how I'd been living, but I prayed, "Lord, if it's you that spoke to me, tell me what I should do. Show me if it really is you."

Bessie and I attended Immanuel Baptist Church. I was a hypocrite. We attended church together even as I was renting room number three at the California Hotel in Monrovia for a rendezvous with one of my girlfriends.

The following Sunday, after the Lord spoke to me, I was shocked when a woman at the church said she had had a dream about me. She dreamed that the Lord wanted me to serve him in the ministry. On top of that, our pastor asked me to help him. Another person was in charge of directing the Bible study, prayer meeting, and Sunday school but wasn't doing a good job. Pastor Emmanuel White needed my help.

As I got more involved at church, I decided to put away my ugly attitudes and behaviors. I was changing. Oddly, I really wanted to please God with my life. No one made me. Somehow, Jesus must have slowly changed my heart from the inside.

We received Comfort, my cousin, on February 15, 1986. The day she was born was the day my aunt died during childbirth. Bessie gave birth to Chester on August 26 later that same year. Bessie and I were officially married in 1987. We were the first marriage performed following the completed construction of Immanuel Baptist Church.

———

Reflecting over these events as I walked the trails, I thought how my life had changed over the past five years. I went from a soccer star and womanizer to dedicated family man. I was a different person.

As we continued our journey from Kakata we skirted past Weala, Salala, Totota, Gbatola, Suakoka, Gbarnga, Gbaota, Palala, Sokopa, and finally arrived at Ganta after fifty days. We still had sixty miles to go before reaching the border. We heard Danané lay inside Ivory Coast another twenty-five miles. We had another decision to make. Ganta was less than two miles from the border with Guinea. There was no refugee camp there, but it was so close. We were tempted to cross there like some other refugees had.

The main tribe in Guinea is Mandingo and Mandingos hated the Mano. At the start of the war, President Doe used the Mandingos living in Nimba County to point out Mano villages. Government troops then massacred the village inhabitants. As word spread of the Mandingos' treachery, the Mano exacted a terrible revenge on them. Guinean Mandingos would remember and kill us at the earliest opportunity. We kept walking.

We arrived in Khanplay by early December, where the United Nations had set up a temporary transit camp for refugees continuing to Danané or other destinations. We thought we were finally safe from the rebels. But in the dead of night rebels came and took away several refugees. Even the United Nations couldn't stop them. That was the last straw. We had to get out of Liberia once and for all.

Our group of thirty had suffered and survived together for seventy days. We hadn't lost anyone. It was a miracle. Now it was time to say goodbye. The morning we left for Danané we exchanged hugs, tears, and prayers for the last time. God had been faithful. He had seen us through the entire journey, sustaining our health and preserving our lives.

I helped Bessie up first into the large, open United Nations truck. Then I helped up Monica, Annie, Kou, Comfort, and finally Gloria. When everyone else was on the truck, I hopped on. As the truck pulled away from the camp, I looked back one last time at Liberia. After all we'd been through, I had no plans to return, ever.

Bessie and the children were all in high spirits. I set my eyes forward to see the road ahead. I held up Monica in one arm and Kou in the other so they could see also. Bessie held up Annie, and Gloria lifted little Comfort so she could see also. They gripped the railing tightly with their little hands and rode like firemen heading off to put out a fire. I couldn't help but recall the similarity with my last crowded truck ride—the one leaving the #72 Soldiers' Barrack, heading for the Duport Road Killing Field, the executioners' ground. The recollection left a nugget of doubt and uncertainty in my mind. But as the black diesel smoke belched out of the truck's tailpipe, I tried to wipe away the negative thoughts. Finally, everything was going to be fine. After all, the United Nations, the world's most powerful humanitarian body, would provide us safe haven in Danané.

The driver shifted into gear, and the truck lurched forward. Surprised, we caught our balance, looked at each other, and then broke out laughing. As we picked up speed, dust from the road kicked up behind us. The transit camp slowly disappeared into the distance.

DANANÉ 18

Crossing the Cavalla River we passed from Liberia into Ivory Coast. After one hour in our slow, rumbling truck, we arrived in Danané. The citizens of Cote d'Ivoire, as it is known by the French-speaking population, were curious at our appearance and stared amazed at the multitude of refugees entering their city.

With the influx of 45,000 Liberian refugees into the Danané United Nations Refugee Camp, the English-speaking refugees were common sights in the markets. Refugees competed for the lowest jobs and could be hired to work harder for much less money than the Ivorians.

While the president of Ivory Coast had welcomed us as brothers and sisters, this sentiment was not shared by the population. Ivorian President Boigny's daughter was married to former Liberian President Tolbert's son. When President Tolbert was overthrown and executed by Samuel Doe in 1980, the Liberian elite fled to Ivory Coast, where they were given asylum. Under the protection of President Boigny, Charles Taylor later trained his small army to begin the invasion of Liberia.

So while there was a close relationship between the ruling elite of the two countries, those feelings did not filter down to the general populace. Nevertheless, with the president's blessing, from 1990 to

145

1992, the United Nations constructed refugee camps all over the country. Eventually, there were 300,000 refugees from Liberia in Ivory Coast.

Along with the refugees came millions of dollars of foreign aid. The refugee camps created an economic boom. Local workers were hired to distribute and warehouse all the refugee supplies. They built and maintained the camps. Thousands of jobs for Ivorians were created by the presence of the camps.

Regardless of the influx of jobs and resources to their economy, the residents of Danané resented our "special" treatment as refugees. They resented the fact that our UN-supplied food, all from America, was higher quality than their local Ivorian variety. They resented our English language. They resented that we did not realize and accept we were second-class citizens. They resented that we didn't keep quiet regardless of how badly we were taken advantage of. After all, we were guests in their country. If we didn't like things, then we should just go back to Liberia. Still, their president had invited and welcomed us. The Ivorians had no choice but to tolerate our presence—for now anyway.

When we arrived at the camp, we registered as refugees and were then taken to the police station for clearance checks. We were asked when we had left Monrovia and what we had been doing from then until our arrival. They gave us UN refugee status and UN identification numbers.

We were given mats to sleep on, blankets, soap, dishes, and pots to cook food. The camp used the same tents as we had in Khanplay, but these had cement floors. Electrical wires and lightbulbs were strung inside the tent and a hand water pump was located nearby. Outside, there were portable toilets but no showers. Considering how we had been living, it was wonderful.

There were two living tents for each kitchen. The kitchen had a corrugated zinc roof but was open on all sides to let smoke escape. Families living in the two tents cooked all their meals over several charcoal grills. I set our pot on the grill and cooked over charcoal or wood. Every meal was cooked in a single pot.

Monthly rations consisted of vegetable oil, cornmeal, rice, sugar, powdered milk, soap, salt, onions, and one can of mackerel or sardines. Anything else we wanted or needed we had to buy in the market.

From the very beginning, there were arguments—and even the occasional fistfight—between the Liberians and Ivorians each time the United Nations distributed food. Because the food was distributed monthly, this ensured that ill feelings were always present. The basic problem with the food distribution was that the refugees didn't get their promised supplies. Each month, the allotment was short. For most families, the monthly allotment was all the food they had to eat. Shortages became matters of life and death.

When we first arrived, the UN provided milk and sugar for the cornmeal. It must have been too expensive, because it only lasted for a few months before being cut off. A few months after that, the rice too was cut off. Finally, they eliminated the cornmeal and substituted bulgur wheat, which we tried to grind up and cook different ways to help it go down better. Nothing worked. John refused to eat it altogether. Many people suffered constant gas and diarrhea as it passed straight through their systems. Bulgur wheat is so high in fiber it's normally only fed to livestock. Without digestion, there can be no nutrition. So whenever we had money, I would buy a little rice to mix with the bulgur wheat for the children and me.

The United Nations hired local Ivorians to receive the shipments of supplies. These workers unloaded the ships and planes, transferring the food and supplies onto trucks. The trucks took the food to warehouses, where it was divided up for the various refugee camps. Finally, they reloaded the food onto trucks and went to Danané and the other camps, where the cargo was unloaded into a camp warehouse. From that warehouse, monthly supplies were given to the refugees.

In short, the process of moving the food and supplies provided numerous opportunities for stealing. We knew the local workers hired by United Nations stole the supplies meant for the refugees. I saw bags of cornmeal and rice along with tins of vegetable or soybean oil in the market every week.

The United Nations switched to bulgur wheat precisely because it was so unpalatable and lacked nourishment. They hoped it wouldn't be stolen. Pigs and horses eat bulgur wheat, not humans. But even the bulgur wheat was stolen. Each bag in the market was clearly marked "Property of United Nations, Not for Sale."

Although our food was stolen and sold openly in the market, the UN seemed incapable of preventing the theft. There was nothing we could do. Our refugee representatives met with the UN officials, but nothing ever came of it. We met with the governor of Danané, but he never did anything. We were powerless.

If a new supply came from the UN, you could see it in the market before it ever reached the refugees. At times, there was nothing for the UN to give out to the refugees. It was all in the market. Then an announcement would be made in the camp, saying there would be no food distribution this month because the warehouse was empty.

At the announcement, oh, the wailing cries of anguish and anger that went up to heaven. I too shed many tears and cried out to God about the unfairness of it all. Many families suffered greatly due to the thievery of the food from the refugees. Some refugees without any other money or resources gradually became weak, sick, and then died.

When we first arrived in Danané, we still had a little money from John's crawfish earnings in Liberia. We had to exchange our Liberian dollars for CFA—Colonies Françaises d'Afrique—francs, the Ivory Coast currency. Unfortunately, due to the war, the exchange rate between the Liberian dollar and the CFA was horrible.

Before Samuel Doe came to power, Liberia used United States dollars as our currency. But United States dollars were being taken out of the country routinely by investors and businesspeople. Our then President Tolbert saw this as a problem and wanted to stop it. By creating Liberia's own currency, the Liberian dollar, President Tolbert hoped to prevent this. Liberian dollars could only be spent in Liberia.

While the new currency solved the first problem, it created a second. The new problem was that no investors would bring money into the country if they couldn't take it back out again. This harmed the economy badly, which led to the social unrest that caused Tolbert to be overthrown and executed. Samuel Doe then assumed power.

Now we bore the full brunt of the almost worthless Liberian dollar. Changing our money to CFA left us almost penniless. Still, we had survived the war in Liberia. God had provided for us so far. We just had to keep trusting that he would continue to do so.

Life in the camp was hard. The tent was very cold. The cold bred sickness, and the children and I succumbed to one bug after the other. We only had thin mats, no mattresses. Lying on the concrete floor, we felt the cold seeping up through the mats and into our bones. Sometimes the infirmary had medicine. Sometimes it didn't. Nevertheless, we prayed over every pill, even if it was just Tylenol or aspirin. We prayed for God to increase and amplify its effectiveness.

None of us had any immunity to malaria. Taking malaria pills in Paynesville prevented the disease but left us with no natural immunity. Now we couldn't afford pills, and they weren't available anyway. Yet, oddly, we had not been stricken like many others.

Stealing in the tents was also a problem. Like our few days in Khanplay, sixty people, or up to ten families lived in each tent. We had to be constantly vigilant to never leave our things unguarded. Two children watched them at all times. Losing the little food we refugees had could spell death as our families wasted away from malnutrition.

With the cutbacks in UN provisions, we had to somehow supplement our diet or slowly starve to death. With the tiny amount of cash we had left, we bought some fish and fried it. We then sold the cooked fish to other refugees for slightly more than it cost raw. My hungry little children never understood why I cooked fish that smelled so good, only to give it away to strangers. With the principal, we bought supplies and could only eat on the small profit we made.

In the same manner, I fried cornbread pancakes, called *frailer*, fried dough, boiled yams, cassava, potatoes, eddoes, and anything else John and I thought we could cook and sell for a small profit.

For ourselves, in the morning, I cooked plantains boiled with oil. In the afternoon I cooked rice with palm butter or greens. I always cooked enough for lunch to save and eat at dinner before bed. We didn't eat much, but we were able to stave off starvation.

With the city awash in refugees, there was little work to be found in Danané. Catholic Social Services operated a farm that employed many refugees, and eventually, John found work there. The farm grew corn, greens, rice, and cabbage. The pay was little and the work was hard—hoeing, plowing, weeding, and harvesting—but it did supply a little more cash.

The children started attending a newly-formed refugee school in the camp, while I kept our belongings protected in a small corner of the tent. John worked the fields all day, but in the evenings, when we were all together again, we praised God for the blessings he'd given us. We were still alive and healthy.

War continued to rage in Liberia with the victors now fighting over the spoils. Week after week, more refugees continued to arrive. The tents grew crowded.

To add to our concerns, I was with child. I became pregnant shortly after our arrival in Danané. Now the baby was almost due. How would I feed it without enough food? How would we survive? We didn't know what God would do. He'd brought us this far. He couldn't abandon us now.

A NEW ARRIVAL 19

JOHN With Bessie's impending delivery, I knew I had to get us out of the refugee camp. The conditions worsened throughout 1991. Refugees flooded into the camp. Tents became dangerously overcrowded and unsanitary. Deprivation and hunger created tensions. Minor disagreements became matters of great weight to be argued over at length. Guarding your place in the long lines for provisions, the stresses of dealing with line jumpers and making sure you were getting your fair allotment, the anger of seeing someone throw trash in the tent near your small marked-out area all contributed to the exhausting, energy-sapping life of the refugee.

Bessie and I began inquiring about renting a house in Danané. We prayed at the camp that God would give us a home like our old home, where we could live without problems. We told some friends that if they heard of any homes to let us know. We also looked around town, not knowing how we would pay the monthly rent. Little did I know plans were already in motion.

In Monrovia we had friends who worked for the Voice of America radio station. As employees of an American company, they were able to leave the refugee camp easily and emigrate to the USA right after the war started.

I called them at the telephone number they gave us before they left. I prayed that God had blessed them financially so they in turn could bless us. When I called, they had indeed gotten on their feet and were able to send us twenty-five dollars via Western Union. While that wasn't much in America, in Ivory Coast, it was enough to pay for rent and food for two months. So armed with prayers and the money they sent, we hoped we would find our own house.

About a month before Bessie was due, a friend located a house near the outskirts of Danané. Within two blocks' walk was the jungle. A teenager lived in the house and was taking care of it while he attended school in Danané. His aunt, who owned the house, lived in a small village about twenty-five minutes' drive from the city. The boy was supposed to take care of the lawn and keep the house clean.

Of course the house was completely filthy. Rather than grass, the front yard had been turned into a cornfield. The cornstalks grew high, but the boy hadn't cared for these either, and weeds grew almost as high as the corn. Behind all this lay the house.

We managed to make our way through the small path in the cornfield and asked him if it was for rent. He told us it was and that his aunt would be in town on Thursday, market day. We made arrangements to meet with her.

Before she arrived, I came out to clean up the place. As a refugee, I wanted to make a good impression and thought this would help. The house was dirty from one end to the other. Tall grass had grown up all around the house. It took three days to clean the house. When I started, we could barely get in the front door for the cornfield.

At the appointment the next Thursday, I said to the aunt, "Please look at my back and my head. Does either look strong enough to tote a house?"

She admitted, "No, they don't look strong enough."

I explained, "We had to leave our things back in Liberia before the war. We were forced to come here. But I want you to know I'm a responsible man. I'm telling you this because as a refugee, I don't have work. I have no income and no job."

"Then how are you going to pay me the rent?"

Drawing in my breath, I silently prayed, then said, "I can pay you rent now and for the next month, but there will come a time in the future when you will see us cooking and eating, but we won't have money to pay your rent. It's not that we don't want to pay you, but we won't have the money to pay.

"But being God-fearing people, we believe God will pay the rent for us. If such a thing comes, we don't want any problems or to be evicted. I don't care how long it will take or how many months we're late, I promise I will pay you every CFA I owe."

I said these things because all over the city, landlords and refugees had continual problems with each other. When the tenants couldn't pay the rent, the landlords tried to evict them. The tenants refused to leave and the police were called. Fights ensued. Arrests were made. Property was damaged and destroyed.

Additionally, I knew the Ivorians would watch us to see what we were doing. They saw other refugees go to Western Union, get money, and then go that same night to the nightclubs to drink and dance. But they had no money for rent and fought with the landlords.

Our neighbors would spy on our behavior to see if that is how we also acted. Without our knowledge, they would inform the landlady. So good report or bad, our landlady would know about us.

Carefully examining her expression, I went on. "If I'm late, I will absolutely pay your rent because it is the right thing to do. If I'm a bad man or we are bad people, you will see that in us. If we're good, you will see that also. Watch us to see how we live, and that will give you confidence." With that, I was finished.

She said she would come back next Thursday to give us her response. We prayed during the week for her favor, and then went to meet her again.

When she came, she accepted our conditions totally. The only thing she said was that she didn't like any family problems and never wanted the police coming to the house for any reason. We were overjoyed. We had a house.

The house was a typical concrete block house. It had a front porch, two bedrooms, a living room but no electricity or plumbing. Common to all Ivorian houses, the kitchen was a little concrete building out back, seventy-five feet from the main house. Between the house and the kitchen was a well for water.

Kitchens were built back to keep smoke from drifting into the main house. The kitchen had two compartments, one for us and one for the next door neighbor with a door each. There was no chimney. Holes in the walls between the concrete blocks allowed the smoke to escape. Everything inside was covered with pitch black soot.

We cooked with two pots over a wood fire and only cooked twice per day. In the morning it was cornmeal, cassava, eddoes, plantains, or yams, all common breakfast foods. For lunch/dinner, we used two pots. In one was rice, spaghetti, macaroni, potatoes, or beans. In the other was a soup made with dried or fresh fish.

If we had money, we would eat beef, but only on Sundays. The beef was steamed in a pot with a little oil and salt. The cooking heat boiled away the blood and water so that the meat dried. This cooking method allowed preservation without refrigeration for up to three days. The oil and salt in the meat replaced the water and kept the meat preserved. Unfortunately, it would be a few months before we could afford meat.

We thanked God that he answered our prayer for a house. Two weeks after we moved out of the refugee camp, Bessie's time for delivery arrived.

When Chester was born, he was so large that she had to have a C-section, and we were both certain, at the time, that once a woman delivers via C-section then all future deliveries must also be with a C-section. If medical care had been adequate, this wouldn't have been a problem. But we were refugees. There wasn't much food to eat, and we didn't know who the doctors were. Were they any good? Was there medicine available for pain, headaches, or high blood pressure after a C-section? What about infections? We couldn't afford antibiotics.

On top of all the worries, Bessie had food cravings for chicken and meat, which were nonexistent for us. She was always suffering from ravenous hunger, and yet there was never enough to eat.

I felt guilty as a man unable to provide for my family and my pregnant wife. But what could I do except to wait on the Lord? Again and again, as distress from our lips reached his ears, he heard and answered our prayers. We were as dependent on him as any human beings could possibly be.

When Bessie's time came, an ambulance called by the refugee camp arrived. It took Bessie and me to a nearby town where they had a hospital staffed by doctors, nurses, surgeons, and gynecologists from Médecins Sans Frontières (MSF), Doctors Without Borders.

Once they examined Bessie, they quickly concluded that she had to have another C-section because of her previous one. They wheeled Bessie into the operating room while I waited outside.

In the lobby, there was suddenly a rush of pregnant women arriving. First one, two, three——nine pregnant women arrived in less than two hours.

Time passed as I paced outside. One by one the other pregnant women gave birth and were wheeled out with their new babies. Bessie had gone in before all of them, and they had all come out— but not Bessie. The last of the nine babies had come out and left thirty minutes before.

I was still pacing back and forth in the lobby. I prayed for God to perform a miracle and somehow allow a natural delivery. I didn't want her to have a C-section, a major operation. A C-section could mean death from any number of things, including a small infection or simply the lack of sufficient nourishment to heal her body.

The prayer team back at our church, Union Baptist, was praying nonstop. They had gathered when the ambulance was called, and I knew that hours later they would still be praying until they heard word of Bessie's condition.

Finally, at 12:45 A.M. on August 19, 1991, a nurse burst out of the operating room holding a baby over her shoulder. Without stopping, she rushed past me and out the front door. I watched her run to another hospital building about a hundred yards away and go inside.

Bewildered, I didn't know what significance the nurse's actions held. Did that baby have anything to do with Bessie? Was that baby mine? I didn't know. Nine babies had come and gone. Could there have been other women inside the delivery room before we arrived? Did the baby belong to another woman? I didn't know.

About fifteen minutes later, the beaming nurse returned and presented me my new son, John Jr. Leaping up and down, I praised God. I couldn't contain myself.

It had been close. When the doctors came to perform the C-section, after finishing with the last of the nine babies, they saw that Bessie was already at the point of natural delivery. Because the nine babies arrived so close together and were delivered one after another, the doctors discovered Bessie's baby had already entered the birth canal. It was too late to prep her and perform the C-section.

Bessie delivered naturally, but immediately the baby was in distress. He wasn't breathing. Furthermore, the delivery room had no oxygen. A crisis quickly ensued. For a moment, no one knew what to do. Then, one quick-thinking nurse scooped up the baby, ran out of the delivery room, and out the front door past a bewildered-looking expectant father. She made a mad dash to the other hospital building, where she knew they had an oxygen tank.

She got there just in time and administered oxygen before brain damage set in. After a few more minutes of oxygen, she determined the baby was fine and strolled casually back through the front door again with a wide grin on her face and showed me my new son, John Jr.

I again leapt for joy and started jumping up and down as she related the close call to save his life and how Bessie had delivered naturally. *God is so good and merciful. Why should He bless us so? How He must love us,* I thought.

The next day, Bessie, John Jr., and I were taken back to the camp. Bessie couldn't yet walk the long distance to our house. From the camp I used a little of our remaining money to hire a cab to take us home.

Reality immediately set in. I couldn't pay the rent and we barely had enough food to last a week. I was overjoyed that Bessie and the baby were healthy, but it seemed our needs were endless. Each crisis just melted into the next.

It was so hard and so humbling. John Gonleh was independent, self-sufficient, and capable. I initiated. I completed. I conquered. By willpower alone, in my business, I had bent circumstances and forced them into compliance with my desires.

In Danané, I was nothing. I was just one of tens of thousands of chirping baby birds with mouths stretched open as wide as possible, hoping to receive sustenance from above.

CRAWFISH 20

Strolling through the market with Bessie and the children was a rarity for me. Normally, Bessie did all the shopping. This day, however, the whole family went. I looked at all the different types of food, and it was painful. Before the war, I'd never given a thought to all the material wealth we had. Food, clothing, our house, our car, electricity, doctors, and medicine were all taken for granted. Now I looked at the plump figs, juicy dates, fresh eggs, and all the different types of meat, chicken, and fish for sale. The sight made me wish I'd stayed home. Stall after stall, the wares were laid out carefully, with the merchants hawking and calling out their products, trying to get our attention as we passed. Half-looking by this time at all the many foods I couldn't afford, my eyes suddenly lit upon a particular type of food.

Crawfish! It looked identical to those I had caught in Kakata. Where had it come from? The nearest river, to my knowledge, was the same Cavalla River we had crossed coming into Ivory Coast. It was at least twenty-five miles distant. How had the crawfish gotten here?

An Ivorian man was selling the crawfish. There were people around talking with him. The language was neither English nor French, yet it was still familiar to me, and I could understand some of what they said.

159

I initiated a conversation with him in my native Mano dialect. "What language are you speaking?" I asked.

"Yacouba," he replied. Yacoubians were a tribe living around the border region of Liberia and Ivory Coast. Their dialect has many similarities to my own, but I didn't know how the two languages might be related. Knowing he was Yacoubian, then, I surmised the crawfish had indeed come from the Cavalla River. But how did he get it here? Fishermen are typically too poor to own automobiles.

"How did you get the crawfish here?" I asked him. He told me by foot, carrying a large basket. He would fish for a week and then carry the crawfish on his head the entire twenty-five miles from Guedoloupleu (Gaytown for short) to Danané. "I would like to buy your crawfish at the river to sell in the market," I explained. "That way you wouldn't have to walk this long distance."

He said he wouldn't be returning next Thursday as normal but gave me directions to Gaytown. He also said a lot of people came from his village to sell their products in the market. If I wanted help to find Gaytown, I should wait for his people leaving the market. They would take a particular road. I should wait for them just after noon at the intersection just outside the city.

As he was Ivorian and I was a refugee, I feared he might harbor some suspicions about my motives. Liberians were universally despised and looked upon as some kind of subhuman species by most Ivorians.

I told him I wanted to be his friend and that he could trust me. As a sign of good faith, I gave him 500CFA to reassure him that I would keep my word. I would come back next week with the returning villagers.

When the next week arrived I went to the junction as instructed. Sure enough, a little after noon I saw a group of villagers coming. I stopped them and asked them in my Mano dialect if they knew Gaytown.

Warily, they all stopped and stared at me with mistrust, sizing me up before answering. A man older than myself, who appeared to be their unofficial leader, finally answered. "Yes, we are from Gaytown. Why do you ask?"

Relief! It was the right group. I asked if they knew the man I had met. Yes they did. That boosted my confidence greatly. With as few words as possible to avoid any misunderstanding between the two languages, I explained my purpose. Going off with a group of strangers to an unknown village in an unknown region could be dangerous if they doubted my story.

We passed many small villages on the way. We followed the road leading from Danané to Gaytown used by the trucks that harvested coffee and cocoa beans from all the small plantations along the route. It was a full six hours' walk maintaining a fast pace. I guessed the distance to be almost twenty miles. We arrived at six o'clock, just as the sun was setting.

No one wanted to be caught in the darkness. The bush has too many unseen dangers at night, ranging from poisonous snakes to larger predators like jaguars, tigers, lions, and bush hogs.

Since my first trip was a site visit, I carried only a small basket. The villagers found the man I met the week before and introduced us once again. I was glad and relieved to see him. He also looked genuinely happy to see me. My gesture of trust and friendship had paid off. The fisherman allowed me to sleep in his hut for the night.

That night I slept like a baby even though I was in a strange village. I was filled with happiness. At just the right moment, something extraordinary had happened to meet our needs.

Drifting off to sleep the words of Psalm 37:23–24 materialized in my mind: "The steps of a good man are ordered by the LORD, and He delights in his way. Though he fall, he shall not be utterly cast down; for the LORD upholds him with His hand."

At dawn the next morning I bought a few crawfish and then made an engagement for the following Thursday. Walking back to Danané, my heart was filled with joy. Hallelujah! I was back in the crawfish business. Now I had a secure way to pay the rent and feed my family.

News soon spread in Gaytown that now there was a man coming from Danané to buy crawfish. With this good news, the fishermen no longer had to make the long trek to the city once a week. Before I started making the long trip, each fisherman accumulated his daily catch for a week and kept them alive inside wicker baskets submerged in the river until market day arrived.

My approach was different. I started making three trips per week. Going from one fisherman to the next, buying up their individual catch for two or three days, I was always able to fill my large basket. With a distance of twenty-five miles to hike each way, three times per week, I never had any competition. Soon I developed a monopoly on the crawfish business in Danané.

Rather than sell my crawfish in the market like the local fishermen had done, I again followed a different approach. I only sold my crawfish to Liberians. The reason for this wasn't out of favoritism or prejudice but my previous experience.

Unlike Ivory Coast, Liberia is filled with rivers and streams where crawfish live. As a result, Liberians absolutely love crawfish. Crawfish have a sweet taste. They're wonderful in soups and sauces, with collard greens, potato greens, butter beans, or anything else. In addition, crawfish have a lot of nutrition. It's one of the most favorite foods in Liberia.

In contrast, with the Cavalla River located so far away, the local people in Danané never developed a taste or love for the little crustaceans. It wasn't that the price was too high; the fishermen sold the crawfish for whatever the market would bear. The problem was that the market just didn't bear much. Ivorians had no great love for this wondrous delicacy and weren't willing to pay much.

The Ivorian fisherman sold a dozen crawfish of any size for 1000cfa in the Danané market. I bought the crawfish for the same price at the Cavalla River's edge. As a result, there was no incentive for the fishermen to make the arduous trek themselves when I was willing to make it for them.

The bottom line was that Liberians would pay more than Ivorians due to their crawfish-craving taste buds.

I split Danané into three zones. Each trip I took my catch to a different zone in rotation. I went from house to house where I knew Liberians lived. I didn't want to sell to only one group of Liberians, since crawfish were loved by all. I spread the wealth, so to speak.

Gaytown was located on the Cavalla River, downstream from where we crossed the border from Khanplay, Liberia. With the river twenty-five miles from Danané, I walked fast to make good time. Daylight broke about six, the basket was filled by six thirty or seven, and then I was off. I never stopped to make sales on the road. I wanted to spend as little time as possible on the bush road.

My wicker basket was thirty-six inches in diameter by fourteen inches tall and held about forty pounds of crawfish. I tied up the basket with big, wide green leaves over the top of the crawfish to keep them alive. On the bottom, I placed plastic to try to keep the water from the crawfish from dripping on my head. Crawfish are filled with water. Believe me, there is nothing worse than walking mile after mile with a slow steady stream of crawfish juice dripping off your nose.

When I arrived in the city, the crawfish were still alive and moving. Not that it mattered much. Liberians loved crawfish so much, they would buy them dead or alive.

I blessed God and the man I met back in Kakata who taught me how to travel to the river villages, negotiate with the fishermen, and sell crawfish in market. From that experience I knew how much Liberians would pay.

Selling in individual Liberian homes, I was able to get from 50% to 100% higher price than my purchase cost depending on size. To make sure I didn't sell the whole batch and forget to save some for my own family, I always filled a plastic bag and tied it shut. In my haste to get my entire product sold, I didn't want to forget that the Gonlehs also loved crawfish.

With the catch bulging out the sides of the basket, I adjusted the cloth *kata* on top of my head, to help balance the load. Then, the fishermen helped me hoist up the heavy basket. All my muscles grew taut at once under the strain. The full basket felt so heavy. I was out of practice. After a few trips, I knew my muscles would respond and strengthen with conditioning. This first time, however, was brutal.

I took one wobbly step, then another, steadied myself and set off back down the path toward Danané. *Only six hours to go*, I thought. *I can do it. I must do it.*

Desperation is a powerful motivator. Without the money this catch would bring, well, I didn't want to think about it. God had made a way for me to get this job. Now I had to do my part with my muscles and strong back.

I wore high rubber boots above my ankles to protect against insects and also snakes. Below the knees were the most vulnerable spots for snakes to bite, so this type of protection made sense. As I walked, I began to sweat. I sweated so much that it ran down into my rubber boots like someone poured water into the boots. By the time I was halfway back, the water inside would squish and slosh around one-half inch deep in my boots. That was a mixed blessing. The water felt good sloshing around my feet and toes, cooling them off, but it also made the boots slippery from the inside and made walking harder.

Occasionally, despite my plans and best efforts, the crawfish dripped on me. Then I had to tilt the heavy basket slightly forward, backward, or sideways to divert the course of the little river to a different path.

By the time I got back, six hours later, I had to wring out my clothes and underwear. They were always completely soaked through.

Traveling to Gaytown three times per week, the villagers I saw gradually grew accustomed to my presence. Though the work was hard, I always wore a smile. I felt God's presence with me. Because of my cheerful spirit, I started to gain favor with the people I passed. They somehow saw my commitment to what I was doing, the smile on my face, and the joy in my heart. In turn, they responded in good ways.

In three little villages they gave me the nickname "Strong Man." I was so strong that I could carry the heavy basket with my arms free. I didn't have to keep one arm up to steady the basket like most people with heavy loads. Normally, only women with years of practice can walk arms free. For a man, it was unheard of.

As I passed, villagers called out to me. "It's the Strong Man" or "The Strong Man is looking strong today." I waved and smiled and greeted them back, never stopping or slowing down.

I responded to these villagers further by bringing a few bars of soap to pass out as I walked through their villages. With small gestures of friendship and goodwill I gained favor with the people. I was free from worry that someone would be plotting, lying in wait for me to pass by, harm me, and possibly kill me and take my crawfish.

This was normally a constant worry. It was quite common to hear of random acts of violence committed against refugees. In the middle of the bush along an isolated road, no one would ever find your body or know who had attacked or even killed you. With the general low regard Ivorians had for all Liberians, we lived with constant fear. Just being out on the trail alone was a dangerous activity. That's why I always walked and moved as fast as I could, especially because I wanted to arrive in Gaytown before evening.

Evening is when big game and big game hunters come out. Being a foreigner, not speaking French, and walking on the road alone in the dark all seemed dangerous to me. I didn't want to encounter a hunter. He might call to me, and if I didn't respond in French, he might feel suspicious. Also, as a refugee traveling at an odd time of day, I didn't want to be singled out for harassment or intimidation. My fear led me to work hard at learning the Yacouba dialect. It would help ensure my safe passage through all the small villages.

As I walked, I constantly prayed for God's favor, for protection from harm, for friendship, and for his guidance. At times, while singing songs or humming, I felt his presence so close. During these times, I was filled with joy and it felt like I wasn't really alone on the deserted road. Other times while sweating profusely in the hot sun, I would get chilled as I felt God's presence envelope my very being.

On some occasions, I had the feeling of being thrilled just to be alive, to be happy, to have experienced God's power so much in my life and to know he would never leave me. Even though I walked through the valley of the shadow of death time and time again, I felt great comfort reflecting on how he was always there, right beside me.

I wondered if David composed his psalms as he tended his sheep all alone in the wilderness. He must have, I concluded. There is something about being alone, with no distractions or people around that turns a person's mind heavenward.

I also wondered during my long walks on the trail, with all the faith possessed by the Christians in Liberia, why could we not overcome the forces of evil that tore apart our beautiful country? After all, the nation of Liberia was started in 1823 by the returning American slaves for the purpose of bringing Christianity to Africa. How could it have gone so wrong? Were we lacking in faith? Did the sins of a few leaders condemn our entire country? Or was it our own sins—or the half-hearted dedication of all lukewarm Christians like I had once been—that had condemned us? I feared I already knew the answer.

Twelve hours of quiet time with the Lord during each trip to Gaytown led me to an idea for a new ministry at my church, Union Baptist, in Danané. The more I thought it through on the trail, the more feasible it seemed to create a midday service like the one I'd led in Monrovia before the war.

From our arrival in Danané we attended the Union Baptist Church, started by the Reverend J. Edwin Lloyd for Liberian refugees. Before starting the midday service, I worked with Reverend Lloyd as a deacon. With the midday service, I would have more responsibility.

Union Baptist Church grew rapidly with the continual influx of Liberian Baptist refugees as well as recent converts. We met under a large circus tent like those in the refugee camp. This was much larger and could hold five hundred people at one time.

I would call the midday service "Lunch with Dr. Jesus." After all, Jesus is the great physician, healing our bodies, souls, and spirits, so it only seemed natural to refer to him this way.

I prayed and then approached the senior pastor, Reverend Lloyd, with my idea. He immediately agreed, and the midday service was born. The service provided another powerful incentive to keep a fast-paced walk. I was leading it. I had to keep going so I wouldn't be late.

Just as the crawfish business and the midday service were coming together, something happened to jeopardize not just these two events but nearly my life.

BLACK STONE 21

BESSIE Our house was like a dream. It was nothing like our old house in Paynesville, but after surviving in the bush for six months and almost a year in the refugee camp it was heaven. No more sleeping on the ground or hard concrete, battling bugs, filth, overcrowding, and thievery.

Now I could actually start arranging our living area. I could add flowers, curtains, and furniture as money allowed! I bubbled over thinking of the possibilities. I would have my own kitchen again rather than sharing with other families. The girls could sleep on beds. Though we had no electricity or plumbing, it was all too wonderful to take in.

In the early years at Danané, rents were cheap. Over time, however, the refugees started a housing boom as those with resources or jobs moved out of the camp and into town. Prices rose, and it was only our wonderful relationship with our landlady that kept our own house affordable.

Our landlady soon became so comfortable with us that she put a second rental house under our control. This house rented individual rooms. She eventually trusted us so much that she gave John her bank account book. He managed the second house for her, collected the rent, and deposited the money into her account. Not only that, but as God blessed us over time with more resources, we voluntarily raised our own rent to bless her for putting her trust in us.

The refugees didn't build just houses and apartments; they also built churches. When we arrived, Danané had only three or four Christian churches. Before long, churches of all denominations sprang up. Methodists, Lutherans, Presbyterians, and Baptists eventually added thirty or forty congregations to the few original churches.

Of all these, Union Baptist was the largest and the one we attended. John became a deacon and helped Pastor Lloyd with the services just as he had at the Immanuel Baptist Church in Paynesville.

When John started the crawfish business, he had to cut the hours he worked in the church. Though he spent less total time there, he focused all his efforts on the midday service. He left right after the service, about one o'clock, and headed into the bush, arriving in Gaytown after dark. The next morning, he had to get up early and be on the trail so that he could return by noon, just before the service started.

There were times he would have liked to have continued ministering longer, praying for people, discussing their problems, or just offering general counsel. But it wasn't possible. He had to get on the trail to Gaytown.

Along the trail, he practiced his sermon for the service, rehearsing it to any snakes, birds, or other bush creatures that happened to be within earshot.

Upon arriving back in Danané he dropped off the basket of crawfish at the house, quickly changed his clothes, and then ran all the way to the church. He usually staggered, huffing and puffing, through the large tent flap that was the front door of Union Baptist Church.

At times, the fishermen in Gaytown were slow, and John wasn't able to get on the road until seven. Then he was late for the service that should have started at noon. John felt bad about being late, but he walked as fast as he could.

Later in the afternoon, then, John made his deliveries to his customers. These were very long days, full of hard work, but we were happy. The financial security provided by the crawfish business made life seem almost normal.

John

We lived on the edge of Danané, and the bush was very close. Because we prepared our food using firewood, I went to a large coffee farm near our house where I knew there would be plenty of branches on the ground. Coffee is grown under big trees to keep the hot sun off the coffee plants. The hot sun would stress and dry out the delicate coffee beans. Shade from the big trees helps keep the beans fresh and plump.

Soon after moving into our house, I went to collect firewood. Leaves that covered the ground were dry and brown. In the background, I heard birds twittering and singing. Using my cutlass, I cut branches and accumulated a good load. Suddenly, I felt something running down my ankle. I looked down and saw a trickle of blood. *How strange*, I thought. *I didn't feel anything.*

Alarmed and a little confused, I left and went back to the main road. As I started to inspect my ankle, a passerby noticed me. He looked at my ankle and said, "Oh, snakebite!" He bent down and saw the two holes made by the fangs, about a half inch apart. The bite was right on the hardest part of my ankle, just above the bone.

How could that be? No pain, no strike, no noise, except the crunch of the leaves and twigs breaking underfoot. Then I suddenly realized how careless I'd been. I hadn't worn my tall rubber boots, which would have protected me up to my knees from snakes.

The man went into the bush and cut a rope vine. He came back and wrapped it around my calf, just below my knee. He made a knot and cinched it up tight to create a tourniquet and told me to get to the hospital right away.

I noticed that the bush birds were still singing, and suddenly I remembered why. They weren't making noise because it was a nice day. Birds twittering and chirping about in the bush always means a snake is nearby. It's their way of warning each other to be careful. I immediately was angry with myself for my stupidity and carelessness. I hoped my mistake would not cost me my life. The time spent in the refugee camp and my home had made my bush survival skills rusty. Snakes stalk frogs in dry leaves, waiting for one to come near. Then they strike and hang on, working their mouths around as they swallow the prey whole. Now I was the prey.

I had seen this firsthand during our bush journey. A green mamba struck and swallowed a lizard. I also saw this drama played out behind our Paynesville house. The victim was a rat and the snake was a cobra.

I breathed a prayer and dropped the branches I was carrying. Where was home?

But first, still hearing the birds' singing, I returned to the edge of the bush. I had to identify the snake that bit me. I was afraid it was a puff adder. They strike so fast that you are bitten and don't even know it. I had to find out, but I dared not walk back in. He might be waiting for me. That was their way.

There was no way I could sneak up on a snake. They live in the bush and are masters of their environment. The moment a man stepped off the main road, the snakes knew he was there, in their domain.

Taking a piece of dry wood I chunked it back into the spot where I had been standing. It worked! The snake was still there. He didn't move until the wood fell near him. Then I saw the leaves rustle as the snake made his getaway. He had a brown back with a pattern and blended perfectly with the leaves. It was likely a puff adder, a member of the poisonous viper family, but I couldn't be sure.

Puff adders are fat for their length. This snake looked just like a moving twig. Perhaps it was his cousin, the thinner and less poisonous Berg adder. I didn't know, but I wasn't going to get closer for a better inspection.

I quickly made my way home. On the short walk, my fear grew with each step. My stomach started churning, and I thought I might faint. I know what snakebites can do. Were my symptoms from fear or the poison trying to get past the tourniquet to my vital organs?

Coming up to the house, but still at a distance, I yelled for Bessie. She and the children all came out. As they stood on the porch, I started telling them about it. They all gathered around and bent down to look at my ankle.

Bessie shouted, "John, you have to go to the hospital. You might die!" Some of the girls started to cry as fear gripped them.

Feeling frustrated and impotent, I didn't know what to do. Maybe the snake wasn't poisonous. I couldn't spend all our money on a false alarm. Even if it was poisonous, maybe only a little venom went inside. Still indecisive, I kept trying to logically analyze the situation. We couldn't tell how deep the puncture wounds went. It probably helped that the bite was exactly on the hardest part of the outside of my ankle. That hard bone or cartilage may have prevented the venom from being deeply injected. We didn't know what to do. We couldn't afford to go to the hospital. We had money to pay for either snakebite treatment or food; not both.

As we were still trying to determine what to do, our Yacoubian neighbor strolled through our yard, returning from the Catholic church where she led the choir. She often took this shortcut to get to her house, which was located directly behind ours. She saw our whole family talking on the porch in worried tones and inspecting my leg. She abruptly stopped, hurried over, and asked in the Yacouba dialect what had happened.

Taking in at a glance the blood caked on my ankle, she said she would send over her teenage son, who knew how to use their "black stone."

"Black stone? What's that?" I responded in my best Yacouba. "I've never heard of anything called a black stone."

She just looked at me with an expression that communicated something like, "You Liberians are really ignorant." Then she carefully explained as if I were a small child or mentally deficient, "It's for snakebites." Then she turned and rushed toward her house.

We all just stood there dazed, bewildered, and looking at each other. I wasn't sure I believed her, but to go to the hospital to be treated for a snake bite would have cost CFA 12,000–18,000, a huge sum. It was either the black stone or the hospital. I chose the black stone.

Whatever the black stone was, I sure hoped it would work. The neighbor lady seemed so confident. I was out of options, and moment by moment the venom was working its damage.

After an interminable wait of ninety seconds, her son ran up with the stone. He just happened to be home and not out with friends. The black stone came from India and was sold in the Danané market. We didn't have one, of course. We'd never even heard of it in Liberia. It was about a one inch wide by three inches long and a half inch thick, and, as you might expect, black and shiny.

My blood was now dried and crusty on my ankle. We went inside and he had me lie down on the bed. With a razor blade he made two shallow cuts straight into the punctures and extending a quarter inch on each side of the two original punctures. Blood started flowing freely.

Next, he placed the black stone on the flowing blood, covering the two razor cuts. To my great astonishment, and blinking to make sure I wasn't seeing things, the stone immediately stuck to my leg like glue. The young man explained that the stone sucks the venom out of the leg.

I got up and walked with it for a little bit, and it remained stuck fast. He left after telling me to keep my ankle hanging down. The stone would fall off when it had completed its work.

It sounded too crazy to believe. How could a stone do this? Bessie didn't believe it at all. It was a shiny black stone. Somehow, though, it defied gravity and clung tightly to my ankle like some inanimate rectangular leech.

I went to bed, keeping my leg bent and dangling toward the floor. Bessie checked the stone throughout the night to see if it was still fastened to my ankle. Between four thirty and five in the morning the stone fell off, its work completed.

When I woke up I didn't feel any pain and could easily walk. There was no sign of swelling. Just then the children ran into our room to see what happened. We all just stared at the black stone lying on the floor, and at my ankle, where it had once been securely attached. Finally, I cut off the tourniquet.

Before the war, Liberian television showed American programs like *Superman*. I thought the black stone acted like some strange anti-Kryptonite. However, whereas Kryptonite sucked out Superman's powers, this stone seemingly sucked the venom out of my leg and restored my powers.

We couldn't imagine how it worked. We gathered for prayer time and praised and thanked God once again for his impeccable timing. He sent our neighbor across our lawn at the perfect moment. Then he made sure she heard us talking about the snakebite and made sure her son was home so he could come over and administer the treatment.

In all truth, I don't even absolutely know for sure if I was bitten by a poisonous snake. It could have been a poisonous Berg adder, or it could have been something else. Adder bites often don't swell right away, so that was no help. Also, with adder bites the poisonous effects are localized rather than dispersed throughout the victim's body. Maybe the hard cartilage caused the fangs to break just the surface of the skin. There were a number of variables, and I never saw the snake clearly, so there is no way to tell.

My snakebite experience wasn't like that of the apostle Paul's on the island of Malta after his shipwreck. A viper, driven out of brushwood by heat from the fire, sank its fangs into the apostle's hand. All present clearly saw it hanging there. Paul then shook the snake off into the fire to kill it. Everyone was convinced Paul was a murderer and that he would die. They waited and watched a long time for him to swell up and fall dead. But nothing happened. He suffered no ill effects. The people then changed their minds and thought he was a god. For me, this entire snakebite episode brought to mind that I have to walk by faith and not by sight.

That very same day I awoke in perfect condition—no swelling and no ill effects—I went back to the bush to retrieve the firewood I had cut. Just to be safe, I threw many sticks in the dry leaves, over and over, until I was sure every last slithery thing had been driven off.

After the close call with the snake, I continued with the crawfish business. Then one day while on the trail, about six months after I started, something happened that changed everything.

The midday service had been underway for two months. I was returning from one of my crawfish trips. I had recently built up the sides of my basket to make it higher, increasing its capacity to hold more crawfish. The fishermen had plenty to sell, and I didn't want to leave a single tasty morsel behind. The basket was so heavy it took two men to help me put it on my head. By now, my muscles were lean and hard. I could handle the extra load.

Along the trail, I struggled to keep my heavy load balanced on my *kata*. Finally, I reached my one and only resting spot—a large boulder on the side of the trail. It stood chest-high with a flat top. Crouching down a little, I slid the basket off my head and onto the rock. Only with this elevated platform could I reposition the basket back onto my head.

Wiping my brow and forehead of sweat, I grasped my water bottle and took a long draw. With no warning, in the middle of slaking my thirst, I heard a voice speak.

"Don't you think I'm able to feed you? Is that why you're suffering with this load on your head and neglecting my people?" the voice said, clearly annoyed. The jolt was instantaneous, as if I'd been struck by lightning on a clear day.

I whipped around, looking for the one who had broken the silence and spoken to me in such a brusque manner. But no one was there. I was standing all alone.

Shocked, I realized it was the Lord. A chill crept down my spine, and the hair on my arms stood straight at attention. It was the same voice I had heard in the bathtub years before. It was the same voice who spoke in the market during my confrontation with the soldier. This was the third time I had heard it. I knew it was the Lord speaking.

I dropped to my knees, my water bottle still in my hand but my thirst completely forgotten. Turning my head to heaven I spoke.

"Father, if this is you speaking to me, then please show me what to do. If you want me to quit the crawfish business, then I'll stop. I won't neglect your people anymore."

Trembling with feelings of excitement, nervousness, anxiety, and wonder, I got up, pulled the load back onto my head, and started walking.

As I walked down the trail my mind was abuzz. Thoughts of all sorts popped in and out of my head in staccato, rapid-fire action. The more I thought about the consequences of obeying this voice, the more negative thoughts invaded my consciousness: *What are you doing? Where will we get money for rent and food? The crawfish business is our only source of income. What will Bessie and the children say? What will happen to us with no income?*

We had just gotten on our feet. We now knew what it was like to know where our next meal was coming from. We weren't stressed about how we could pay our rent, food, and expenses totaling fifty US dollars a month.

After a few minutes of this, I finally rebuked myself and tried to sweep the thoughts out of my mind. God wasn't giving me the benefit of clarity or understanding how he would work everything out. He had spoken to me clearly and told me what to do. There was no mistaking his voice. Yet I also knew that if my will insisted, then my mind would eventually fabricate an explanation to negate his clear command.

He had left me with only two options: obedience or disobedience. Did I or did I not trust him? It was such a simple, yet hard, question.

After distilling my entire future down to this one question, I made my choice. My job was to be obedient. If he called me to do this, then he would provide a way.

Just then I remembered that old hymn "Trust and Obey." The hymn was right, I concluded; there was no other way. So, armed only with a faith that I hoped would be sufficient, upon reaching Danané, I set down the crawfish basket and never picked it up again.

Note: For information on the mysterious "black stone," use an Internet search engine with the following keywords: "blackstone snakebite treatment." Modern medical testing has demonstrated that in actual use, the black stone has no value in treating snakebites. Of course, we didn't know that at the time of this incident. We've concluded that the snake was either nonpoisonous, or the fangs were unable to inject the poisonous venom because of the bite location on the ankle. While the black stone did not save my life, it did save my money.

UNION BAPTIST CHURCH 22

BESSIE Market days always drew the biggest gathering of people in the city. It seemed like everyone came to the open air market on Thursdays and Saturdays. People strolled up and down the aisles looking at everything to buy even if they didn't have any money.

Food products were arranged by type and there were entire sections devoted to nuts and dried fruits, fresh fruits and vegetables, slaughtered domestic meat, bush meat, dried products like rice and beans, fresh fish, dried fish, and cans of this and that with fascinating labels.

Wistfully, we walked past tins of Campbell's soup and Chicken-of-the-Sea tuna clearly marked "Property of the United Nations, Not for Sale." We could only look, feeling a touch of bitterness and indignity, at the delicious food provided freely by the United States of America. I wondered if their citizens knew it was being used to feed corruption rather than the refugees.

And not just food. It seemed you could buy half of Liberia there, since much of what was sold in the market had been pilfered and scavenged by the rebels and sold for pennies on the dollar. There were hubcaps by the hundreds but few cars in Danané. There were street lamps for sale that had been wrenched from the tree-lined boulevards of Monrovia. There were twisted coils of copper cable, the veins and arteries of modern civilization, ripped mercilessly from

179

Liberia's dying body. There were the disparate skeletons of unidenti-
fied machines needing the detective skills of a team of paleontologists
to reconstruct them to identify their original purpose. Once-thriving
factories, businesses, and houses were all fair game for the warring
rebel factions to plunder.

The market was a menagerie. When we first arrived in the refugee
camp, we longed for the day when we could taste with our lips some
of what our eyes feasted upon. That glorious day came when John
started the crawfish business. It lasted only six months.

John walked in the door that day but didn't speak to anyone. At the
time I took no notice of his unusually quiet demeanor. Like always,
he took his shower and then got something to eat.

It wasn't until our devotional time that evening that he announced
he had something to discuss with the entire family. He started slowly.
He mentioned the trail. He mentioned the resting rock. He mentioned getting a drink. Then he spoke of it: the Voice—the voice of
God.

With that, he had our full attention. All eyes were set on John,
examining his facial features as he spoke. He repeated the words,
having committed them to memory for just this moment: "Don't
you think I can feed you? Is that why you are suffering with this load
on your head and neglecting my people?"

The children didn't yet understand where this was heading, but
I knew. The voice was telling John to give up our only means of
income and work full-time at the church.

John was still talking as questions and objections bombarded my
mind: *Are you sure God spoke to you? Was it audible? Could you hear
the voice with your ears or just inside your head? Maybe it was just a
thought. How do you know it was him? What if it was your own desire
due to the hard work of carrying the heavy basket? Maybe it's just your
guilt convincing you to quit. I know you want to spend more time at
church.*

All of these thoughts exploding in my head screamed at me to
shout them out loud, to demand some explanation, some rational
answer. *This is our money we need to live! How can you just stop?*

But I remained silent, the thoughts accumulating pressure inside my skull. I let John continue talking. Before he finished, however, first my left hand and then my right started to shake with nervousness and a creeping fear. I clasped them involuntarily, hoping the children wouldn't notice my agitation. *That crawfish business was our only source of income. We were finally standing on our own feet, and now John was suggesting going back to just depending on God.* I suddenly listened to my own thoughts: . . . *just depending on God.* I felt ashamed for thinking this way. After all God had done for us, how could I respond like this?

John finished talking. I looked at the children and could tell by the expressions on their faces they were stunned and didn't know what to think except to wonder about what he said. Next we all prayed and asked God for guidance. Finally, after the prayer, John asked, "Well, . . . what do you think?"

After a few moments of silence, Monica said, "I think we should listen to God."

One after another, all the children agreed with Monica.

Finally I spoke. "I agree. We should listen to God and obey him." It was settled. From now on, God would have to feed us. It was what he called us to. "He will do it," I said, trying to sound convincing, even as I sought to reassure myself.

John

From the start of the midday service, I took no pay or offering of any kind as a salary. The crawfish business supplied our needs. I couldn't change now and ask for a salary from people who had no incomes and owned nothing.

God's command was simple: Stop the business and trust him to feed us. For this reason, I never returned to reclaim money I'd left with the fishermen as my guarantee for their next catch.

From that point in time the midday service took off like it was an African fish eagle taking flight off the Cavalla River, its powerful six-foot black wings pulling it upward toward its nest with its catch securely held by large talons. Truly God's blessing was upon me.

Hearing and obeying God's command to me seemed to set off a chain reaction of events. Not only did the midday service at Union Baptist Church soon become widely known in Danané, news spread to other cities. Before long, there were midday services in Liberian churches all over the Ivory Coast.

The presence of God was in our midst. News spread all over Ivory Coast about the results of healing and protection we were seeing. I believe God worked miracles in the lives of people because of my testimony and my obedience in stopping the crawfish business.

One lady in our church was bitten by a snake. She went to the hospital, received antivenom shots, but still suffered great pain in walking and was forced to use a cane. She came to my office after the service to request prayer.

The other pastors and I scoured the Bible and saw that the apostle James said to anoint the sick with oil and pray for their healing. For this reason, we took olive oil and consecrated it by praying over it. We prayed that whenever the oil was used, it would accomplish the purpose that God willed. By doing this we were following the biblical example.

I rubbed oil on her left foot in the name of the Lord. I told her that the oil had no inherent power to heal her; it was just olive oil. "Don't believe in the oil," I said. "Believe in the Lord."

I prayed for her, and then we chatted a little while longer. As she rose to leave, her face registered a look of amazement. She said she was feeling better, clearly surprised. She walked around the office a little and then left, carrying her cane. She hopped into a taxi and went home.

The next day she came back to the midday service still without her cane and without pain. She shared her testimony in the service. From that day forward, she never again used a cane. She continued coming to midday for several years, and all of us could see that the healing was genuine and permanent.

Then, there was a horrible traffic accident in the city. Body parts were strewn all over the street. It was a horrible scene of carnage. Everyone on the bus involved in the accident died, except one woman. She suffered only minor scratches. God saved her life. She was a regular attendee of the midday service, and everyone attributed her miraculous survival to God's protection.

After she shared her testimony in the midday service, I invited her to my office. It seemed quite clear that God had spared her life for a reason. I told her this and encouraged her to remain committed to his service. Then I prayed that God would reveal his plan and purpose for her life.

A few days later, she approached me after the service and said she needed to talk to me. When she stepped into my office, she closed the door and proclaimed she wanted to kiss me and make love to me. Shocked, I told her that this was not the reason God had saved her life and she should not let the devil use her to tempt a pastor into sin.

"What are you trying to prove?" she asked. "Even right next to my house, a deacon brings his girlfriend over when his wife is gone. And in the house on the other side, a pastor has a girlfriend who visits all the time. What makes you so different?" she demanded, now angry and scorned.

"I cannot be like them."

"Why not? Everyone else is doing it!"

"Because the Spirit of God lives in me, and I have devoted my life to him. There is no turning back for me."

I arose and opened my office door so she wouldn't scream and then lie, telling people I had tried to molest her. At that, she stood up and stomped out.

She came back two more times and asked why was I so stubborn. I refused to yield to her advances, and after that she stopped attending midday and Sunday services altogether.

I wondered why this woman came to tempt me. Then I realized it was a test. I belonged to a pastors' council with all denominations. We met every Saturday morning for breakfast and to counsel each other. I was very hard on the other pastors. I urged them to always be on guard in how they lived, what they did, and where they went.

As pastors we were visible examples to everyone else. If we set good examples, then the people would respond to God's Word.

So many people from Liberia didn't know how to read or write and didn't know the Bible. They could only look at the pastors' example to illustrate biblical teachings. If we failed as moral examples, then the Word of God we spoke would fall on unhearing ears.

People came to the midday service with migraines, stomachaches from parasites, joint pain from malaria, fevers from unknown jungle diseases, and diarrhea from dysentery. Rather than rub oil on every person's hurting body part, I wanted to devise another means for them to know and experience the power of God. But I wanted them to know that any healing came from him and not me. I had no desire to become an idol.

I felt led to use a cup of water. God didn't tell me audibly to use a cup of water, but without my thinking about it, the idea just popped into my head to do this.

Jesus spit into dirt to make mud for the blind man's eyes. God caused the water in the Pool of Bethesda to have healing powers when it stirred up. Elisha healed Naaman, the commander of Syria's army, of leprosy after dipping seven times in the Jordan River. Water was a tool God used often to demonstrate his power.

Usually I had them drink the water. Other times they poured the water on the injured body part. If a healing occurred, then the person knew it was God's doing, because a cup of water has no power on its own.

The healings were all relatively small in restoring the person's health. No hacked off limbs were regrown, no blinded eyes began to see. To unbelievers and even some Christians, these healings could be easily denied or passed off as mere coincidences. To the people involved, however, they were real and were living testimonies of God's power and evidence that he truly cared for them individually.

Though not all were healed, I believe the healings that did occur were real. They were not the result of the power of suggestion or a temporary emotional high that masked symptoms of an illness or injury. The midday service at Union Baptist was not an emotionally-driven spectacle by preachers claiming to have miraculous powers of healing. I claimed no powers for myself, and the people involved attended the church regularly for many years. Any false claims were easily identified.

I don't know why God didn't perform large miraculous healings any more than I understand those that he did do. God keeps his own counsel and doesn't consult me. To me, the healings showed that God cares about us, but he rarely removes the large problems we face in life.

As refugees, we had no resources other than God himself. There was no health or life insurance, no recourse against injustice. God was our only hope. But rather than using his unlimited power to fix our problems, he helped us pass through the problems. He offered brief glimpses of himself along the way to encourage us, to develop our character, building our faith gradually, and teaching us to totally depend on him.

Next, we started midday services at the hospital and the prison. At each location, we used a prayer box. People wrote their requests to God, needing solutions to their problems or asking for healing, on slips of paper and placed them in the box. No one read the prayers other than the people who wrote them.

Each week we fasted, taking water only, from Wednesday to Friday. Then on Fridays, the prayer team and I opened the box and emptied all the contents into a basket. We surrounded the basket, prayed, and then dumped it in the middle of the floor. We lit the papers with a match, and as the flame grew, the smoke drifted up to the Lord.

I myself wrote a secret prayer, put it in the box, and, like all the others, it was consumed by fire with the smoke going to heaven. My prayer was to emigrate to America. But we didn't have anyone in America to file the necessary documents. There was no one I could ask other than God himself.

Bessie had cousins living in America, but in order to be allowed to come, we needed to be sponsored by immediate family. Cousins would not do.

Each week I watched as the smoke slowly curled upward, lazily spreading out and filling under the crown of the church tent, creating a holy haze of prayer—full of hope, despair, and longing.

VIOLA 23

BESSIE

Usually one or two of the girls accompanied me to the market. When John had the crawfish business, we enjoyed the energetic atmosphere in the market as merchants and customers conducted animated negotiations. With money in my pocket, I felt like we qualified to be part of this. If I wanted, then I too could buy the luxurious sweet sticky buns or the expensive cuts of beef.

As it was, I never bought any of those expensive items, just the basics. We had learned to not splurge, for we never knew what tomorrow might bring. But just having the money made me feel different. It felt good. Just knowing I could buy something didn't mean I had to, but I could if I wanted to.

Having money eliminated the stress of having to get the absolute best price for every last item. With money, I was more relaxed, not having to ensure the merchant didn't short us even one kernel of rice. I could take my time picking out the plumpest chicken and stopping to enjoy the pungent aroma of fresh fish. Money allowed me to negotiate harder. After all, with food reserves at home, time was on the side of the buyer instead of the seller.

This morning I was alone. I came to buy a few meager rations. After John quit the crawfish business, we had to cut back. Meat, chicken, and fish were rarities, but thankfully we weren't starving like some of the other refugees.

Strolling through the familiar market, looking at the wares carefully arranged on blankets, cardboard, or woven baskets, I glanced up. I noticed a woman who looked vaguely familiar. I was sure I recognized her but couldn't place her immediately. She was alone also and displayed the sad look of resignation so common to Liberian refugees.

We had all lost so much from the war—family, possessions, jobs, our entire way of life. Furthermore, many people looked different after significant weight loss or trauma that actually changed their personalities. Even old friends seemed different than before, aged, worn.

I was still looking at the woman as she made her way through the market. She almost passed by with her head lowered but then looked up. She saw me looking back at her, and recognition and surprise spread across her face. "Bessie!" she cried out, running up to me.

It was Viola, Monica's mother! It had been almost two years since I'd seen her last. Monica was with us when the rebels attacked, and there had been no way to contact Viola for this entire time. We didn't know if she was dead or alive, and she had no idea if Monica or any of us were still alive. We hugged and cried as I told her that Monica was fine. We cried again when I told her Chester was dead.

I gave Viola directions to our house, and she said she would come and bring her other children with her to see Monica that afternoon. We hugged again, and then Viola scurried off to tell her family the joyous news.

Lately we had been wondering about and discussing Viola. Monica was worried about her mom and mentioned her frequently during our daily devotions. Over and over she brought up her mother to pray for her, for her safety, and that one day God would reunite them.

After getting the items I came for, I set out for home. As I walked, I pondered how far we had all come. If was hard to comprehend how God had changed us all.

I knew Viola had grown up in a strict religious household. Her family attended the Inline Church, where men and women sat apart during the services. Women had to wear head coverings and dresses below their knees. They weren't allowed to drink, smoke, or even participate in recreational activities such as playing video games, listening to music, or even attending soccer matches. The leaders thought that almost any sort of fun would cause their members to backslide. For committing fornication, they would first talk to you and then expel you from the church if you refused to change your behavior.

Viola rebelled against her rigid upbringing. She cast off her strict rules and eventually met John while he was a soccer star. One thing led to another and she was one of his girlfriends. Monica was born as a result.

When it happened and for months afterward, the pain had felt like a hot knife penetrating not only my heart but my stomach also. Night after night, the anguish flooded my soul and overflowed into wracking sobs. John and I fought over first one and then another and another of his girlfriends.

Recalling all of these memories as I walked home, I turned them over in my mind to examine them for traces of residual pain and resentment against this woman. There was nothing there. I only experienced joy and an abiding sense of grace and God's providence that reunited us in the market.

Back in 1984, all of us were Christians but living worldly lives. We were still spiritually blind. Though we heard sermons about God every week in the church services, we didn't really know him. We didn't know what it meant to trust him with our lives. We were believers, just not very strong. As a result, we fell prey to temptations and sinful behavior.

Viola, pregnant with Monica, was kicked out of her church. That drove her even further away. Her parents were important leaders in the church and became embittered against her. They expected their child to set an example for other children. When she couldn't, they expelled her.

Before the war started, she, like John, repented, married, and had other children. Even so, back then, I had trouble completely forgiving her. Then the war came.

The rebels tried to execute John. But what they intended for evil, God used to save John's life, shielding him under a stack of bodies from the bullets. How did the Gonlehs deserve such divine favor?

In some mysterious way, though we were stripped of all possessions, God provided food, shelter, health, and guidance until we reached Danané. We lived each moment as baby chicks, seeking shelter under his wings. It was then we truly found life. It was then we truly experienced God and Jesus interceding for our benefit. Now I was a stronger Christian. God had forgiven us and so had I. Nearing home, I concluded that I had no animosity whatsoever toward Viola. She was my sister in Christ and I loved her.

Viola arrived in the afternoon with her other children. Monica ran out of the house screaming, and both of them started bawling. It was a wonderful reunion. Monica's prayers were finally answered. Loud wracking sobs came forth with the release of years of pent-up tension. This was followed by laughter and then more tears.

Monica and Viola weren't the only ones crying. Tears steamed down our faces as the children and I witnessed this scene. We all remembered our own reunion with John. Now it was Viola's turn.

After everyone calmed down, Viola told us about her own harrowing journey and how she had reconciled with her parents. They joined with her for the long, difficult bush journey to escape Liberia. The entire family was living in the refugee camp, but they hoped the parents would soon be emigrating to the USA.

We learned from Viola that her older brother lived in the USA. He had attended a university and, after graduating, stayed and became a citizen. Now, he had applied for their parents to come live with him.

We inquired delicately as to why her brother had only applied for her parents to come to the USA and not her and her children. Was there some problem between her and her brother? Viola laughed and explained the process. Under the strict rules of the USA's Family

Reunion Resettlement Program, children can apply for parents and parents for their children, but not siblings.

After a long visit, Viola and John decided that Monica should stay with us and visit back and forth. Our house was a healthier and safer living environment than the tents, but Monica would go every week to visit. This arrangement reminded me of our life back in Paynesville.

John

The prayer team at Union Baptist Church was composed of several women and two men. For months, we devoted ourselves to weekly fasting and prayer. We began our fast on Wednesday and ended on Friday night. I believe that this was why God answered our prayers in powerful ways. Fasting in addition to prayer seemed to break invisible barriers and allowed us to see results not seen previously. During our fasts, we prayed for ten minutes each hour all day long, during work or whatever else we were doing.

One pastor friend related his story about fasting. Before he fled the country with his family, they were completely out of food. Everything inside the house was gone. Outside were gunfire and rockets. The phones were out. They couldn't leave the safety of their home.

He told the family to turn all the cups, dishes, and glasses on their kitchen table upside down. This meant that the whole family was fasting, even their little baby. This gesture was his way of signaling to God that he still had faith, that his family was only fasting as compared to starving to death. He had faith that God would provide food for his family to break their fast that evening.

They prayed all day for deliverance. Around six o'clock a knock sounded at their door. Sure enough, it was a friend bringing them food, food to break their fast. The pastor knew his friend had no knowledge of their need, but somehow God had mysteriously revealed it to him.

I also experienced a similar incident. Each day, I passed by another refugee minister's house on my way to the church. It was a Friday morning. I had already begun my fast two days before. When I stopped by to say hello, they confessed they had no food and asked me for help. I told them I was broke and had nothing to share. I suggested that all seven members of their family and I pray together. After the prayer I told them that before evening, God was going to work a miracle. That day they came to the midday service. I prayed with them again. Their plight wasn't publicized. It was only written on the paper as a prayer request and deposited in the prayer box. No one knew.

The family returned home after the service. Midafternoon, a mutual friend knocked on their door. When they opened it, the person said, "I'm led by God to be a blessing to you." This friend gave them a bag of bulgur wheat, a tin of oil, and a little money. Then he left.

At the end of the day, I decided to go to their house to break the fast together with them. This also was an act of faith on my part because I knew they had no food. By the time I reached their yard, the children were outside singing and jumping up and down. They were singing the familiar hymn, "My Lord Has Done it Again." I immediately realized God had indeed answered their prayer, and I joined my voice with the children's to finish the song: "He heals the sick, He raise the dead, He has power to save, He never change, God has done a miracle, He has done a miracle, And he will do it again."

I went inside and could barely make out the entire story through all the praising, shouting, and dancing. Together, we broke our fast just as I had predicted that morning.

Every so often, an act of God occurred to offer us encouragement, a little glimmer of hope that we weren't totally alone. And yet there seemed no way out of our refugee status. We were unwanted strangers in Ivory Coast. The local people spoke French. They are wary of strangers in general and hostile toward refugees. They resented that the UN was taking care of us. It made them jealous.

The refugee council voiced our complaints to the governor regarding unfair food distribution. But the outcome never proved satisfactory and provoked violence. Many evenings, in retaliation for complaining, roving gangs stalked the refugee camp. Any refugee found alone was severely beaten.

While I was working at Union Baptist under our large tent, I heard a commotion up the street and stepped outside to get a better look. A group of refugees was running toward the church. They were coming from the UN administrative office.

As they grew closer I realized they were heading toward me. I tried to close the tent flaps so they wouldn't seek refuge in the church. I could not allow my church to be involved in a street riot.

Close on their heels were security personnel armed with rubber hoses, beating whomever they could catch. I tried to roll the church flap down to cover the entrance. With my back turned, wrestling with the flaps, I suddenly felt the sting of rubber hose against my back. A rush of panic swept through my mind as I recalled my own torture. I was hit several more times before I could get the flaps down, dash inside, and tie them shut.

We allowed refugee meetings to be held in our church tent, since it was the largest in the city and could accommodate many people. But the fleeing refugees sought sanctuary I could not afford to provide. Gasping to collect my breath, I listened as the riot eventually subsided or moved on down the street. Thankfully, I wasn't hurt badly.

This incident only increased the hostility and distrust between the refugees and the locals. Danané authorities accused Union Baptist of inciting the riot because we allowed them to have meetings there. Smoldering anger and hatred on both sides kept relations bad.

In 1994, the United Nations cut off all supplies. Clothes, bedding, dishes, food, and even medical care were eliminated. In a meeting with the UN officials, they told our representatives they were no longer in a position to support or help us.

One blessing was that Viola's parents' emigration documents were finally approved. They could now live with their son, Viola's brother, in the USA. They left the camp just in time to prevent their elderly bodies from succumbing to the deprivation.

The news of the aid cutoff was devastating for the refugees. Many relied totally on the handouts as their only means of survival. On top of this bad news, another incident threatened the fragile life we had carved out in Danané.

A Liberian refugee accidentally shot and killed an Ivorian citizen while hunting in the bush. In revenge, Ivorian mobs raided the refugee camp. They beat men to death and raped women and girls. To protect the refugees, the government declared a curfew, keeping all Liberians indoors for several days and allowing tensions to cool down.

Faced with the risk of starvation or being beaten to death or raped in the UN camp, thousands of refugees returned home to Liberia. A fragile and tenuous cease-fire was in effect between Mr. Taylor's soldiers and his enemies. Daily life proved so hard in the camp that the chance of dying in war weighed less on their minds than waiting for death in the camp.

As for the Gonlehs, we would never return. The suffering and torture Bessie and I endured could never be erased. We would only go forward, never back.

Furthermore, within a few months, the cease-fire failed, and the sides started fighting again. All the refugees who returned to Liberia were trapped. Many died. Those who managed to straggle back to Danané brought fresh stories of torture and death. These stories rapidly circulated, were retold and embellished, and thereafter few refugees could be forced to leave the refugee camp regardless of the hardships.

Other refugees escaped to the Mandingo tribal areas of Guinea near the border with Ganta, but they met with disaster also. Because of atrocities committed early in the war, the Mandingos hated Liberians. Some of the refugees who made it safely out of Liberia to Guinea were murdered. Their bodies were thrown down into wells. Unlucky victims were thrown into the wells alive, head first.

Bessie and I paid little attention to the stories; we had our own concerns. She was pregnant again and having a difficult time. Birth control pills and other means of contraception were unavailable. So amidst the abject poverty of the refugees, babies were as plentiful as were their deaths. The doctor treating her made plans to perform a C-section. Even so, we had no money to buy drugs for pain or antibiotics should an infection develop.

Death among refugees was a common daily occurrence. Diseases like malaria claimed many. Women and their babies routinely died during childbirth. For men, heart attacks and strokes from high blood pressure were common as they succumbed to indignity upon indignity and sorrow upon sorrow.

Several days before the C-section was to be performed I had a dream. In my dream, people were passing in front of our house. I was outside with them. Together we saw blood running out from under the front door. They asked about the blood, and I replied, "Don't you know that my wife is undergoing a C-section?"

I suddenly woke up frightened and nervous. Sharing my dream with Bessie during our prayer time, I knew I had to stop the C-section. The day before the C-section, I called three members of the prayer team to join me in fasting and prayer for a normal delivery.

We prayed the whole day and broke our fast at seven o'clock that evening. Shortly thereafter, labor pains struck Bessie. In the middle of the night, I rushed Bessie to a midwife's house. After hours of labor, the baby came out with the umbilical cord constricting its neck. With weathered and wrinkled hands the midwife quickly unwrapped the cord from around the neck just as the baby started to turn blue.

I waited in the living room, praying up and down against everything I could think of that could go wrong. Early October 29, 1994, Miracle Gonleh was born healthy as could be. Slowly but surely, God was leading us step by step to trust him completely.

By God's grace we survived, albeit barely. We bought used clothing and charcoal or wood instead of gas for cooking. When there was extra money we bought soap and other household things. If we had money we would buy it; if not, we went without.

Once in awhile friends who had left Danané and emigrated to the United States sent us money. No one sent us money monthly, however. Sometimes we were late paying rent for four or five months.

At times we fasted for three days so God would touch hearts before I phoned our friends in the States asking them for money. Several times, even before our fast came to an end, a friend in the USA called to tell they had sent us money via Western Union.

Once we were so broke that everything was empty in our house— no food, no money, rent due, and bills piling up. We were down to brushing our teeth with the little detergent soap powder we had left just to make our teeth feel clean.

We knew Bessie's cousins lived in Montgomery, Alabama, but we hadn't spoken to them since the war started. We'd lost their telephone number during our flight from Paynesville. If we had known that there was such a thing as Directory Assistance, it would have been easy. But we were ignorant and had no idea such a service existed in the United States.

In desperation, I called for a three-day family fast. By this time Bessie and I normally fasted only once per month. But this was a dire emergency. The whole family had to participate.

We had a tiny bit of food, but only enough to feed John Jr. and Miracle. They fasted until noon each day, but the older children, Bessie, and I had nothing for the entire three days.

"We all have to pray," I explained to the family. "You are not babies anymore. You know the condition we're in and what we're going through. We have to trust God for help because he's the only one who can save us."

So we started our fast on Wednesday and would end it, God willing, on Friday. The children prayed at first, and then complained, and finally cried and whimpered, because they were so hungry. It broke our hearts, but what could we do? Our fate was solely in God's hands.

Nothing happened on Wednesday. Nothing happened on Thursday. But then on Friday we received a call from Vicky and Arthur Siaway, Bessie's cousins, in Alabama. We were shocked and dumbfounded! "How did you find us?" we asked Vicky.

Vicky explained that one of her Liberian friends living in Philadelphia had just received some relatives arriving from Danané as part of the Family Reunification Program. Her friend knew Vicky had been trying to find us and asked the new arrivals if they knew John and Bessie Gonleh. Her friend called her on Thursday evening to tell her she knew our whereabouts.

Because I was pastor of the midday services, I was widely known by the congregation, and these refugees knew us also. Friday morning Vicky called the Union Baptist Church phone number that the newly-arriving refugees had provided. Union Baptist then gave Vicky the telephone number to our home and *voilà*, she found us.

We explained our situation and the shape we were in. As soon as we ended the call, she wired us one hundred dollars. That evening in our prayer time, we couldn't contain our praise for God who hears and answers prayer. We marveled at the years of preparation that went into God's answering this specific prayer in the manner he did.

The arriving refugees had waited for years for their chance to go to the USA. Their arrival, the phone calls between Vicky and her friend, and our emergency fast all came together in perfect timing. What a miracle! We praised God for both the giver and the gift. And we prayed that God would replenish the money they had given us and bless them even more. Then we took ten dollars out for a tithe.

The next day was Saturday, market day. Bessie and the children bought a bag of rice, one gallon of vegetable and palm oil, dried fish, dried meat, salt, greens, pepper, okra, tomatoes, sweet potatoes, eddoes, eggs, powdered milk, a pack of tea, sugar, butter, bread, and charcoal by the bag instead of just several pieces, bath soap, laundry soap, toilet paper, and toothpaste.

Bessie and kids came home walking alongside a man with a "push-push," a makeshift wagon made of old tires, an axle, and a wooden box with a handle that could be pushed. They had so many groceries they couldn't carry them.

Our uncomfortable, subsistence existence continued for several more years, until one day, we received exciting news that Monica's mother had been sponsored by her parents to emigrate to the United States. They lived in the Philadelphia area with their son, Viola's brother. So in 1999, after five years, all the paperwork was approved, and Monica went with her mother and other siblings to the final emigration interview.

They were approved. Before they left, we held a party for them, though the food we ate was the exactly the same as every other day. This occasion was different, however, because we didn't know if we would ever see Monica again. With sadness and tears we wished them well as they left for the United States.

As she left, Viola promised that when they arrived, she would help Monica fill out the forms to help the rest of her family join them. I remembered the rising smoke from my prayer.

Their departure was well timed. Shortly after they left, storm clouds of political and civil unrest began to appear on the horizon. Month after month they grew darker and more ominous. Following the clouds in the distance was the threatening low throaty rumble of hatred and revenge. Faint flashes of lightning appeared as Liberians clashed with Ivorians over accumulated grievances. The same dark cloud that had appeared over Liberia now cast its shadow over Ivory Coast.

We were familiar with this type of storm. It had been just such a tempest that swept us to Danané so many years ago. Now it was coming again. I could feel the winds strengthen amid the whispers in the market. Bessie sensed it in the urgency and fear in prayers. Rumors swirled in every corner of the city.

Friends living in the capital, Abidjan, heard the thunder in loud distinct tones as politicians blamed all the country's ills on foreigners. We knew who they were talking about.

The president who had once welcomed the refugees to Ivory Coast died, and another president took over. Then there was a coup, an assassination, and yet another president came to power. And this president hated the refugees. Like the Israelites in Egypt, a new pharaoh came to power and treated the people harshly.

ATTACK ON DANANÉ 24

JOHN

The civil war started near the capital city of Abidjan. Like Liberia's war, this war began as a fight between rival political leaders. First there were charges of stolen elections. Then a coup d'état and an assassination followed. Finally, each side resorted to force rather than peaceful political means.

Factions formed along tribal lines. Everyone was forced to choose a side. Because the government in power controlled the army, they won the initial skirmish. Following the battle, many rebel soldiers were taken prisoner.

That was when the president discovered that many of the rebel fighters were Liberian mercenaries. Greatly alarmed by this turn, he concluded that the Liberian government of Mr. Taylor had conspired with his political rivals to invade Ivory Coast.

The president's fear wasn't completely farfetched. Mr. Taylor and his fighters had destroyed Liberia and its economy. To keep his power, Taylor needed money to pay his fighters. Otherwise they would turn against him.

But Mr. Taylor was shrewd. He allowed foreign companies to come into Liberia and strip the rainforest of timber and other natural resources. But still he needed more money. He required a guaranteed revenue stream. He found it in the diamond mines of his northern neighbor, Sierra Leone.

Mr. Taylor exported the only product he had—weapons and fighters—to Sierra Leone in support of rebels opposed to the government. In return the rebels paid him with uncut, untraceable stones from the lucrative diamond fields. These he turned into hard cash by selling them to unscrupulous dealers all over the world. The diamonds had no identifying markings and proved the perfect currency.

Brutality ruled the day in Sierra Leone. Hands, arms, and legs were routinely hacked off ordinary citizens by rebels with machetes or axes. Without one or both arms it was impossible to fight back, so this proved an effective method of disabling, terrorizing, and controlling potential foes. The diamonds became known around the world as "conflict diamonds" or "blood diamonds."

So Ivory Coast's president could be forgiven for mistakenly thinking that Mr. Taylor had now set his sights and ambitions on his southern neighbor.

In reality, however, there were many warring factions in Liberia. And not all of these were on Mr. Taylor's payroll. These other fighters needed employment also. Liberia's economy was in shambles. There were no jobs to earn money. The only marketable skill possessed by mercenaries was fighting. So they simply went where they would receive pay.

It was easy to identify them as Liberian. They spoke English, whereas the language in Ivory Coast was French.

As a result of this threat from Liberia, the president decided to send troops to Danané, the nearest border city. Danané was filled with Liberian refugees. And the now-paranoid president could only imagine what sort of mischief the refugees might be planning together with Mr. Taylor's Liberian army. And so it was that one day in September 2002 we awoke to a Danané we had not previously known.

Overnight, the president replaced all the soldiers in Danané with new ones who he was certain were loyal to him. Their numbers had swelled, and soldiers were everywhere—on street corners, in the markets, all over town. The previous soldiers had never gone to any of these places.

Also, none of the new soldiers spoke English, only French. Many of the previous soldiers had been in Danané for years. We knew them and they knew us. All of them spoke some English. Now they were gone.

This action struck terror into our hearts. We had no idea what was going to happen next. Fighting was intensifying throughout the country between the rebels and the government. Things got very tense. Roadblocks were set up on the highway between Danané and Abidjan. For a few weeks, refugees were forbidden to travel. We started fasting and praying for God to intervene so they wouldn't kill us if that was their plan.

Shortly after the arrival of the new soldiers, all of the foreign doctors, nurses, and aide-workers left. We were isolated and completely alone. The foreign relief workers had given Danané a window to the outside world. Affluent doctors and other skilled professionals were like our eyes. Other nations could look into our world. We could look out through the reports these workers filed with their countries and home agencies. Their departure meant that both we and the rest of the world were completely blind to what happened in Danané.

Our prayers grew in intensity and urgency. Fighting hadn't yet reached Danané, but we were caught between the two warring factions. Because some of the mercenaries were Liberian, it concentrated the burning hatred many Ivorians felt for us.

A few weeks after the new soldiers' arrival, citywide meetings commenced for all Ivorian citizens of Danané. Soldiers led the meetings and directed the agenda. Other than that little piece of leaked information, we had no idea what the meetings were about. Some of our refugees tried to attend but were turned away. They were told the meeting was for Ivorians only.

We were very suspicious, wondering what they were plotting. They had never had secret meetings like this before. Now they were meeting every week. Some refugees got so frightened, they packed their belongings and left. None of us knew what to do. There was nowhere to run. We just prayed.

By November, rumors circulated confirming our worst fears. The Ivorians were planning to massacre us. The rumors described a plot by the Ivorian soldiers and citizens to kill the refugees in our churches. The Ivorians were supposed to bring their knives, garden machetes, picks, shovels, and anything else that would serve as weapons to kill the Liberians once and for all. Because almost all the Liberians were Christian and were in church every Sunday, we would be wiped out.

This was the rumor, but many of us couldn't believe it was true. Surely our Ivorian neighbors wouldn't kill us in cold blood with no provocation. Surely, our neighbors wouldn't harm us. Our family had tried to cultivate our neighbors' friendship over the years.

We shared our food with them when we could. When we moved to our rental house in 1991, the entire neighborhood was pitch black at night. I was instrumental in getting running water and electricity to my house and then our entire neighborhood.

In past years, our neighbors had looked out for us. They warned us when they heard about problems in the city. Sometimes a neighbor needed a loan. We shared what money we could with them and told them to keep it as a gift. They didn't have to pay it back. We wanted to be their friends. Surely, after more than ten years, these neighbors saw us as their friends also.

Furthermore, schools were operating normally. Teachers hadn't said anything to our children. Everything seemed to be normal. How could these rumors be true when life carried on as it always had?

Then a date leaked out. The attack was to be on Sunday, December 1, 2002. Again, there was no hard evidence, only rumors. Who was getting this information? And from whom? And how did they know if it was correct?

Finally, at church I heard that some of our refugees heard this information from Liberian soldiers, those working as mercenaries for the Ivorian rebels.

"Liberian soldiers!" I shouted. "They are the last people I would ever trust. Why are we listening to them? And how do they know what the Ivorians are planning?"

The person was shocked and hurt at my response. After all, he was just telling me what he had heard. He was just trying to help.

A few days before Sunday, we could feel the tension in the air. It seemed like my Ivorian neighbors avoided eye contact when I passed them on the street. Or did they? I couldn't be sure. Maybe I was just being paranoid. Perhaps I was just imagining things. Did they know something? What were they thinking? I wanted to stop them on the road and say, "Friend, we are not your enemies. We want to live in peace, just like you." But I never did. We both passed by quickly and quietly, neither acknowledging the other.

On Thursday morning, November 28, the attack came. The rumors had been right all along; just the date was wrong.

It started at nine thirty A.M. in the market. Next to Saturday, Thursday was the largest market day, and the aisles in the open-air shopping center would be filling with merchants and customers.

We heard the distant gunfire as fighting broke out. Soon the rapid staccato of automatic weapons filled the air. The frequency seemed to rise and fall, pulsing faster, then slower, as if some unseen conductor of death was directing the symphony.

When the gunfire erupted, our hearts stopped as an awful realization hit. "Comfort!" shouted Bessie. "Comfort is at school!"

I assured her that the teacher would keep the pupils inside and safely away from the gunfire. Silently, I prayed that this was true as the words escaped my lips.

Thank God, little John and Miracle were home. On Wednesday, their teachers at the Catholic school sent a note home that there would be no school on Thursday. Now, we realized that the teachers feared something would happen. *Why didn't they say something?* I thought. *Why didn't they tell us their fear?*

I wanted to blame the teachers, but now I could feel my own conscience shifting the blame back onto me, accusing me: *You didn't want to believe the rumors because they came from the Liberian soldiers. That's why you let Comfort go to school today.*

I countered: *But there was no way to know. We've been hearing rumors for months.*

But my argument and pleading innocent didn't stop the accuser from getting the last word: *You should have known. You should have known.*

I tried to swallow. My tongue felt like it took up my whole mouth. I couldn't believe it. This couldn't be happening. Bessie couldn't speak. She was in shock.

I pulled the blinds and made sure the door was locked. Then Bessie, John Jr., Miracle, and I huddled together inside our house like helpless, uncomprehending creatures trapped in the fury of a raging storm. And Comfort was outside, exposed and completely vulnerable to the lethal elements.

I mentally took inventory of the rest of our family. Annie and Kou, eighteen, had graduated the year before and were with Prince and Dennis in Abidjan visiting friends. Monica lived in the United States with her mother. Gloria was now married but living apart from her husband while studying in the United States at the University of Minnesota. John Jr. and Miracle stayed home from school. Only Comfort, sixteen, was unaccounted for.

I was wracked with guilt over Comfort. We should have kept her home. We should have been more aware. We should have sensed the danger, but we didn't. Now she was stranded, and we couldn't reach her.

Fighting spread out all over the city. For the first three hours, the sound of gunfire filled the air from the fierce firefights taking place.

Comfort was supposed to come home between twelve thirty and one P.M. She never made it.

The noise slacked up the afternoon, and by three o'clock, we only heard scattered, random gunfire. In the lull, an eerie quiet pervaded the city.

Then something happened that shocked us. Our phone rang! It was Gloria, calling from the United States. She blurted out that she had been watching CNN and a reporter said an attack on Danané was occurring at that very moment. Details were scarce about who was fighting and what was going on.

We confirmed the truth of the news report about the attack and that we were trapped inside the house, except for Comfort. Gloria said we had to get out of Danané at once. Otherwise there was a good chance we would all die.

Looking through our blinds, we noticed that our Ivorian neighbors had ventured outside and were talking in small groups. Fighting had stopped, and since our neighbors were outside, we went out also to see what had happened.

Soldiers on patrol appeared in groups of two. As some drew near, we heard them speaking—in English! What was going on? We had expected the Ivorian soldiers and citizens to attack us. Why were they speaking English? Only Liberians spoke English.

Our neighbors heard the soldiers also. They first looked surprised, and then their surprise turned to extreme anger. One neighbor noticed Bessie and I standing outside our house and walked toward us. His eyes were wide, his jaw clenched in anger. Glaring at us, he shouted in broken English, "You, who we have taken care of and hosted all this time. Now you come and make war on us? We are going to kill you like dogs as soon as your soldiers leave!"

COMFORT 25

Bessie and I were terrified by the words from my neighbor. We didn't say anything back to him but knew he was serious. Years before, a single hunting accident had led to riots and attacks on refugees. What would the people do to us now that their city had been attacked by Liberian mercenaries?

Bessie and I went back inside and assessed our situation. We decided to heed Gloria's advice and leave. Bessie quickly prepared something for us to eat. I retrieved the old weather-worn satchel with the important papers. Then I counted all the money we had. That's all we would take, other than one small plastic bowl of dried rice kernels. With two small children, we couldn't carry anything else.

Our plan was to first go to the school, find Comfort, and then flee Danané. Then, despite the risks, we would head for Guinea. Guinea's president had earlier incited a campaign of terror against refugees from Liberia and Sierra Leone. Hundreds of refugees died at the hands of neighborhood vigilante death squads.

But going back to Liberia wasn't an option, even though it was closer. Once they arrived in the USA, Viola had helped Monica file for Bessie and me to go also in the Resettlement Program. If we returned to Liberia, the UN authorities would remove us from the list for emigration consideration. We had to take our chances. Hopefully, God would protect us one more time.

Guinea was close compared to our first bush trek. Our journey to the UN refugee camp would take only three days if everything went as planned. Once there, we hoped we'd be safe.

At five o'clock, we unlocked and opened the front door. We peeked outside to see what was happening on the street. Satisfied there wasn't a neighborhood mob waiting for us, we stepped outside. The street was a flurry of activity. People had loads on their heads and were carrying armfuls of household goods. A crowd of Liberian families moved slowly but steadily up the street toward the highway that went to Guinea.

Our objective was the opposite direction. Comfort's school was located near the market where the fighting had started. I feared that we could be in danger by going back to where the fighting was heaviest, but we had no choice. Comfort was near there. We had to find her.

Slowly, we made our way past the throngs of people flowing like water out of the besieged city. Keeping a safe distance away, we passed armed soldiers standing like boulders in a river as the crowds swirled past them.

They wore different uniforms from the new Ivorian soldiers who had recently arrived in Danané. They were clearly Liberian. But whether they were mercenaries for the Ivorian rebels or the regular Liberian army I didn't know. One thing was clear: They were as dangerous here in Ivory Coast as they had been in Liberia.

We were still far from the market when we stumbled into a friend, a woman who attended Union Baptist Church and taught the children. She was wide-eyed and gulping air. She exclaimed, "I've just come from the market. Liberian soldiers . . ." She had to stop and catch her breath. "Liberian soldiers started shooting everyone. There was an attack." She was repeating herself in her excited state. "They were shooting and stealing everything. Fighting was heavy in the market." Still panting, she gasped out, "I saw Comfort's body there."

Bessie interrupted her. "Comfort's body? What do you mean Comfort's body?"

Shocked back to reality, the woman suddenly cast a sober expression. She realized that in her adrenalin-charged state of mind, she had just shattered the world of her good friend.

Bessie drew in a sharp breath as the meaning of the words penetrated her heart like a knife.

I asked resolutely, "Are you sure it was Comfort?"

The woman was distracted now and staring at Bessie.

"You have to be sure," I said seriously, getting her attention back on me. "We are on our way to her school right now to find her."

The woman looked as guilty as if she had killed Comfort herself. Then she started to cry. "Yes, I'm sure. I've known Comfort for nearly her entire life. She had on her school dress. I looked closely at her. I love Comfort. I'm sure it was her."

The woman would no longer look at me but kept her head bowed as if I were a vengeful god ready to pronounce judgment on her. After a moment, I spoke. "God bless you, sister. Thank you for telling us. I know how difficult it was for you."

She didn't reply but continued looking down. I then hugged her. She mumbled something I didn't understand, and once I let her go, she moved away, disappearing in the flowing current.

I didn't know what to do. *Should I believe this woman? Is there any way to be sure?* My mind raced through the possibilities. The odds were very high Comfort was indeed dead. Bessie and I had known this woman for many years. *If I make us go to the market to check for ourselves, will even more of us die?*

I made my decision, then I turned to Bessie. She was blank. Her mouth didn't move but remained open like she was about to say something. Her eyes were dead. There was no emotion. Just dull shock.

Gently, I held her shoulders, turned her around, and said, "Come on, Bessie. There's nothing more we can do. We have to go."

Holding the hands of the two little ones who were now crying, I led us into a sea of souls and joined the thousands of other unfortunates being swept away.

We made our way through the crowded streets toward the main highway. I saw only Liberian soldiers on patrol or standing at the ready. All of the hundreds of Ivorian soldiers had vanished. Where had they gone? We were totally confused.

We eventually left the city behind and were in a group with hundreds of other Liberians all walking together. By now everyone was silent. The emotional excitement of the day's events had decayed into weary dread and anxiety. *Where will we sleep? How will we eat?*

We watched the sun start to set behind a threatening sky. Soon, it would open up and we would all be soaked. But we couldn't stop. We had to reach the first village. There, we'd be able to get shelter. I mentally tried to recall our first bush journey years before and the lessons we learned that could perhaps help us now.

It was hard to think, to accept, that so many years later the same thing could be happening all over again. I tried to imagine what sort of plan God had where all of this would make sense. But there was no way. Any plan was completely beyond anything I could decipher.

As I came to this conclusion, I heard the rare noise of a plane approaching, a sound I hadn't heard since we left Paynesville before the war. There was no airport in Danané, so to hear a plane way out here was very strange indeed.

The plane approached from the east, from the direction of Abidjan. I saw only a little bright spot against the clouds, illuminated orange and yellow by the setting sun. Closing the distance, the plane circled. And then it swooped down.

A mile behind us, we suddenly heard bombs exploding, followed by the sound of machine-gunfire. The plane was a fighter jet and was attacking someone on the road! We were a good way from the city, so it couldn't be shooting at Liberian soldiers.

No, I suddenly realized! It was shooting at us!

We felt the rolling shock waves from the concussion. Everyone else suddenly realized what was going on. In unison, refugees broke and scattered as if a rock had been dropped on an anthill. A cacophony of screaming erupted all at once as people panicked and scattered.

The sound of the bombs snapped Bessie out of the stupor she'd been in since Danané. Like everyone else, we grabbed the hands of our children tightly and ran for the bushes. Within thirty seconds, the road was cleared of people. Only belongings dropped helter-skelter littered the highway. The refugees ran under trees, lay down in the grass, or crouched down in the bushes to hide. With hundreds in our group, every possible hiding place was utilized.

Bessie and I simultaneously spoke our prayers aloud. The words in God's ears were the only weapon we had against the bullets and bombs of the jet. We were determined to make any projectile that might be headed our direction pass through a blanket of prayer that shielded us.

We remained hunkered down, hiding from the winged predator stalking us. We waited five, then ten, and finally twenty minutes to see if other planes were going to join the initial fighter. The time passed slowly, but we just huddled close together, trembling, and prayed.

Thankfully, the fighter jet never did turn toward our group. It must have exhausted its munitions on the first group of refugees and headed back to its base. No other planes appeared either, so we emerged from our hiding places. Everyone retrieved their few remaining worldly possessions. The march continued.

The first village lay another hour along the highway. We arrived just as the rain began. Following the pattern we used going from village to village in Liberia, I sought out the first large house in the village. Very likely it belonged to the village headman. A few chickens milled about the house pecking at the ground.

I knocked on the door. The door opened and a man answered.

"*Bon-nuit* [Good evening]. Sir, we are refugees from Danané. Please, can we stay in your hut for the night?" I asked.

He didn't answer but just looked at us now getting soaked from the rain. I wasn't sure if he understood me at first. But then, without a word, he stepped back inside, closed the door, and locked it. Standing on his small wooden porch, I heard only the soft rain.

It felt like I'd just been kicked in the stomach. I had failed. I thought the same approach would work here as it did back in Liberia. I thought people would show a little compassion.

I was wrong.

Then the lightning flashed. A few seconds later the corresponding boom followed. And the sky opened. It was now too late to try to find a place to stay the night.

I went over to Bessie, John, and Miracle. I didn't need to say anything. They had seen it all. I gathered them on the porch. Off the porch a sea of mud was developing. Though there was no roof, at least we could sit leaning against the locked door.

Chickens gathered with us on the porch. I had to shoo them away so we could sit down and huddle up. Lightning filled the sky and thunder shook the house as chickens came running back to seek shelter with the humans.

We were soaked and shivering as water flowed like streams off our heads, necks, and shoulders to regions below. With only the briefest illumination, I looked toward heaven and wondered how God could ever make this right again.

We got John and Miracle to stop crying after about fifteen minutes. They'd been quiet only a few minutes when Miracle exclaimed, "Something is on me!" She started wiping her legs and arms and stomach with revulsion and tried to stand up. Just then we all felt them. Lice!

The chickens who shared the porch with us also shared their lice. With that final straw, we all started to cry.

"God, it's just too much to take!" I wailed. "Lord, have mercy on us," I pled between the cracks of thunder.

"I cry to you, O Lord; O Lord, hear my voice . . ." The words trailed off as I finally submitted my will to the fate preordained for us.

For everything there is a season; a time to be born and a time to die, a time for weeping, and a time for mourning. Tonight was a night for mourning and misery. No reprieve was forthcoming.

Comfort was gone, dead in the market. Only God knew if more of my children had died.

"Your will be done Lord . . ." I said, and I drifted away.

THE DARK NIGHT 26

BESSIE In the darkness, the torrent of rain and thunder burst from heaven with the same intensity that tears and wails emanated from my own eyes and mouth. Everything had gone so wrong. The first hour produced the usual cracks of lightning and corresponding peals of thunder. Each new fury was met with a fresh round of sobs. Fear, grief, and misery on the cold open porch had taken its toll.

Two hours later, the storm matured into a steady, drenching downpour. The only sound to be heard over the deluge was the occasional squawk of a disturbed chicken. We humans, curled up and huddled together, weren't really asleep. The lice saw to that. But we were spent and totally exhausted from the day's events.

At some point during the long night, I no longer cared that the bugs crawled all over me, under my wet clothes and in my hair, trying to get warm and dry. My grief overwhelmed and swallowed me whole. Another child was dead and more were trapped in Abidjan.

At least God smiled on the lice. These creatures were just trying to escape the rain, and the sanctuary provided by the surviving Gonlehs was much preferred to their old hosts, the chickens. They had no knowledge of the horrendous tragedy that brought them their good fortune.

I envied the lice. This night their Father in heaven had blessed them with ease and comfort. Warmly tucked away, they couldn't feel the depth of pain crushing my soul.

But for the beings created in his image and likeness, it was a different story. None of us would ever forget what we'd lost today—our daughter, their sister. How could God allow this to happen?

The day had started ordinarily enough. Sixteen-year-old Comfort went to school as usual. Little John and Miracle stayed home. Their teacher had sent a note home the day before, saying school was being cancelled the following day. The note contained no explanation, so John and I didn't think anything of it. Now I know differently. The school must have suspected something or heard a rumor and taken this precaution. But why didn't they alert us to the danger they felt? They hadn't told us anything to raise our concern. My twins, Kou and Annie had graduated from high school the year before and were in Abidjan with Dennis and Prince staying with other Liberian friends. I had no idea how we would find each other now.

I couldn't believe it. After twelve years and everything we had gone through, it was all happening again. But this time was worse. I lost Chester during the first evacuation. Now, I'd lost Comfort and possibly more. How many more of my children would the Lord allow to die before our ordeal was over?

"Father, take me instead. Please, not my children," I pleaded. My words were only met by the constant sound of a steady drizzle. "Lord, please protect the others wherever they are."

I couldn't bear the thought of losing more than one child. Maybe the older children were all right. Maybe the situation was different where they were. I hoped there had been no coordinated attack on refugees in Abidjan.

My tears started flowing once again as John shifted his position to wrap one arm around me tighter with his other still secure around Little John and Miracle.

"I didn't even get to see her," I sobbed to John.

No answer.

"Now, I'll never see her again and we can't go back."

My pain and anguish couldn't be consoled. I knew Comfort was dead. Our church friend told us clearly that she had seen her body in the market. She was certain it was Comfort. She had on her familiar school dress uniform. There was no doubt. It was Comfort.

"But still, I didn't get to see her," I whimpered. "I didn't get to cradle her in my arms one last time."

I felt like those unfortunate refugees in Guinea who were thrown down into wells still alive. Deep inside my own well, it was pitch black with cold dank walls that pressed in on all sides, suffocating me. Looking up, there was nothing but black. I was trapped and surrounded. Blackness obscured the true light that gives light. Darkness was trying to extinguish the last ember of hope and faith from my broken heart.

John finally answered, "I know, Bessie. I know . . ." Then he started crying, too, and gripped me harder.

ESCAPE TO GUINEA 27

BESSIE

At daylight, we struggled wearily to our feet. The rain and my tears had ceased sometime during the dark hours. The night had left us exhausted, but we had to get going. Hundreds of refugees clogged the small village.

"Momma, I'm hungry," Miracle said as she reached to scratch her legs. After a night with the lice, her tender skin was raw from the itching.

"I know, baby, I know," I replied. "But first, we have to reach another village before we can cook our rice."

"But I'm real hungry. Will it be a long time?"

"I don't know, baby; I don't know . . ." What could I tell her? We had never gone to Guinea. We were following other refugees.

Other than our satchel and the clothes we wore, the small plastic container of rice was our only possession. We would have to stop at the next village to borrow a cooking pot. With the calloused treatment we received last night, I didn't want to even ask here.

I would have shaken the dust from my feet if we hadn't slogged through ankle-deep mud leaving the small village. In all our years of hardship, I had not encountered such a lack of hospitality to people so desperately in need.

In Liberia, even in the midst of war as factions slaughtered each other with impunity, there remained a kindness and generosity that bush villagers extended to strangers passing through. Now it seemed that only tribal and national affiliation determined friend or foe. This cancer had killed Liberia, and now it was doing the same thing in Ivory Coast.

Before we left, amid the lice and chickens on the soaked porch, we had our daily devotional as we always did. John and I would not allow the tragedy from the day before to destroy the relationship we had built with God over the years.

For this devotional, John turned to Psalm 91 and read it out loud. Then, as we did every morning and evening for our daily devotions, we recited together, "May the words of our mouths and the meditations of our heart be acceptable in your sight, O Lord, our strength, our Redeemer, in Jesus' precious name. Amen."

John Jr. said, "Why is it that you are always praying and asking God to help us? Yesterday, Comfort was killed. We had to leave all our things, our home, and run away. Why didn't God stop this and protect her?"

John gazed at his son for a moment. I admired the directness of the questions. John Jr. is so much like his father—inquisitive, determined, and to the point. He was small for his age, but when playing sports, he compensated for his size with intensity and competitiveness, again just like his father. Finally, John collected his thoughts.

"You cannot ask God questions the way you and I are sitting here talking," he said. "You can't see God, and if you ask him a question, he won't answer like a person. The only way we have to talk to God is by asking things in prayer. Do you understand so far?"

"Yes. I've always wondered why people sing about walking with God and talking with God when he doesn't have a body. How can you walk and talk with someone who isn't there?"

John answered, "It's not that God isn't there. It's just that he's different from us. Everything that is good comes from God, and everything that is bad comes from the devil. God had to allow Satan to have his way and use evil men to kill Comfort. Otherwise it would not have happened. John, Miracle, it seems wrong, because you love your sister and will miss her terribly. But we are not God. We don't know his plans or agendas. Nothing can happen in this world without God allowing it to happen. Many times, we don't agree with what God allows to happen because it hurts us or those we love, and we can't understand his purpose. Sometimes, he allows our own sinful behavior to cause us harm. Other times he allows the evil that others do to harm us, like for Comfort."

Then I jumped in. "But you have to believe the Bible. It says that for believers, all things—including good things, bad things, and even horrible things—work together for the good or God's best purpose for each Christian. That is God's promise to all of us who believe in Jesus. That's why we don't have to live in fear. Even though we can't see God face to face, we can know that he will allow us to live as long as it is good for us. He allows us to finish the work he planned for us to do just like he allowed Jesus to complete his work before permitting evil people to kill him. Remember how God protected Jesus as a baby from evil King Herod? But remember also that he allowed many other innocent babies to be killed."

John added, "John, Miracle, God loves Comfort so much more than we are capable of, and she is now with him in heaven. Do you understand?"

"Yes, Dad, we understand," answered John Jr.

"It's just that I miss Comfort so much," added Miracle, as tears began to well in her little eyes.

I held her tightly and said, "I know, baby. I know. We all miss her."

John then announced it was time to get on the road. We had three days of walking ahead of us.

We carried two empty plastic gallon milk containers to fill up with water. We used the hand pump in the village before leaving. Then we set out. I knew we wouldn't have anything to eat until that night, but I couldn't bear the thought of telling poor hungry Miracle.

To save time, we took a bush trail through a swamp to join up with the main road that went to Guinea. This route we learned from some other refugees would save an hour on the trip.

Like the bush trails in Liberia, this path was only shoulder width. The dirt trail was swept clean of leaves and broken branches. When we saw this, we were relieved. The villagers must use this trail often. A clean trail meant there was no place for snakes and scorpions to lie in wait for passing frogs. It would be safe, I thought.

We walked for quite a distance and then saw our trail disappear into a small river. It reemerged on the far side. Obviously, we were supposed to ford this river. I didn't like it. None of us except John could swim, but it was too far to turn back and go around the long way to the main road.

We had to cross here. John said a prayer for safety and one by one, we waded into the water. John first, followed by Miracle, John Jr., and then myself.

At first John led through a shallow section. Then it got deeper. He was up to his armpits. Miracle stepped a little to the left of where he had gone. Suddenly she sank into a deeper hole and was submerged. Frantically she bobbed up, screaming and flailing her arms as the current began to sweep her downstream. John turned just in time to reach out and snatch her waving hand before she went under again and the current swept her off.

He got her steadied but then realized he'd lost the satchel in the water. We all saw it floating downstream. John quickly helped Miracle to the other side and then jumped back in and swam until he caught it. Fortunately, the satchel was waterproof and protected our important papers, a few family photographs, and money.

He rejoined us on the bank, where I was tending to Miracle, who was still shaking with fear and excitement. John smiled at Miracle. "See, God intervened to save you. At just the right time he allowed me to grab your hand."

"But why did God allow me to go under the water in the first place? So you could rescue me? Why didn't he rescue Comfort in the market?" she asked. "Does he love me more than Comfort? Is that why he rescued me?"

John responded. "I have told you before that God never gives us a burden too great for us to handle. Yesterday, Comfort was taken from us. Today, we almost lost you, Miracle. But God knows it would be too great a burden to lose you the very next day. That is why God made it possible for me to save you. Obviously, God has a plan for your life. So today, God saved you. He wants you to know he can save you again and for you to trust him."

We reached the two-lane dirt road that went all the way to the border. We passed through dense forests with tall trees. John and I were careful to keep the children in the middle as we walked. With all the branches and leaves littering both sides of the road, I was sure there were poisonous snakes about.

Talking to other refugees, I learned that a woman had died while crossing the small river at another location. There were logs across the river for people to walk on. While refugees were crossing, the logs broke, and the woman drowned. They buried her right there at the side of the river.

Along the side of the road, people who didn't have jugs like ours stopped to get drinks out of the running streams. We always tried to just drink well water from our jugs. We didn't know what type of microbe might be in the stream water that could make us sick.

During our first bush journey, we never drank from the streams. Dead bodies lay in every stream we passed, and the water was totally contaminated. But I didn't know why so many bodies were congregated in the streams. Later I learned that when people are shot they can get very thirsty. When bullets enter the body, it feels like a fire inside and makes the person very hot. For this reason, many people with gunshot wounds are thirsty. I concluded that this must by why the bodies were in the water. The injured people made it to the stream to drink and then died right there with the water running over them.

We stopped periodically for the children to rest. Then finally we stopped in a village to spend the night. Like the first village, there was a hand pump, and there were hundreds of refugees. We said a family prayer before knocking on the first door.

Praise God, the man and woman at this house spoke both French and English and were more hospitable than the other man had been. Intermarriage was common in this area nearer the border with Liberia. So as a whole, the people seemed much more sympathetic to our plight.

We asked if we could use their fire and cooking pot to make some rice. We all appeared a bedraggled mess. John Jr. and Miracle looked especially pitiful. The man said yes, so I began to prepare our meal.

I carefully measured out a portion of rice. The one container had to last three days at least. John said, "*Vien, manger* [Come, let's eat]," inviting the people to eat with us. When the rice was finally ready, the kind family politely declined to share our meal but let us borrow their bowls. When I had served everyone, we all held hands, and John prayed.

"Father, today we give you thanks for this food. We thank you for the kindness of this family to share their fire and pot and bowls with us. Father, we thank you for the life of our daughter and sister, Comfort, who is now safe. Just like our Savior Jesus, you preserved her life until her work on this earth was done and she was ready for heaven. Protect our other children in Abidjan. Command your angels concerning them. You are our only refuge, O God. In the name of Jesus Christ, your only Son. Amen."

While stress, grief, fear, and exhaustion had sapped our energy, the food helped revive us. We offered to clean up, but the kind man wouldn't hear of it. They also agreed to let us sleep just inside their front door on the floor. We were so thankful that God had led us to these kind people. The woman gave us a second surprise by producing mats for us to sleep on.

We got up the next morning and ate the extra rice I'd prepared the night before. Then we were off once again after devotions. The day passed uneventfully, and once again God led us to kind villagers who shared their fire and house with us. Only one more day and we would start another new life in Guinea.

Mid-afternoon the third day, we reached the St. Johns River marking the border between Ivory Coast and Guinea. There was a ferry that took cars and trucks across the river. Normally we would have had to pay to cross, but by producing our Danané identification cards to show we were refugees, we were able to cross for free.

On the other side was a UN truck receiving refugees from Ivory Coast. Once again, we registered as refugees, and, as the four of us stood in the truck, I remembered twelve years before. Then, all of my now-grown children were small and we'd thought we'd reached the Promised Land, Ivory Coast.

Now we were leaving this place also. I thought of the Jews wandering for forty years in the desert, dying off one by one until the entire disobedient generation was gone. Other refugees in our truck talked of riots and attacks on refugees in the Guinean UN camps. Even the president of Guinea incited hatred and attacks against the refugees.

The fear gnawing at my soul grew as our truck penetrated into the heart of Guinea. "Lord," I prayed, "don't let us die one by one in this wilderness. Deliver us, for you and you alone are our refuge."

THE ENDING 28

JOHN

The Liberian mercenaries didn't stay long in Danané. Within a few days the Ivorian president mounted a counterattack and sent troops from Abidjan to drive them out. From other refugees, we learned that the only purpose of the attack was to save Liberians from the impending attack by the Ivorians on Sunday, December 1. So, ironically, Comfort was killed in a battle that was designed to save us from our Ivorian neighbors. The Liberian mercenaries had learned about the impending attack and decided to strike first. Whatever their plan was, it had not been thought out sufficiently. For as soon as Ivorian troops arrived from Abidjan, the hunting down and slaughter of any remaining Liberians began.

The few Liberians who did remain were married to Ivorians. Their marriage status guaranteed them personal protection, but they were offered bounties to point out other Liberians. The Ivorian citizens would handle things from there.

When the fighting eventually subsided, some of the Liberian refugees went back to Danané, intending to collect their belongings. These unfortunates learned firsthand the sad truth of the bounty, and a number were killed by mobs. Survivors staggered back into Guinea with stories of horrific deaths at the hands of the angry crowd. Some were set afire and burned alive. Others were tortured with their arms pulled back behind them until their joints popped before they were murdered.

Needless to say, Danané was no longer a safe place for Liberians to live. Eventually all the Liberian refugees left.

Then the economy collapsed. Houses stood empty. The Western Union office closed down for a lack of Americans sending money to their refugee relatives. With no refugees to make deposits, the only bank in the town shut its doors. Ivorian businesses didn't need loans to build rental houses or to expand their services.

Bushes grew up around all the vacant homes once there was no one to rent them. The open-air market was bare of many customers. Lost was the vibrancy of frenzied buying and selling that characterized our twelve years of living there.

Danané reaped what it had sown. Its citizens wanted to kill the refugees and finally their wish came true. The unintended consequence, however, was that they destroyed their own city as well.

In the aftermath, the Ivorian citizens burned down a few churches and looted the rest. They stole anything of value, including musical instruments, books, pews, chairs, benches, speakers and public address systems, school books and supplies, and dishes from our orphan-feeding program. Houses rented by Liberians lost furniture and all the household items and personal belongings.

Now, all of this took a few months to unfold in Danané, but arriving in Guinea, Bessie and I had more immediate concerns. We were out of rice, and we needed food and shelter for our two little ones.

The truck carried us to the transit camp in the town of Lola. The camp was located in a large, empty community meeting hall like a huge barn. It had two large garage doors that slid together. All of the newly-arriving refugees were issued mats, blankets, and drinking cups. Food was cooked on the premises by local people hired by the United Nations.

In the beginning we were near the front doors that were always open. Dust blew into the building and swirled in small eddies, like miniature cyclones, covering our belongings. Each day as other refugees were assigned to the main camp and left, we steadily moved toward the rear. Each day delivered more refugees from Danané, and the building became extremely crowded.

We were next to a pathway, and people accidentally kicked us or our belongings as they passed by. Day and night we heard, "Oh, I'm sorry; excuse me; I'm sorry," as they apologized. We appreciated their politeness, but sleeping was almost impossible.

Once, Bessie and I left to buy some food in the town market. We also had to cook it before returning and left Miracle to guard our things. The transit camp had cooks to prepare food for the refugees, and sometimes we even smelled the wonderful aroma of beef cooking. The aroma, however, was the closest we ever came to the actual beef, fish, or chicken.

Just like in Ivory Coast, the food intended for the refugees was stolen by the local hired help. Audaciously, the cooks used the camp's own kitchen to cook meat that was intended for the refugees' soup. Then they took the meat to their own homes or sold it in the market. The soup we refugees ate contained no meat whatsoever—no beef, no fish, no chicken, no pork. It was mostly broth with some beans or rice, and that was all.

That was why we had to buy and cook our own food in the town. Upon returning from our excursion to the camp building, we looked all over for Miracle. We couldn't locate her in the huge hall. Where was she?

We looked where we thought our spot was but couldn't immediately make her out. Finally, we saw a small figure sitting nearby, completely covered in dust. It was Miracle! She was still guarding our things, but as people walked by, the dust they stirred up had completely covered her and made her unrecognizable. Her hair, arms, face, skin, and clothes were all just one shade: dust.

After seven days, we finally left Lola for the refugee camp in Laine. On the eighth day, a violent storm came up, and a tornado tore through the transit camp building. It was so strong that the rear concrete-block wall gave way and was blown over.

Thankfully, the wall fell outward, saving hundreds of lives. Most of the injuries to the people next to the wall were caused by falling debris and people trampling each other trying to escape. Bessie, the children, and I realized that just one day before, we were directly next to the wall that collapsed. It was as if God was reminding us that his hand was still on our lives.

The Guinea Laine Refugee Camp had been hastily carved out of the high forest. Trees were felled. Bulldozers leveled the ground, and large tents were erected in a matter of days. The camp was huge, housing upward of twenty-five thousand refugees from several ongoing wars in Sierra Leone, Liberia, and Ivory Coast. It had sections from A to Z, with Z being the cemetery. The joke going around was that when they took you to the end of the alphabet, you were dead.

Refugees had flooded into Guinea from Ivory Coast and now also from Liberia, where fresh fighting had broken out. The Liberians had their sections of the camp. Armless and legless refugees from Sierra Leone had their sections. And even Ivorians escaping the escalating civil war were given their own sections.

Housing was in large tents, just like in Danané, except these tents had only dirt floors, not concrete. In the UN's haste to respond to the humanitarian crisis, there was no time for proper construction. The camp had no electricity.

As a result, cold from the ground seeped into fragile refugee bodies. Sickness in its many forms quickly spread throughout the camp. Contagious diseases flourished.

Bessie came down with malaria. Carving the camp out of the high forest provided anopheles (mosquitoes carrying the deadly plasmodium parasite) with an abundance of victims. Environmental conditions were ideal for an epidemic. Hard downpours during the summer rainy season keep the mosquitoes down because it's difficult for them to fly in the rain. It is during the dry season in the fall when they flourish and breed in pools of standing or stagnant water. Early December is one of these ideal times.

Bessie started out with flu-like symptoms: fever, shaking, chills, muscle aches, headaches, diarrhea, and nausea. As the parasites multiplied, they attacked her red corpuscles. The corpuscles burst, releasing hordes of parasites to travel unobstructed throughout her bloodstream. Bessie's body was wracked off and on with a high fever. One hour she was sweating profusely; the next, shivering uncontrollably. The only medicine available was paracetamol, known commonly in the USA as acetaminophen or Tylenol. That was it. Typically chloroquine or the older drug quinine was used to treat malaria. Both were available . . . for those with money. But we had none. Surrounded by her helpless family, Bessie would likely die.

She stopped eating and could only lie on her mat day after day. The children and I prayed over her hot, feverish body even as she lay shivering. We committed each pill to the Lord before giving it to her.

As she grew weaker, I had to do something. Our prayers alone were not going to save her. In desperation, I set out and foraged through the forest searching for "bitter leaves" or the herb known as "Jologbo." Jologbo was a vine in Liberia that wrapped itself around trees. The leaves were a brilliant green color. This was our traditional malaria medicine prior to the arrival of western medicine and modern drugs.

I didn't know if this vine grew in Guinea but it was my only hope. Each morning after prayers, pleading with God to spare Bessie's life, I set out into the forest. Late morning on the third day of looking, I found it! The leaves were a dull green, perhaps due to the dryness of December. I pulled one off, and carefully rubbed the leaf between my thumb and forefinger crushing it to break it up and release its juice. Then slowly, I licked my fingers.

An incredibly bitter taste puckered my mouth even as my lips broke into a wide grin. Quickly I plucked as many leaves as I my pants pockets could hold. I raced back to the camp praising God as I ran. I had to believe and trust I wasn't too late to save her.

Arriving, I quickly placed leaves in a pot of water and boiled them to make a strong tea-like potion. Bessie was so weak. Kneeling down, I gently slipped my hand under her head and propped her up. Lifting the cup towards heaven, I spoke to God.

"Father, you directed my steps and led me to this vine. I ask you now to bless this liquid so that Bessie will be healed."

Then, I held the cup of liquid to her lips and sip by sip encouraged her to drink almost two full cups. We repeated this three times per day for several days, each time offering the cup to heaven with a prayer before giving it to her.

After over a week of sickness, her fever finally broke. She steadily grew healthier. Gradually, she could eat and regained her strength. The Lord had spared her life. We thanked the Lord over and over.

I wondered how it was that one person was saved when another was lost. Other malaria victims in the large tent weren't so lucky. Even as I shared the Jologbo herb and where to find it, some victims still died. Often, malaria comes with infections that require an antibiotic in addition to the chloroquine for treatment. The most virulent variety travels to the brain.

Those with cerebral malaria were removed from the living tents and cared for in the clinic tent, centrally located in the sprawling camp. The poor victims are driven out of their minds as their brain tissue is attacked by the parasite. At times it travels down their spinal column. The lucky ones finally lapse into a coma. For others, convulsions and seizures ebb and flow like the tide before death finally washes them away.

Thankfully, with the massive size of the camp, it was only the areas closest to the clinic tent that were subject to the screams of pain and agony. Their weakened voices don't carry all that far in the tropical air. After a few days, they eventually succumbed. Like a cool breeze that passes once and is no more, so too were they.

As the camp swelled with new arrivals, cholera broke out from the cold, the overcrowding, and the latrines located too close to the tents. Flies around the latrine transported the germs of human waste to the nearby food areas and the result was inevitable. More died.

Other diseases spread throughout the camp. The children came down first with measles, and then with chicken pox. Then Bessie got sick with malaria again and her treatment with Jologbo was repeated and she recovered.

In addition to diseases that plagued the camp, it was not safe. Many of the Liberian mercenaries had joined the refugees fleeing Ivory Coast. Gunfire late at night from their smuggled weapons belied their criminal activities of armed robbery and theft.

Local Guinean security guards were supposed to protect the warehouses filled with food for the camp. But often the guards connived together with the mercenaries or rebel soldiers from Liberia to steal the supplies. It was just like in Ivory Coast, where injustice and corruption stole the very life from the refugees.

Many refugees died from chronic fear, stress, frustration, or depression. Officially, the cause of death was recorded as a stroke or heart attack, but those weren't the real causes. Even those approved for emigration to the USA, those who had a reason to hope, fell prey to these killers. For many, waiting day after day, hoping and praying for things to improve, to have fair food distribution, to be treated with a little respect proved too much. Refugee life was just too hard. The only journey many of these refugees made was to the end of the alphabet, Area Z.

Despite the grim daily realities, there was hope. Christians in the Guinea Laine camp dressed up for Sunday services as if they were not refugees, as if they had enough to eat and decent medical care. After all, we are children of the King. And as such it was not befitting our high status that we should remain depressed and downtrodden, wearing sackcloth and ashes. Rather, church was our sanctuary and oasis, where we worshiped our Father, the King. For us Christians, our entire social life of the camp revolved around church services, Bible study meetings, and potluck dinners. There we encouraged and built each other up to face the long and difficult days.

Once we were settled in the camp, it didn't take us long to learn that all of our children, except Annie, had been accounted for. In Abidjan, Kou and Dennis traveled with one group of refugees and safely made it to Ghana. Annie, however, was staying with different friends. She went with another group.

After multiple failed efforts to find Annie through the Red Cross, we concluded that she must have been killed. We have never made contact with her, and only God knows what happened to her. Yet our grief is not total. We still hold out hope that somehow, somewhere, she is alive and will one day be found.

After almost a year in the camp, we moved to N'Zerekore, about four hours' drive away from the refugee camp. There, we had access to telephone and Internet service where we could contact our family and friends in the USA and receive their monetary gifts via Western Union.

After moving, our health improved and we were able to focus on our efforts to emigrate. We had come so close in Danané. We had completed our prescreening interview and casework and had filled out all the required forms in three days, starting August 13, 2002. This was right before the Ivorian civil war broke out in September. All that remained was our final interview before we could go to the United States. With the Ivorian civil war, that day never came, and now we were forced to start over. We were never given an explanation of why.

Nevertheless, we repeated the entire process on October 27, 2004. All four of us went to the first interview. John Jr. and Miracle waited outside with the other children while the adults went inside the tent. Shouting loudly, the officials announced a new policy regarding children. Apparently, previous refugees were allowed to bring their children even if their names didn't appear on the official affidavit filed by the sponsoring relative in the USA. Only the parents' names were required. Some of these refugees mysteriously acquired ten, fifteen, or even twenty more children to take to the USA. Emigration officials promptly ended the practice. Now each individual's name was required. The affidavit Monica filed in 2000 under the old rules had only my and Bessie's names.

When it was our turn to be interviewed, we appealed over and over for the children to come. "They are small and need their parents," we pleaded. The officials wouldn't budge.

When we persisted too long with our arguments, they became exasperated and exclaimed, "If you insist on trying to bring your children, then we will close your file permanently and be finished with you. You can apply for the children once you're in the United States. So, do you two want to go, or would you rather all four of you stay here?"

There was nothing more we could do. We would go, and John and Miracle would have to stay with friends until we could send for them. The interview itself consisted of emigration officials asking us questions about the information on our documents, why we didn't want to go back to Liberia, and what we went through during the war.

Next, we had to know everything about Monica to prove she was my daughter. If the officials doubted our answers, they would immediately call Monica to verify our claims. If we had been lying, they would have found out quickly.

When we went outside, we had to break the terrible news to John Jr. and Miracle. They started crying, then Bessie and I joined them. If we were ultimately approved for emigration, then a future day was sure to be one of great joy and even greater sorrow.

Finally, after months of waiting for the emigration officials to review our files, they arrived at the camp in February 2005. They had a large list of prospects. From Monday to Thursday, they interviewed each principal applicant, generally the head of the household.

Then on Friday, February 11, 2005, they called, one by one, all the people they had interviewed into the office. Because I was the principal applicant, Bessie stayed home in N'Zerekore with the children in a prayer vigil.

Each person received a Notice of Eligibility for Resettlement letter with the decision. If the letter had your picture on it, you were approved. No picture meant your application was denied.

Waiting in the line for my letter, I began to get very nervous. Many people receiving their letters immediately ripped them open. They shouted for joy and screamed for happiness or wailed with anguish and shed tears of sorrow. Standing in line, listening to the commotion of the emotional extremes was unnerving. But then the Holy Spirit reminded me, "Fear not, for I am with you." The Spirit's voice helped, but I was still nervous. After suffering so much for so many years, I just didn't know what I would do if we were denied. This had been my prayer for fifteen years. I had no alternate plan.

Then they called my name. Trembling, I went into the office. The official seated at the desk nonchalantly handed me my letter, contained in a common, light-brown envelope, made from recycled paper. It remained unopened as I looked at it. Then I knew what I had to do.

I rejoined the emotional maelstrom outside the office. My mood was suppressed as I made my way through the jubilation and devastation. I proceeded directly to the church. Once inside, I placed the letter carefully on the altar. My heart thumped loudly beneath my shirt, damp from perspiration.

I took deep breaths, trying to calm myself down and concentrate on what I wanted to say. A few seconds after gaining my composure, I started. "Lord, I have come to present the result of the emigration process you allowed us to go through. Whatever the result is in this letter; help us to accept it. But because you made a way for this to occur, I brought it you so that you will in turn interpret the result to us. Amen."

Retrieving the letter, I stared at it once again. I couldn't do it. Esther Gleeplay, one of my assistant pastors from Danané, was there in the church watching me. I called her over and asked her to open it for me.

Taking the envelope from me, she carefully tore it open, removed the letter, and gently unfolded it. Then I looked.

There it was! I saw my photo on the first page and Bessie's on the second. A huge sigh of air escaped my taut lungs.

"Thank you, Jesus! Thank you, God! Lord, I praise your name! You are faithful! You are a God that hears and answers prayer! Your Word is from everlasting to everlasting."

Sister Esther was overjoyed for us. Our acceptance gave Esther renewed hope that she too would soon be approved for emigration. She had waited so long.

Then I turned to her and asked something Bessie and I discussed before I came for my interview.

"What is it, John?"

"You know that we cannot take John and Miracle with us when we leave. Will you take care of them until they can join us in the United States?"

She didn't hesitate a moment. "Of course I will, John. My children are all grown. I love John and Miracle."

"Thank you so much, Esther. You are a good friend."

Then, as quickly as I could, I left the camp and paid my fare for the four-hour ride home in a minibus. My joy mingled with sadness. Now it was decided. We really were going to have to leave our children behind.

Typically, when I got home from the Laine camp, I had my own familiar knock on the gate. From inside, I would hear John and Miracle shouting, "Paapy's home, Paapy's home." Then I would come in and hug and kiss everyone. Today was different.

As I walked up to the gate, I started singing, "He has done it again; my Lord has done it again . . ."

Bessie and the children came running out, and all together we sang the song all the way through while we jumped up and down, hugging each other.

Another month went by until we were scheduled for medical exams. Bessie and I went by bus to Conakry, Guinea's capital, while the children stayed with Esther. There we were given physicals and blood tests to check for HIV and STDs, and had a chest X-ray for tuberculosis. Everything was fine, and we returned to the Laine camp and then to N'Zerekore.

It was another five months before our names were posted on the camp's bulletin board with our departure date. We would leave from Laine on August 31, 2005. We had one week's notice.

The church hastily called a revival meeting. They wanted me to preach for three nights starting on the twenty-eighth. For those three nights the Spirit moved mightily. On our last day, the church arranged for a jazz band. People were dancing and praising for all God had done.

Late in the afternoon, it was time to go. The dreaded moment had arrived. In all the festivities, as children do, John Jr. and Miracle had forgotten what was about to happen.

Then they remembered. Miracle started pleading. "I want to go. Take me with you, Mommy. I want to go, Paapy." Then she started crying. The bus honked. It was time.

John Jr. started crying. "Please don't go. Don't leave us. We'll do anything. Please don't go." Now, we were all bawling. Miracle was clinging hard to Bessie's waist, trying to keep her from moving toward the bus, all the while crying and pleading.

Our friends tried to talk to the children, to reason with them and console them. But the children were having none of it. Full panic set in as they desperately clawed to keep hold. The impatient driver honked two more times.

Now everyone was in tears—the children, Bessie and I, and all of our friends. It wasn't fair. They were just children. But there was no way out. There was no turning back. With our friends restraining our screaming children, we climbed onto the bus. It started moving even as Bessie and I were trying to get seated. We looked back. Our children were terror stricken. John Jr. and Miracle wailed and writhed to break free from the grips of our friends. Then we turned the corner. They were gone.

ANOTHER BEGINNING 29

I t took another half hour before I could help Bessie stop crying. The bus spent the next day and a half driving to Conakry, Guinea's capital. We stayed there a few days for physicals and other medical matters. Continually, we grieved over leaving the children. They were safe but my guilt whispered I should have done more, fought harder. Finally, we were told our flight would leave Guinea on September 6, 2005.

Sixty or seventy refugees from the Laine camp were heading to different cities in the USA where they had family. Our Air Brussels flight was scheduled for a late evening departure. It was near time to leave, and all the other passengers were already on the plane. At the last moment our emigration papers arrived. They hastily called our names and handed us a plastic bag with our documents. We hurriedly boarded as the engines started up.

The last-minute scramble seemed designed to hide one last injustice. Beforehand, Guinea officials told us we would receive fifty dollars each for travel expenses to the USA. In the haste to give us our documents and get us on the plane, none of us received any money. All the travel money was pocketed by the corrupt officials.

All our remaining funds stayed with Esther Gleeplay to care for the children. We left Africa without a penny to our names. But by this point, we didn't care about the money. Fifteen years had passed since our ordeal began. Bessie and I were filled with excitement and anticipation. I glanced over at her to see her smile as the idling engines roared to life. Then out the corner of my eye the smile slowly faded and a faint melancholy sigh escaped her lips. I could read her mind. She was thinking of the children. How long would it be before we were a family again? Months? Years?

The engines roared to life as the plane rolled onto the tarmac. It was really happening! The long dark night was almost over. I couldn't thank and praise God enough. The plane lifted off the ground.

We flew throughout the night and arrived in Brussels about seven the next morning. Bessie slept for most of the flight, but I never slept a wink. One part of me was so excited but another part worried about the children. Upon landing, our emigration representative navigated our bewildered group through the large airport toward the Continental Airlines departure lounge. The next leg of our journey would take us to Newark, New Jersey. From there, we would travel to Charlotte, North Carolina, and finally to Birmingham, Alabama, where Monica would meet us.

Bessie and I had dressed in our Sunday finest for our journey. She wore a bright yellow suit, and I wore my best suit and my stiff, white clerical collar. We each had one duffel bag with the few clothes we owned.

God had performed miracle after miracle for us to arrive at this point. We were certain he would continue to provide for us. I reflected and marveled how God brought good out of my affair with Viola. Monica, the child from that affair, was now the means God used for our salvation out of the refugee camps. Eventually, her brother and sister would join us also.

Our group sat down in the departure lounge area to wait the one-hour layover before our flight would leave. A few other passengers were already in the waiting area when our group was seated. Refugee parents tried to quiet restless and squirming children. Other little ones played with newly-made friends, as kids do so easily. Bessie and I just sat calmly, waiting and watching the children while thinking of our own.

How I wished John Jr. and Miracle were with us also. They would be playing with the other children. But God's plans are different from man's, I reminded myself.

I noticed another passenger, a man with crutches. He glanced in my direction and saw me looking at him. Seeing that I noticed him, he raised himself carefully to his feet, retrieved his crutches, and made his way over to Bessie and me.

"Hello," he said. "Do you speak English?"

"Yes, we do."

"Are you refugees from civil wars?"

"Yes, we are Liberian, but we come from Guinea and before that Ivory Coast."

The man looked puzzled. "Is your group all together?" he asked. "Going to the same place?"

"Yes, we are together, but we don't know these other people in our group. And all of us are going to different cities in the USA." Again, he looked puzzled, so I changed the subject. "By the way, I'm John Gonleh, and this is my wife, Bessie."

"Hello. My name is Bruce. Oh, I noticed your cleric's collar. Are you a Catholic priest or an Episcopal minister?"

"No, I'm a Baptist pastor." When I said that, his eyes got wide.

"Oh, that's interesting. In the United States, only Catholic priests and Episcopal ministers wear collars like that, I think. Also, I'm a Baptist myself. That's quite a coincidence," he said, looking surprised. "Well . . . where are you traveling to in the United States?"

"We have a daughter in Montgomery, Alabama, and we're going to live with her," I replied. With that answer, the man looked more confused than ever. Now, I could see he wanted to end the conversation.

"Well, it was nice talking with you," he concluded. "I hope you have a good flight and a good life in Montgomery."

Bessie and I both said, "It was nice meeting you." Then he hobbled on his crutches back to his seat.

Finally, it came time for the passengers to board, the crew to perform their checklists, and finally to taxi onto the runway. The engines roared to full power as we gained speed. As we lifted off the ground a Bible passage came to mind:

> IF I RISE ON THE WINGS OF THE DAWN,
> IF I SETTLE ON THE FAR SIDE OF THE SEA,
> EVEN THERE YOUR HAND WILL GUIDE ME,
> YOUR RIGHT HAND WILL HOLD ME FAST.

We were traveling to a place where a man's success was only determined by God and his own hard work. Long ago, Liberia had been such a place for me. Now it would be the USA, a place without civil war.

The flight to Newark would take eight hours. Our group was situated near the rear of the plane. The flight attendants served a meal that was the best food I can ever remember eating. Given that we only ate refugee food for years, perhaps my judgment and taste buds were skewed.

Two hours into the flight I looked up. The man with the crutches from the departure lounge was working his way back toward us. It took him a while because the aisles weren't wide enough to accommodate his crutches.

He stopped at our row, looking relieved that we were the only two in the middle section with five seats across. Then he asked if he could sit down.

"Yes, of course," Bessie replied. "Please sit down."

"Thank you," he said, lowering himself gingerly. "I hope you won't think I'm crazy, but God told me to come back and help you." He paused, looking, it seemed, for some indication that we did indeed think he was crazy. When he didn't get one, he continued.

"I was sitting in my seat reading a book, when suddenly I heard a soft voice in my head. It said, 'Bruce, you need to help them.' So here I am. I hope you don't think I'm crazy."

"No, not at all," I answered. We then shared just a little of our story with him. I told him how I had been tortured and escaped death and how we had spent six months in the bush.

Bruce mentioned the organization, Bill Glass Champions for Life, he volunteered with. Perhaps, he said, we possibly could be speakers at one of their prison events. His organization could pay two or three hundred dollars to speak at a weekend prison event, and even though it wasn't much, it was something.

He didn't understand how we were emigrating from Guinea to live with a daughter already in the USA. But politely, he didn't pry for more information. He took out his wallet and gave us $160. Then he gave us his phone number and e-mail address in Houston. We gave him Monica's number in Montgomery. Bessie concluded our ten-minute conversation with a prayer.

Bruce said, "I'll call you in a week or two. I'm not sure how else I can help you, but if God wants me to, then I'll try."

With that, he went back to his seat. Bessie and I could hardly believe what had just happened. He was the first American we met and God had spoken to him and arranged for us to be blessed by him.

Our flight landed in Newark. Bruce came over to say good-bye again and then went to his gate for Houston. After several hours in customs and emigration, our plane left for Charlotte.

We were greeted in Birmingham by Monica and Bessie's cousin Arthur Siaway and his wife, Vickie. We were finally home. Amid all the hugs and kisses and greetings, we shared with them about Bruce. They were all astonished by the story and the money.

We settled in at Monica's apartment. The only money we had to our name was what we'd received from Bruce. The next day, we called the Bethel Church at the Guinea Laine Refugee Camp and told them also what happened. Then, we took fifty dollars and sent it via Western Union to the church in Guinea as an offering. Everyone at Bethel was praising God for the blessing we received and were able to share.

After four weeks in the USA, rising tensions threatened safety and security in the Laine Camp. The children were in danger. There were rumors circulating of ethnic cleansing and murdering the Liberians in the camp. Further, John and Miracle had been sick for weeks as diseases circulated in the overcrowded conditions. Duration and severity of illnesses were exacerbated by the camp's poor design and location. We asked Kou, now living in Monrovia, to make the three-day bus trip to the Laine Camp to rescue her brother and sister.

It would not be easy. The children's official UN documents stated they were to remain at Laine. Taking them out of the country involved risks to Kou. Nevertheless, she made the trip, slipped the children out of the camp, bought bus tickets, and then fast-talked her way past several checkpoints during the return trip. It didn't take much convincing the Guinean soldiers. They were quite happy to allow any Liberian to vacate their country. One in and three out was just fine.

Bruce visited in early November 2005. He was going to a prison event in Birmingham and drove down to Montgomery to spend some time with us. He was thinking that perhaps our story could be made into a magazine article.

We spent time telling him our story Friday afternoon. He was so intrigued that he decided to stay Saturday in Montgomery instead of driving back to Birmingham for the prison event. When he arrived Saturday morning at Monica's apartment, he was very excited.

He told us he had a dream overnight. This story, he said, is too deep and rich for a magazine article. In his dream he realized that this story should become a book and that he should write it.

Bruce confessed that he'd never written a book before. But that wasn't going to stop him. If God wanted him to write a book, then that was God's business. God would make a way. Also, it would be up to God to get it published, since Bruce knew absolutely nothing about how to go about that. He added that he'd never started a business before he did it in 1987. The business grew and became very successful before he sold it to a large company in 2004. The weekend ended and Bruce returned to Houston.

Meanwhile, life in Montgomery grew tense. Monica lived with her boyfriend in the apartment and Bessie and I were their guests. Just as Liberian culture had encouraged my behavior resulting in Monica's birth, now American culture encouraged young people to live together without marriage. I explained to both of them that this was not right nor was it God's plan. They wouldn't listen to me, just as I hadn't listened to Bessie when she complained of my behavior. I was wrong years ago and Monica was wrong now. But there would be no resolution. After several weeks, in a fit of anger, the boyfriend threw Bessie and me out.

Even with this sad turn, however, God came to our rescue once more. Guan Tompkins, a friend of Arthur and Vickie, agreed to take us in as his houseguests.

We couldn't work as we didn't have driver's licenses or work permits. We applied for them and then waited for two months for them to arrive. It was awful just to sit around Guan's house and before that Monica's apartment.

In late November, a few weeks after returning from the Laine camp with her siblings, Kou was married. William Selmah, the groom, instantly became a surrogate father and inherited nearly full-grown children, ages eleven and fourteen. He'd had one month's notice to prepare. Thankfully, he loved Kou so much that two more members of her family were joyfully received.

With the happiness of the children's arrival in Monrovia and Kou's wedding came sadness mixed with joy. My father, the old *zo*, left his home in Garnwe to receive treatment in Monrovia for a stubborn infection. He grew worse in the hospital as treatment proved ineffective. My cousin Joseph and his wife, whose house sheltered us in Kakata, visited my father. Joseph's wife shared about Jesus with the old chief and at long last he believed and accepted the Lord's gift of eternal life. Just before he died, an old friend visited and wanted to discuss the old times and stories of the bush devil. With a wave of his wrinkled shriveled hand, he declared, "That is in the past now. Today I am a new person." He died in his sleep a short time later.

We started attending the First Baptist Church in downtown Montgomery. The church owned several old inner-city homes that they were refurbishing. In return for helping to fix up one of these homes, they permitted us live in one house rent free.

As church members began to hear our story, they donated furniture, appliances, a television, beds, a kitchen table, pots and pans, dishes, and silverware. In short, we went from owning absolutely nothing in September to living in a furnished house by Christmas.

Bessie and I truly felt like Job. After Job suffered such tremendous losses, God restored to him everything he had before and more.

When our driver's licenses and work permits came through, I got a janitorial job, working the night shift at the Air Force base, and Bessie began working at the First Baptist day care.

A lawyer at First Baptist, Douglas McElvy, agreed to help us file the necessary paperwork to apply for John Jr. and Miracle to join us. Like so many others, he too offered his services free of charge.

I eventually left my night job and went to work in landscaping at Faulkner University. Our lives were moving forward. We sent money back for John Jr. and Miracle every month and called weekly. After almost a year in the USA, slowly life was getting better.

Then a new crisis broke. In May 2006, I was at work, trimming trees using a chain saw. I was on a ladder nine feet in the air. I came to a limb I couldn't reach with the chain saw, so I climbed down, got a handsaw instead, and went back up. As I started on my final cut, the large limb sounded a loud crack and began to fall. It fell and as it did struck another limb, the one my ladder rested against. The ladder wobbled. I desperately tried to steady it.

Too late! As if in slow motion, my ladder slowly stood up on end. It tilted ever so slightly towards the rear. I knew at that moment I was going to fall. I clawed fruitlessly for the limb. It was just out of reach. I picked up speed, hurtling to the ground. I slammed down with a thud onto the beautifully-manicured lawn, directly on my back. Thankfully, neither the chain saw nor the handsaw I still clung to impaled me.

I lay stunned and dazed for a few moments. Slowly, I forced myself to stand, collected the tools, and took it easy the rest of the afternoon. I was sore but thought once more I must be extremely blessed and lucky to have escaped serious injury. That night at home, however, pain attacked with a vengeance.

The next morning I could barely struggle in to work where I told my supervisor what happened. I was taken to the hospital and X-rayed. Three vertebrae were crushed, the doctor informed me, as I writhed in pain on the examination table.

"God, I know you have a plan here," I prayed. "Help me understand it, or at least give me the strength to endure it, Lord." How amazing! I had survived brutal civil wars, torture, my own execution, deadly diseases, and the cruelest deprivations only to break my back in a fall off a ladder.

Just as the wheels of bureaucracy were stuck in mud in the children's emigration, so too were they stuck in getting the proper treatment for my back. The doctor started with therapy, wanting to avoid surgery. But it never worked and never alleviated any discomfort. So despite excruciating pain, I had to report to work each day and perform my job as best I could.

In July 2006, Bessie's father died. He was stricken with malaria and grew weak as the disease progressed. By the time he made it to the hospital, he hadn't eaten for several days. The hospital injected him with powerful medicine to attack the malaria parasite, but he was too weak to receive it. It was the cure that killed him. Bessie grieved with many tears. The godly old man had taught Bessie to read the Bible in their native Krahn dialect while she sat on his knee as a small child. He had taken her to church and instilled in her his love for the Lord. Our lives were moving on and yet we longed for our family to be together. His death only emphasized the sorrow we felt being apart from the children.

Another Christmas came and went with no progress towards getting approval for the children. The wheels of bureaucracy turned as slowly as a cart stuck in the deep Liberian mud after a monsoon. It seemed like they would never come.

After ten months of failed treatments, delays, and red tape, the doctor finally had me stop working in February 2007. I had back surgery in April, nearly one year after the accident. Three discs were replaced and a steel rod was inserted. At long last, I started the slow painful rehabilitation of my body.

Kou was pregnant and expecting in May 2007. Just before her time, she came down with malaria. No one knew what effects the treatment would have on the fetus. There was no choice. Without treatment, both Kou and the baby would die. Complicating this was two different doctors telling her she would need a C-section. The baby was positioned breach and could die in the birth canal. Yet a C-section in war-ravaged Monrovia was almost as dangerous to the mother as it was in the Danané refugee camp. Bessie and I fasted and prayed for three days, just as I had for my own two children, John Jr. and Miracle. Kou not only responded to malaria treatment but the baby turned around. She had a normal delivery and a healthy baby girl.

In early summer, Bessie's mother contracted malaria. Prayers like little missiles were aimed towards heaven, pleading for divine intervention. She made it to the hospital in time. The same powerful medicine that killed her husband a year before now healed her completely.

Life was so hard and difficult in Africa and in some ways it was much easier in the United States. Yet even here, life was a constant battle. Bessie and I realized that the Father was well aware of the difficult trials and circumstances we faced. Yet we also knew that each of these trials was a test to see what kind of relationship we had with him. Would we turn away? Would we blame him for not doing what we wanted? Would we curse God and die, as Job's wife advised? Our hope was that the Lord would use each obstacle to make us into the people we should be. Our confidence was that at the end of our test we would have a testimony more precious than gold or silver. This hope and confidence were our only weapons to fight the continual assaults life kept launching against us. Without these, we would have been totally overwhelmed.

Miracle was hospitalized in Monrovia with asthma attacks. Thankfully, however, the treatments were effective. With each occurrence of illness or problems in school, our frustration with the emigration process mounted. It had been two years since our arrival and the children seemed as stuck as ever in Liberia. Our lawyer could get no news out of the embassy in Conakry, Guinea, regarding their status. In desperation, he wrote the governor of Alabama to ask for his help. Every letter or inquiry raised our hopes that finally something would happen. It was to no avail. All were met with silence.

At last in early December we received good news. The lawyer received notice the emigration had been approved. This was wonderful news. Perhaps the children would be here for Christmas! Mr. McElvy's secretary called the US embassy in Conakry to inquire about the emigration procedures. The children had to depart from Guinea since they were never officially living in Monrovia. We dared not risk the long delay trying to get the paperwork changed.

Bad news again. The next time the lawyer called, the embassy wasn't answering the phone. Day after day the lawyer called but the phone just rang unanswered. Days passed. The time zone difference of seven hours didn't help. Weeks passed. The lawyer called the State Department to try to get another telephone number. No luck. Christmas arrived and still no information and no contact with the embassy.

At last I called a friend who lived in Conakry. This friend was able to supply a fax number and an e-mail address for the embassy.

Finally, a few days after Christmas, the lawyer made contact via e-mail. No explanation was ever provided as to why the phone wasn't answered. It just wasn't. That's the way things work in Africa. The children were to report on any Tuesday morning to the embassy in Conakry to start the emigration process. Medical tests, paperwork, and so forth were required.

On January 10, 2008, William Selmah, Kou's husband, traveled with the children on a three-day bus ride from Monrovia to Conakry.

They went to the embassy on Tuesday as instructed and met with an official. The meeting was extremely short. Their instructions were to return in two weeks, January 29th. In the meantime, the embassy would pull their files together and start the process upon their return. Delays . . . delays . . . delays. Welcome to Africa.

February came. The children had to get DNA testing to prove they were our children. DNA testing crawled slowly forward, calling for appointments, waiting, appointments made, waiting, samples taken, waiting, send results to Africa, waiting, embassy review of results, waiting. May passed by.

Suddenly, Conakry burst into violence. Reuters news service reported "four days of violent protests in Conakry, [Guinea] and some other garrison towns by rebellious troops, who fired indiscriminately into the air to press their demands [resulted in] . . . several people, mostly civilians . . . killed and dozens wounded, almost all by stray bullets raining down on populated areas during the protest shootings in the air."

The children were trapped along with our friend, Frederick Dixon, from the Danané refugee camp. Frederick sang in the choir in Danané and now helped care for the children in the two-bedroom apartment I rented for them. No one dared venture out, they told us, for fear of the mutinous soldiers. The US embassy remained closed. A desperate phone call arrived. Frederick had run out of food for himself and the children. He had no money. We rushed to Western Union to wire $200 only to find out the office in Conakry was closed due to the violence. There was nothing we could do except once again to pray, pleading for peace and protection for our children.

After several tense days of standoff, the president agreed to meeting with the renegades demanding pay raises. That cooled things down enough for life in the city to return. Thank God, our children and Frederick only went without food for four days.

Bruce decided to try to use the violence in Guinea to our advantage. Douglas McElvy, our attorney, sent an e-mail and press release created by Bruce's publicity company, B&B Media Group, to the Embassy. The press release started with, "Displaying compassion not normally associated with large bureaucracies, the United States Embassy in Conakry, Guinea, has moved quickly to finalize documents required to reunite two teenagers with their parents following years of forced separation."

It worked! Whether we were put to the top of the pile of applications, I don't know but we definitely believe it influenced the officials in the embassy because right after this e-mail, the process sped up. The embassy contacted the Catholic Social Services Refugee Program in Mobile, Alabama. This organization checked out our living situation to make sure the children would arrive at a good place to live and be cared for after school and so forth. Bessie and I had a phone interview followed by a home visit. A report was filed and slowly made its way back to the embassy.

The children received notification that they could go and get their immunization shots, a sure sign that we were getting close. As July drew to a close, we finally received the joyful news. The children were scheduled to leave Conakry, Sunday evening, August 10th.

HOMECOMING 30

BESSIE

August 11, 2008

"Bessie, isn't it exciting!" exclaimed a woman I recognized from our church. I couldn't remember her name.

"Yes," I replied, "our prayers are finally answered." I tried to sound cheerful but felt a nervous tension and rising anxiety. I'd waited so long for this day to come and something deep inside me held my emotions prisoner. *What if something goes wrong? Their plane could be delayed or crash. What if on the happiest day of my life, I lose my entire family? Stop it, Bessie!* "Everything will be fine," I whispered, reassuring myself.

Montgomery Regional Airport buzzed with excitement and anticipation. Nearly a hundred people were gathered. Friends and church members eagerly awaited the flight from Atlanta. Only John was missing.

He'd left early this morning to fly to New York to meet the children at JFK airport. They'd departed the evening before from Conakry, Guinea, and flew to Paris and from there to JFK. The government required John's presence to help get the children fingerprinted and to fill out Customs and Immigration forms. All three were due to arrive back in Montgomery at 8:16 P.M.

"Are you excited?"

"What are you feeling?"

The questions from the reporters covering the children's arrival taxed my already stressed mind. Along with the local newspaper, crews from CBS and NBC were filming and asking questions. Homemade posters, balloons, and American flags were poised to welcome the children. It felt like a historical event was about to unfold. I still couldn't believe I was in the center of it all.

I recalled our final phone call with the children just before they boarded the flight. Kou flew from Monrovia to Conakry to see them off. John and Miracle insisted on describing the clothes they were wearing. They wanted to make sure their dad would recognize them in the JFK airport. I laughed, "Don't you think your father would recognize you, anyway?" As a final declaration before we hung up, Miracle exclaimed, "I'm so hungry, Momma. I want Jellof rice (a Liberian concoction of rice, tomato paste, chicken, shrimp, and spices served at celebrations). Oh! And spare ribs too."

"Okay, Miracle. I'll fix you plenty to eat," I reassured her. The children had been hungry ever since their arrival in Conakry last January. Money we wired the children for food, rent, utilities, and other expenses didn't go far in the high-cost capital of Conakry. Growing children need plenty to eat. I pictured them small, when John was taller than Miracle, as we fled from Danané. Then Miracle had a growth spurt and was taller than John when we made our excruciating departure from Guinea. Now, three more years had passed. I wondered what they would look like.

Annie flashed into my mind as I remembered what she looked like. Before her disappearance in 2003, she used to mother John and Miracle. With strong maternal instincts, she fed them, helped with schoolwork, and made sure they took their baths and brushed their teeth. She even mothered Kou, her twin sister. Now, Kou was pregnant with her second child while Annie was missing and presumed dead. She was one more victim among millions, but in my mind she was still a blossoming beautiful young woman who sung soprano in the church choir and hoped one day for a large family.

"Delta flight 4352 is in range and will arrive at Gate 2," an announcement blared across the loudspeakers. Flashes from cameras started up anew. Friends crowded a little closer to ensure seeing John and the children the moment they came through the revolving door.

"What will be the first thing you do when you get home?"

"Will you take a family vacation?"

"Are you worried about the children's adjustment?"

All the things we need for the children. My mind was overloaded with details. A checklist ran through my brain. Register at the Social Security office. Register for school. Get vaccinations. Go shopping for school supplies, groceries, shoes, clothes.

Clothes . . . Comfort. Comfort sewed beautiful clothes for her dolls. Even at sixteen after she lost interest in playing with them, she still sewed dresses and outfits from scavenged scraps of cloth. She mended tears in little John's pants from his roughhouse playing. A self-taught aspiring seamstress, quiet, easygoing Comfort could always entertain herself in her room sewing. A tear rolled down my cheek. I never got to see her body, never got to see her one last time. Pangs of guilt. *We never should have let her go to school that day.*

"Bessie, the plane just landed. They'll be here any minute. What emotions are you feeling now?" asked Madiyah Mosley, CBS Channel 8.

Madiyah had spent most of the afternoon at my house interviewing me. She was so sweet and kind and made me feel comfortable. I felt like we'd been friends a long time. Before I could answer, the last of the three children, Chester, appeared in my mind's eye.

What a daddy's boy! I was second rate compared to John. Whenever John took a bath, Chester had to have one too, even if he just had his. When John ate dinner late from work, Chester needed to sit in his lap for a second dinner right off John's plate and fork. When John left for an errand, Chester cried and rolled around on the ground wailing. He wanted to go with his dad.

"Madiyah," I answered, tears shining, trying to see her through the camera's spotlight. "I am so happy right now, but I have mixed feelings. Three of my children will never come home."

Madiyah lost it. Tears rolled down her beautiful, slender cheeks. She visibly stiffened, blinking hard, as her fingers rose to stem the flow. It seemed like a battle raged between her human emotions and her professional demeanor. I grasped her hand and gave it a tender squeeze. She squeezed back.

Suddenly, they were coming! My feet started to move, slowly at first. They're outside! All at once, I broke and ran to greet them, bouquets of flowers in each hand. Miracle was first, then John Jr. We clutched each other desperately. I could barely let them go to see their faces. I stroked their hair, then their faces, caressing their cheeks, lips, eyes, and forehead to prove they were real.

I glanced to the side and saw John dancing and singing praises to God. Once again, I buried my head against the children. All the fears, anxiety, and repressed emotions flooded out like a torrent. I clawed to hug and grip both children as tightly to myself as my adrenaline-charged strength allowed. We cried and laughed and cried some more before finally calming down. What joy! What wonder and happiness filled my body, my soul, my spirit!

Then I heard singing. Our church friends and pastor from First Baptist were praising God. More interviews, more conversations, and more posed photos occupied everyone as if a celebrity wedding had occurred. Eventually, almost an hour had passed. Throughout the entire time, Miracle seemed overwhelmed by the attention. She didn't smile much but her huge, brown, soulful eyes, wet and shining, took in everything. She never once left my side or my touch. John Jr. however, was made for these moments. He was just like his dad. John Jr. gave interviews to the reporters like it was the most natural thing in the world. He was so confident and his huge smile never left his face.

What great and mighty things the Lord has done. My heart could only ponder the events of nearly twenty years. It could never understand them.

Finally, it was time to go home. I was exhausted and asked about the children's luggage. John replied softly, "Bessie they don't have any. They just came with the clothes they're wearing." Tears wet my cheeks once more. We climbed into Guan's car that would carry us home. I sat in the back seat between John Jr. and Miracle, her head resting on my shoulder. A few minutes passed as we made our way slowly past the orange barrels of the perennial freeway construction zone. With soft breath and periodic sighs of contentment, I thought she must be falling asleep. All at once, she jerked her head up, turned and looked me straight in the eye.

"Momma," said Miracle, "I'm hungry." I just smiled at her. "We're almost home now, baby. Supper's waiting."

AFTERWORD

Three years have passed since my experiences in the Dominican Republic prison, La Victoria, and my first acquaintance with John and Bessie. I never set out to write a book about total strangers I met in an airport departure lounge in Brussels, Belgium. It was a small act of faith heeding the words, "Bruce, you need to go help them," that I should tell the Gonleh's story.

As a mechanical engineer by profession, I possessed neither the education, experience, nor the talent for this undertaking. However, God saw in me something he could use. I had the time and some financial resources. Only a few months earlier I sold my engineering business and was effectively retired at a young age. I had a willing heart and a desire for a deeper relationship with God. Even being president of my company ultimately did not provide me the sense of purpose and happiness I sought. I was still hungry for more.

Rarely did the words flow easily. I struggled to understand and organize their myriad stories, snippets of long-ago conversations, painful memories returning in emotional floods, and reflective ponderings. With almost every chapter, weeks of stagnation and writer's block led to frustration followed by desperation, which led me to cry out in prayer for help. Only then did the Lord come to my aide with epiphanies of clarity and direction. Like manna from heaven, the Lord nourished me and the book slowly took shape.

My prayer throughout has been "Lord, help me not to mess up John and Bessie's incredible story." Now, the task for which I was chosen and appointed is complete. God bless you.

To order additional copies of this title call:
1-877-421-READ (7323)
or please visit our Web site at
www.winepressbooks.com
AMAZON
If you enjoyed this quality custom-published book,

drop by our Web site for more books and information.

AMAZON
www.winepressgroup.com
"Your partner in custom publishing."